Friendship's Bonds

Friendship's Bonds

Democracy and the Novel in
Victorian England

Richard Dellamora

PENN

University of Pennsylvania Press
Philadelphia

10 9 8 7 6 5 4 3 2 1

Published by
University of Pennsylvania Press
Philadelphia, Pennsylvania 19104-4011

Library of Congress Cataloging-in-Publication Data

Dellamora, Richard.
  Friendship's bonds : democracy and the novel in Victorian England / Richard Dellamora.
    p. cm.
  Includes bibliographical references and index.
  ISBN 0-8122-3813-3 (cloth : acid-free paper)
    1. English fiction—19th century—History and criticism.   2. Democracy in literature.   3.
Politics and literature—Great Britain—History—19th century.   4. Literature and society—
England—History—19th century.   5. Judaism and literature—England—History—19th century.
6. Political fiction, English—History and criticism.   7. Citizenship in literature.   8. Friendship
in literature.   9. Mentoring in literature.   10. Jews in literature.   I. Title.
PR878.D377D45   2004
823'.809358—dc22   2004043009

In Memoriam
Alan Bray,
scholar and virtuoso at friendship

This image combines three elements that converge in this book. One is Jewish national and religious sentiment focused on God's Covenant with Abraham and his seed. The second is Anglo-Saxon idealization of Dorianism, the institution of Spartan military pederasty, discussed by Walter Pater in a chapter of *Plato and Platonism* (1893). The third is the tendency in emergent male homosexual culture to find the basis of citizenship in male friendship rather than in blood connection.

The subject is the covenant sworn between David and Jonathan. The moment that John Singer Sargent chooses to illustrate is especially important, affirming as it does a covenant "between me and thee, and betweene my seede and thy seede forever" (1 Sam. 20:42). In biblical terms, the verse affirms a link of kinship (David was Jonathan's brother-in-law) between two young warriors. But in the absence of weapons and in Jonathan's physical vulnerability, the image suggests a sublime understanding of citizenship that depends neither upon family ties nor divine authorization but rather upon the covenant of friends. The image resonates further among sexual dissidents at the turn of the century. Radclyffe Hall's lover, Mabel Veronica Batten, for example, in adopting "John" as a pet name for Hall, had the heroic pair in mind. Batten reserved to her own use the name of Jonathan (Sally Cline, *Radclyffe Hall*, 66).

This drawing is one of a number dealing with the narrative of David and Jonathan that Sargent in 1895 submitted for consideration as possible contributions to a new illustrated edition of the Bible. When the three-volume work appeared in 1899, however, neither this nor any other of Sargent's images were reproduced. The Sargent scholar, Trevor Fairbrother, accounts for this absence by the defensiveness about male romantic friendship that was prompted by the conviction of Oscar Wilde on charges of gross indecency in 1895. During the trial, Wilde had defended his friendships with young men specifically by instancing the biblical example of David and Jonathan. In its survival, this drawing indicates how thoroughly a hellenizing English culture had become saturated with homophilic and semitophilic sentiment by the end of the century (Trevor Fairbrother, *John Singer Sargent* [New Haven: Yale University Press, 2000], 161, 220).

John Singer Sargent, *The Parting of Jonathan and David*, Illustration for 1 Sam. 20:42, c. 1895. Courtesy of the Fogg Art Museum, Harvard University Art Museums, Cambridge, Mass. Gift of Mrs. Francis Ormond.

Contents

Introduction

What is the connection between citizenship and friendship in Victorian fiction? And why do Victorian novelists use the portrayal of relations between mentors and protégés as a way of meditating on the possibilities of democratic governance? In the following pages, I revisit the classical (and Victorian) dream that a just society would be one governed by friends. In the actual struggles over who should or should not be eligible for the rights of citizens, however, the ideal of male fraternity was troubled by anxieties about the possible conversion of intimacy into sexual anarchy. This ambivalence is historical. In classical republican rhetoric in seventeenth- and eighteenth-century England, the concept of the virile citizen/soldier was contrasted to that of the sodomitic monarch, courtier, prelate, cleric, or political agent.[1] Linda Dowling has argued that the notion of the politician as sodomite, adapted by Tory polemicists in their attacks on the Whig oligarchy in eighteenth-century England, has a further life in morally and politically conservative attacks on poets in the romantic and Victorian periods (12–31).[2] For Victorians, moreover, anxieties about the corruptibility of male relations are indexed in the appropriation to English Protestant national ideology of the biblical narratives dealing with God's Covenant with the Chosen People, especially the story of Lot.

Focusing in particular on the writing of Benjamin Disraeli, novelist, polemicist, and prime minister, as well as that of his leading political rival, William Gladstone, in this book, I consider how sodomitic intimations inflected debates over the civil, political, and social rights of artisans, women, Jews, and Irishmen in Victorian England. Beginning with Charles Dickens's angry response to the denial of the vote to manual workers in the Reform Bill of 1832 and continuing with studies of two little-known works by Disraeli that focus on the relationship between male friendship, Jewish culture and religious belief, and citizenship in the imperial nation-state, the study continues with an excursus on Karl Marx's classic essay on the Jewish Question. The central chapters deal with novels by Anthony Trollope and George Eliot that respond to Gladstone's attacks on Disraeli and other English Jews following the further extension of male suffrage after 1867. The book ends with chapters on works by Henry James and Oscar Wilde that reflect critically on the implications, for both art and male intimacy, of the advent of mass democracy. By the mid-1890s, Wilde had good reason to wonder whether belief in a positive relation between friendship and expanded rights of citizenship could be sustained.

In a democracy, citizenship is an individual matter. But both in political action and practical legislation, the rights of citizenship are usually legislated and practiced by individuals as members of groups. The two groups that I am particularly interested in are Jews, who gradually won political rights during the century, and Irishmen, whose burgeoning and on occasion violent efforts to achieve autonomy were continually baffled. Resistance to rights for members of these two groups was in part religious in character: namely, fear of theocratic tendencies in both groups. In *The Wondrous Tale of Alroy,* Disraeli had to put these doubts to rest before he could have a chance of entering the parliamentary scene. In this Introduction, I will have a good deal to say about the religious character of Victorian politics more generally. The condition of Jews and the Irish is, moreover, linked in a yet further way that the late twentieth-century focus upon subaltern subjects has tended to keep out of view. Unlike natives in the Indian subcontinent or others brought under colonial rule during the nineteenth century, Jews and the Irish were not subordinated subjects living outside the metropole. They figure as what Jonathan Boyarin refers to as "internal Others," that is, groups who are regarded as other even though they live within the boundaries of the imperial nation-state.[3] Resistance to recognizing the rights of both groups is at times motivated by a fantasy of the negation—Boyarin would say "the obliteration"[4]—of internal Others in the name of national purity. During the Victorian period, writers such as Thomas Babington Macaulay and Matthew Arnold addressed the problems they associated with internal alterity by recommending political and cultural assimilation, respectively, of Jews and Irishmen.[5] After 1850, such calls were increasingly rationalized in racial terms that called for English hegemony not through the total exclusion of others but by fashioning a hybrid nationality in which Jewish and Irish difference would be sublimated in the formation of a composite national subject.

Victorian writers were passionately engaged in the attempt to connect personal intimacy in friendship with the experience of democracy. In considering the linkage as it appears in novels, what impresses even more than utopian aspirations, however, are the anxieties that attend the linkage.

These anxieties have points of origin both in classical and Judeo-Christian tradition. In ancient Greece, mentor-protégé friendships were a source of moral solicitude. It was thought that the improper exercise of friendship, especially between a citizen and a male on the verge of manhood, had an effeminizing, devirilizing effect that could undermine the very existence of the commonwealth. During the late medieval and Renaissance periods, royal and aristocratic governance depended on the public institution of male friendship, both between equals and between patrons and clients. In these relations, the line between ardent friendship and a sexual relation was indistinct enough to be crossed with relative ease. In particular circumstances, however, such a relationship might be recognized—less likely by its participants than by their antagonists—as a sodomitical one.[6] Since sodomy was deemed to be a form of both blasphemy and treason, such allegations were as threatening to the political order as they were to the individuals thereby singled out. Friendship was both necessary and potentially dangerous to the existing order.

Attacks on sodomy are a standard feature of classic republican discourse from the mid–seventeenth century onward. Tory opponents of Sir Robert Walpole, for example, condemned political patronage as a form of "luxury" and "corruption" that was metaphorically and (at times) literally sodomitic (Dowling, 5, 9 n.). The patterns of patronage and dependence, often between an older man and a younger one, in which parliamentary politics in England were played out could be equally construed under the rubric of friendship or sodomy, depending on one's choice of lens. Jonathan Goldberg argues that these relationships were part of the tradition of aristocratic hegemony.[7] Equally, however, as Dowling reminds us, they were a necessary means whereby eighteenth-century Whigs practiced their "modernizing" politics.

Dowling charts the shift of anti-sodomitc rhetoric into the realm of aesthetics in the nineteenth century, where it becomes part of a general Tory onslaught against innovative and, later, vanguard cultural practices. She places in this context the attack on John Keats in *Blackwood's Edinburgh Magazine* for the "emasculated pruriency" (15) of his writing. It would be incorrect, however, to conclude on the basis of Dowling's discussion that classical republican rhetoric, shunted into aesthetics, disappeared from politics in the nineteenth century. One has to think only of the liaison between the Liberal prime minister, Lord Rosebery, and Viscount Drumlanrig, Alfred Douglas's older brother, in the 1890s, to be reminded of how the interweave of class, party, and sexual affiliations continued during the Victorian period.[8] Indeed, one would be wiser to consider the sexual connotations of, say, *Punch*'s satiric representations of male aesthetes in the 1870s and 1880s and the innuendoes of the Newman-Kingsley controversy in the 1860s as struggles, within aesthetic and religious terms, that intersect at times with explicitly political questions.[9] In Chapter 2, I argue that the connection between William Beckford and Benjamin Disraeli provides a crucial switch point for the continuing influence of earlier anxieties about the contamination of political friendship by intimations of sodomy amid the much more complex politics of ethnicity and the imperial nation-state that Disraeli faced as a Jew and an Anglican at the outset of his political career.

These complications are further overwritten by the place of the Hebrew Bible in Christian tradition. Here the account of the destruction of Sodom in Gen. 18–19 is apropos. The story of Lot—or of Sodom, it being referred to interchangeably as both[10]—is an important link in a series of narratives that deal with the history of the Israelites as God's Chosen People. Three aspects of this narrative as ideological construct are particularly pertinent to this study. One is the genealogical concept of group chosenness, the conviction of a covenanted relationship with God, which proved to be key to the survival of the Israelites. In the modern period, this notion was transferred to the constitution of Protestant Englishmen as national subjects, a process that, as we will see, continued in the imperial present of Victorian England. Second is a potentially annihilating othering of those against whom chosenness is defined: in the Bible, the citizens of Sodom; in Christian times, Jews and Muslims; after the Protestant Reformation, Roman Catholics; and in the period of colonial expansion, heathen idolaters. The exclusion includes Lot's own line of descent, who failed to share in the patrimony of Abraham. Perhaps because of the violence of this feature of Lot's story, accounts of the translation of Abraham's covenanted relationship with God into the ideology of Western nation-building often tend to ignore this particular linking narrative.[11] The third feature of particular interest is Lot's unseemly cosmopolitanism. Victorian commentators quail at his choice of Sodom as a place to live (Gen. 13), an error that seems to lead implacably to the incestuous relations with his daughters with which his story ends. Resistance to God's word shows as well in the perverse turn back to the condemned city taken by his wife. The effects of these lapses is to subvert the clear-cut distinction between what biblical commentators in the eighteenth century referred to as the "unnatural" desires of the men of Sodom and the behavior of God's Chosen.[12]

Finally, a word about genre. Literary writers pursued questions about what citizenship means and who is entitled to it particularly in the form of the novel, a popular literary genre entrusted with the responsibility of representing contemporary actuality. In line with Sir Walter Scott's contribution to the genre, the Victorian realist novel was closely associated with attempts to conciliate religious, economic, regional, and national differences within the United Kingdom.[13] The form, however, also offered a means of registering dissent from general maxims about the rights supposedly enjoyed by the inhabitants of the British Isles. And, after the successful passage of the Reform Bill of 1867, novelists such as Eliot, Trollope, and James explored in their fiction some troubling implications of the gradual expansion of political rights.

Performing Citizenship

The most striking fact about political rights in England in the nineteenth century is that they were slow in arriving. General male suffrage was not accomplished until the mid-1880s; and women had to wait even longer, until World War I. Major legislation in 1832 and 1867 that expanded male suffrage was limited in scope. The Reform Act of 1832, which enfranchised two out of every ten adult males in England, in effect created an expanded oligarchy of male property-owners. The Reform Act of 1867 increased the number to more than three out of ten. Within this long, slow process, parliamentary maneuvering and debates tended to be short on moral high-mindedness and long on tactical considerations.[14]

Out of these discussions emerged a property qualification for the vote and an emphasis on its masculine character that excluded the vote for women from consideration while exacerbating concern about the devirilizing, effeminizing effects of political influence. Performing citizenship meant performing masculinity, both in the sense that suffrage was one expression of achieved middle-class masculinity and in the sense that the continuing denial of political rights to manual workers arguably prevented them from achieving "manly independence."[15] In 1832, the vote went specifically to male heads of households. Their rights subsumed the claims that could be made on behalf of other dwellers: women, children, other males in the household, and servants. Precisely the fact that male householders exercised authority over dependents at home as well as employees of a lower class validated their claim to the vote.[16] In contrast, single gentlemen who rented were excluded. Prior to passage of the 1867 bill, Edward Cox expressed concern about "'intelligent, unsettled lodgers, who dislike an order of things in which their merits are not sufficiently recognized,' and who might be prone to revolutionary ideas" (Clark, 242).

The emphasis on the gender performativity of political rights also figured in debates about extending the vote to working men. Those in favor contended that achieving suffrage was necessary if they were fully to achieve virility (Clark, 232). The flip side of this view was the anxiety expressed by novelists such as Eliot in *Felix Holt, the Radical* and Trollope in *Ralph the Heir* about how party agents could demoralize rural and industrial workmen at election time. Trollope's resistance to the introduction of the secret ballot stemmed from the same sort of concern. Voting in private wasn't manly.[17]

Religious belief, and in particular Bible reading, was another mode of masculine performativity. In the "family Bibles" that figured prominently in commercial publication during the period, the male head of household reappears as "the Master of the family" (M. Carpenter, 18). As such, he was responsible for both supervising the reading of the Bible aloud in the circle of family, dependents, and servants while at the same time reserving from other members of the household exposure to troubling Jewish or "Oriental" material that editors of the Bibles believed should be kept separate for private reading by "the Master" in his "CLOSET" (44).[18] This religious role has a significant political function insofar as "the English Bible" was understood, in Mary Carpenter's words, as "the Law on which the British nation is founded"(42). For this reason, the editors of *The Illustrated Family Bible* (1871–76) include as frontispiece an illustration of *Latimer Presenting the Bible to King Henry VIII* (Fig. 1). Protestant religious affiliation underwrote one's status as a British subject.

The Sin(s) of Sodom

With their extensive commentaries, Victorian family Bibles are valuable repositories of what Pierre Bourdieu might term the "common sense" understanding of the sin of Sodom in the nineteenth century, that is, an understanding so thoroughly diffused and infused among a particular population that it scarcely required explicit formulation.[19] I've already suggested that within the series of narratives dealing with God's Covenant with his Chosen People, the story of Sodom is especially significant in defining God's People in contrast to an abjected Other, fully worthy of divine con-

Fig. 1. Leighton Brothers, *Latimer Presenting the Bible to King Henry VIII*, from *The Illustrated Family Bible* [1871–76]. Used by permission of the British Library.

demnation. Just as importantly, however, the infidelity of Lot and his family indicates that the people of Israel are as liable to be condemned by God as are the other inhabitants of Sodom. As one commentator puts it, the destruction of Sodom "was designed for a standing revelation of the wrath of God against sins and sinners, in all ages: it is, accordingly, often referred to in the Scripture, and made a pattern of the ruin of Israel."[20]

Reading Victorian Bible commentaries can help one understand the many and complex ways in which the Jews themselves were associated with the sinfulness of the inhabitants of Sodom. While especially attached to Jews, moreover, this animus could be directed as well at members of other groups, such as Irish Catholics. The commentaries throw light on why internal Others were potentially so disturbing to Protestant Christians for they show that the barrier between Sodomites and Christians could be easily breached. In the eyes of commentators, the internal Other is not only the Jew but likewise the sinful will and desire of the Christian him- or herself.

Commentators find three major types of sin in Sodom: sins against faith, sins against charity, and sins against nature. Among these, the most important is the sin of "unbelief" or infidelity. The figure of Lot himself poses special difficulties, first of all because he chose to settle in the plain of Sodom despite the fact that his uncle, Abram, thought it better to remain in the mountains (Gen. 13). When Sodom is condemned and the angel tells Lot to flee to the mountain (Gen. 19:17), Lot begs to be permitted to flee to Zoar, another of the otherwise condemned cities of the plain (Gen. 19:20). The editor remarks:

Lot was forbidden to look behind him: as this would indicate great reluctancy to leave his property in Sodom, and to quit the fertile plain which had so long ensnared him. Indeed, his attachment was so strong to Sodom, and his lingering so criminal, that it was an instance of *special indulgence* that he was not left to loiter till it had been too late to escape. And at last, through unbelief and undue valuation of worldly things, he was unwilling entirely to quit the plain, and flee to the mountain: yet mercy prevailed; and Zoar, a small city, was spared in condescension to his infirmity, and in answer to his request! (*Portable*, 16n.)

The situation is even worse with reference to Lot's wife, who, one commentator remarks, may have been "a native of Sodom": "This unhappy woman, contrary to God's express command, in unbelief, and love to Sodom and its riches, regretting what was left behind, and probably purposing to return, 'looked back'; and, as some think, actually attempted to return. . . . She was therefore instantaneously struck dead and petrified, and thus remained to after ages a visible monument of the Divine displeasure" (*Portable*, 16n.).

The allegation of unbelief sets in train a series of associated terms: the sins of infidelity, blasphemy, and idolatry, all of which can be observed in the behavior of Lot, of members of his family, or of his descendants. For example, Lot soon leaves Zoar for the mountain in fear that Zoar too will be destroyed. Once there, his daughters, whose gentile fiancés chose to remain behind in Sodom, get their father drunk, then have sex with him. According to the editor, Lot "died under a dark cloud; all his substance and part of his family perished in Sodom; his wife in looking back lost her life; and it might almost have been wished, that his daughters had been taken away too, to have prevented his and their sin and shame" (*Portable*, 16n.). Lot's progeny by his daughters are cut off from God's Covenant: Ammon and Moab, the offspring of this incestuous coupling, "were nations accursed."

Their descendants became both "idolators" and "enemies to the children of Abraham."[21]

Infidelity, blasphemy, and idolatry are all sins against faith. Notice, moreover, how the commentary links these offenses with sins against charity, that is, the turn of faith away from God and toward material goods and the desire to possess them. Lot is guilty of "undue valuation of worldly things." His wife "looked back" "in unbelief, and love to Sodom and its riches." Lot and his wife give to earthly goods the faith and love they owe to God; they covet riches for themselves instead of sharing them with others. This set of offenses is an important switch point in efforts to link Jews with the sin of Sodom. For example, in his essay "On the Jewish Question" (1844), Marx first identifies *Judentum* or Judaism, as he puts it, with capitalist acquisitiveness, then argues that Jews are both anti-human and sexually perverse because they violate the defining "species-relation itself, the relation between man and woman, etc."[22] This phrase refers to what, in a moment, I will describe as the central sexual offense of the men of Sodom. Their sins against charity likewise served the purposes of Liberals and Radicals in the 1870s and later who attacked Disraeli and Jewish financiers as well as upper-class men with sexual and emotional ties to other men. For Gladstone's campaign against Disraeli and Henry Labouchère's against men such as Wilde and Lord Rosebery, sins against charity nicely overlap the set of offenses connected, in classical republican discourse, with the vice of "luxury" (Dowling, 5). In Victorian as in earlier uses of this discourse, corruption or effeminacy is seen to subvert "the health of the polity," which is identified in turn with "the *virtus* or virility of an ancient warrior ideal" (Dowling, xv).

Thus far I have not spoken of the sin that a reader today is most likely to associate with Sodom: namely, sodomy or buggery, more particularly, male-male anal intercourse. This sin is referred to in circumlocution by the editor of the *Portable Folio Family Bible* when he says that the demand of the men of Sodom that Lot's angelic visitors be turned over to them "conveys more forcibly an idea of the extreme and unparalleled wickedness of Sodom, and all ranks and descriptions of its inhabitants, than the most laboured descriptions and rhetorical declamations could have done; and is a most beautiful example of giving intimations concerning practices, too shameful to be mentioned, in language which excites no other sensation than horror and indignation" (16n.). In contrast, editors of earlier family Bibles had not shied away from being direct. For example, the earliest family Bible, published in 1735, reads:

Before it was time to go to rest, the inhabitants of the city, both young and old, being informed that Lot had strangers with him, and, in all probability tempted with beautiful forms, which the angels had assumed, encompassed the house, and demanded of them to deliver them up, that they might abuse them. That is, in an unnatural and preposterous manner, which was afterwards expressly forbidden in the levitical law, and made capital. This vile sin continued among the gentiles even in the apostles [sic] time (as may be gathered from Rom. 1:27 and 1 Cor. 6:9) and was so generally practiced among the people of Sodom, that from thence it took the name of Sodomy, and the practisers of it are called Sodomites, both in the holy scriptures, and our English laws, which (as did the law of God of old) do still make the punishment of it to be death.[23]

It is important to bear in mind, however, that male-male anal intercourse is only one meaning of sodomy. English statutes outlawing "buggery," for example, criminalize other acts as well.[24] More generally, in the writing of Saint Augustine, "the root sin of the Sodomites is not the desire of same-sex copulation. It is rather the violent eruption of disordered desire itself."[25] This sense appears to be seconded in the passage in the commentary to *The Portable Folio Family Bible* in which it is argued that the fiery destruction of the cities of the plain was fit punishment for the "burning lusts against nature" of their inhabitants (16n.). In medieval theology, the sin of Sodom is "the vice or sin against nature," namely, "when someone spills semen outside the place specified for this."[26] Both in the commentary to *The Portable Folio Family Bible* and in other Bibles, there is a tendency to combine references to particular sexual offenses with general contrasts between procreative sex and sexual practices that deviate from this standard.[27]

One way or another, Lot, members of his family, and their descendants may be associated with all three sorts of sins of which the gentile inhabitants of Sodom were guilty. At first glance, the story of Lot seems to be a story about how God protects Abraham's nephew and destroys the ungodly. Violence toward those who don't fall within the terms of the Covenant seems to be a basic feature of the story of God's election of a chosen, biologically related, few. But the story actually operates differently. Lot's family consists of both Jews *and* Gentiles. And the latter, Lot's wife and his daughters' fiancés, have an opportunity of coming to know the true God and of being saved by him. But they refuse or fall away from the proffer of faith. Likewise, the Jewish people, whom God has claimed as his own, are not saved by that fact alone. They must maintain their faith and act accordingly; and, if they do not, they will lose both the promised land here below and eternal life in heaven after death. Accordingly, while the story of Lot seems to make a binary distinction between the faithful and heathens, in fact the two categories are interfused. What this fact means is that the Chosen People are always at risk. Promises of providential protection are only as secure as the faith of the Jews, Christians, or Englishmen who see this promise as being directed toward themselves. All are capable of joining the ranks of Sodom. The promise of the Covenant, then, brings with it a demand for continual moral armament.

Lot and his family do appear to be reserved from male sodomy. Indeed, commentators go out of their way to dissociate Lot from excessive interest in the beauty of the angels who visit him.[28] And well they might, since a skeptical reader may wonder why Lot was willing to sacrifice the virginity of his daughters to the men of Sodom in order to protect his male guests untouched. On this score, there are theological explanations available.[29] On another, however, it is evident that Lot does fall into unnatural vice as a result of his fatal error in making Sodom his home. For example, one commentator explains Lot's incest with his daughters in the following way: "The truth seems to be, that, though preserved from gross crimes, they [that is, Lot's daughters] had been accustomed in Sodom to hear and witness wickedness, till their consciences were become unfeeling, and their sense of shame blunted. No sufficient excuse can be made either for them or for Lot; and, indeed, scarcely any account can be given of the transaction, but this, that 'the heart is deceitful above all things, and desperately wicked; who can know it?'" (*Portable*, 16n.).

Judaism, the Irish Question, and the Post-Confessional State

The linkage of sins against faith with sins against charity and unnatural vice, including male sodomy, in the story of Lot is important in understanding latter-day prejudice against Jews. Although one needs to maintain distinctions between the three sorts of sins, it would be a mistake to ignore the linkage in Judeo-Christian thinking between religious unbelief, materialism, and a range of sexual acts regarded as unnatural, including male-male anal intercourse. Anti-sodomitic rhetoric tends to conflate the differences. Accordingly, it is both surprising and, on second thought, not so surprising, to learn that the political pamphlet in which Gladstone first learned how to mobilize Nonconformist, male, working-class voters after 1867 is entitled *Bulgarian Horrors and the Question of the East* (1876).[30] Likewise, when, in the following national political campaign of 1879–80, he rallied huge crowds with accusations of mammonism and infidelity lodged against his political opponents, those who heard him were well aware that he was implicitly comparing contemporary London with Sodom and the converted Jew, Disraeli, with the inhabitants of that condemned city.[31]

At the beginning of the nineteenth century, England was a confessional state, which means that, in order to enjoy political rights, one had to be an Anglican. The removal of civil and political disabilities from non-Anglicans in the nineteenth century took almost as long as it did to win the vote for the majority of male adults. In a detailed account, Gauri Viswanathan shows how, beginning with the repeal of the Test and Corporation Acts in 1828, Protestant Dissenters, and then, a year later, Roman Catholics, achieved civil emancipation. Although these reforms were enacted under the leadership of a Tory, Sir Robert Peel, following passage of the Catholic Emancipation Act, Macaulay and other liberals campaigned unsuccessfully for the removal of civil disabilities against English Jews. In the following years, Jews gradually won rights such as eligibility to run for municipal office; but it was not until 1858 that they were admitted to Parliament.[32] Disraeli's career as a parliamentarian was possible only because his father had arranged for him while still a youngster to be baptized as an Anglican.

The motives that prompted efforts to remove the civil disabilities of non-Anglicans were mixed. Since the eighteenth century, attempts in western Europe to create civil societies had found the question of Jewish emancipation to be a particularly challenging one. Jewish belief and practices, dietary and otherwise, were understood to be expressions of a commitment to social and cultural exclusivity. Since democratic states were founded on a principle of universal brotherhood, how was it possible to enfranchise a group whose very existence appeared to negate this proposition?[33] In the excursus on Marx, I consider how, as a young theorist and political radical, Marx responded to current debates among left Hegelians over what was referred to as the Jewish Question. In effect, Marx found the problem to be insoluble. The Jewish Question would be resolved only when Judaism ceased to exist. In less extreme terms, Macaulay held a cognate belief. Macaulay argued on behalf of civil and political equality for Jews on the grounds that it would lead to their assimilation.[34] At this point Jonathan Boyarin's view that "annihilation" and "assimilation" are different means to a shared end is highly pertinent (*Storm*, 83, 82). Both Marx and Macaulay assume both the immutability of Jewish culture and the desirability of creating an integral body politic. The former must be sacrificed if the latter is to be achieved.

When Boyarin uses the word annihilation, he does so in part as a way of bearing in mind the actuality of the Holocaust. In light of the extermination of millions of European Jews in the twentieth century as an exercise of state policy, Marx's apocalyptic desire for the end of European Jewry, on the one hand, and Macaulay's confidence in the eventual absorption of English Jews into the population at large are disturbing phenomena. The narratives of the Covenant in Genesis, and in particular the story of Sodom, indicate how culturally embedded such desires are. The conviction that nonbelievers are sinners who deserve to be annihilated is perhaps the single, most negative legacy of Judeo-Christian tradition. Moreover, this legacy is not only religious, it is also philosophic. As Moshe Halbertal and Avishai Margalit argue in their book, *Idolatry*, the monotheistic principle in Judaism, Islam, and Christianity has frequently resulted in the condemnation as idolaters of those who do not share one's beliefs. In nineteenth-century writers such as Marx and Macaulay, the belief is attached to such secular principles as the commitment to socialist transformation and to the modern, liberal state, respectively.

Peel, for his part, saw the emancipation of Roman Catholics as a way of relieving continuing dissatisfaction in Ireland over the loss of self-government in 1800. Unfortunately, until the very end of the nineteenth century, the political class in Great Britain proved to be unable to rectify the injustices done when, fearful that Ireland would be used as a base by Napoleon and his allies, the British disbanded the Parliament at Dublin and absorbed Ireland and its population into the United Kingdom. From that date forward, the relationship between Ireland and Great Britain was not only colonial but also internal. Being Irish and being Roman Catholic in effect threatened the practical incorporation of Ireland into the British state and the psychic incorporation of Irish subjects into a phantasmatic British national subject.[35] In the course of the century, this relation came to be coded more and more in terms of racial theory within the disciplines of biology and anthropology.[36]

At mid-century, Jewish difference too began to be theorized along racial lines. Disraeli made an important contribution to this conceptual shift in his discussion in *Coningsby* (1844), subsequently continued in his 1852 biography of Lord George Bentinck. The leader of the Protectionist party in the House of Commons, Bentinck joined Disraeli in supporting the Whigs' call for the removal of civil disabilities against Jews in 1847 despite opposition from the rest of the party. Disraeli argued that Arabs and Jews both belong to "the Bedoueen race," a particular subtype among what he referred to as the Caucasian races.[37]

By the late 1860s, the scientific character of racial theory was widely accepted. In his volume of Oxford lectures, *On the Study of Celtic Literature* (1867), Matthew Arnold appeals to the findings of modern "ethnology" in an attempt to solve the Irish Question in cultural terms.[38] In the study, he develops a racial, cultural, and moral typology of the inhabitants of the United Kingdom. Arnold points out that Englishmen tend to associate themselves with "strong sense and sturdy morality" (xv).[39] In contrast, Celts are associated with sentiment, emotion, passion, and enthusiasm. Arnold values these qualities as capable of contributing to the development of a new British nationality that will surmount Anglo-Saxon matter-of-factness. It is the "nature" of the Celt, he says, "to be up—to be sociable, hospitable, eloquent, admired, figuring away brilliantly. He loves bright colours, he easily becomes audacious, overcrowing, full of fanfaronade" (84).[40] Arnold calls for an admixture of this Celtic "spirit" to leaven the dullness and self-complacency of English philistinism. "The hard unintelligence, which is just now our bane, cannot be conquered by storm; it must be supplied and reduced by culture, by a growth in the variety, fulness, and sweetness of our spiritual life" (150).

Arnold frames this discussion of culture in political terms, which he persists in understanding in terms of moral psychology. He attributes the failure of British policies in Ireland to flaws in the English character (xv). English errors have provoked the republican revolutionary violence of "Fenianism" (150). The remedy that he proposes is cultural: namely, the promotion of Celtic studies at English universities and the reformation of both the Celtic and the Anglo-Saxon characters. Arguing against earlier theorists of race, who contended that the Celts are not Indo-Aryan, he cites recent research supporting the view that Celts and Teutons are part of the same human family. He also argues that the pattern of Anglo-Saxon invasions of England after the fall of the Roman Empire implies the assimilation of the Britons living in Great Britain at the time. The resulting English type is already a composite of Teutonic, Celtic, and other blood. "A great mass of Britons must have remained in the country, their lot the obscure and, so to speak, underground lot of a subject race, but yet insensibly getting mixed with their conquerors, and their blood entering into the composition of a new people, in which the stock of the conquerors counts for most, but the stock of the conquered too, counts for something" (75).

Arnold's recognition that the English are already a cultural hybrid might be seen as countering the tendency to demand that citizenship be based in a phantasmatic ethnic purity. But hybridity, in Arnold's cultural ideal, is in service of the subsumption of lesser nationalities in the dominant (that is, English) one. He calls for a new hybrid nationality—but also for the continued dominance of England within the United Kingdom. These two calls are contradictory in terms since a transformed England would no longer see itself as needing to be the dominant partner. Moreover, although Arnold emphasizes cultural hybridity, the basis of this cosmopolitan culture is blood cousinship. By means of ethnology, Arnold prophesies the emergence of "a new people," who will be blood "brothers" (18). Cultural hybridity is endorsed in the name of political unification: in turn, unification is endorsed because of the cosmopolitan culture that it will produce. The relation is continually reversible. Moreover, the Anglo-Saxon element remains preponderant within the racial/cultural hybrid. As political corollary, Arnold opposes Irish home rule. When he refers to our "Welsh and Irish fellow-citizens" (xvi), he means citizens subject to government from Westminster. In this context, citizenship means subjection. In Arnold's words, "the fusion of all the inhabitants of these islands into one homogeneous, English-speaking whole, the breaking down of barriers between us, the swallowing up of separate provincial nationalities, is a consummation to which the natural course of things irresistibly tends; it is a necessity of what is called modern civilisation, and modern civilisation is a real, legitimate force; the change must come, and its accomplishment is a mere affair of time" (10).

The Religious Character of Post-1867 Liberalism

In her discussions of conversion to minority religious beliefs in Victorian England, Viswanathan emphasizes that the rejection of Anglican belief was perceived by Anglicans to be subversive of the state and its subjects. She makes this argument both about John Henry Newman's conversion to Roman Catholicism in 1845 and Annie Besant's conversion, late in the century, to theosophy. By the state, Viswanathan means the modern state, with its liberal policy of tolerance of religious minorities. There is, however, an important lacuna in Viswanathan's thinking, namely, recognition of the extent to which the imperial nation-state can itself be the vehicle of religious conviction and belief. In Liberal party politics after 1850, this happens in two ways. First, religious affect and belief is transferred to the state. Second, politics is often directed by religious fears and commitments.

In the 1850s and 1860s, English Protestant Nonconformists infused the Liberal party with the idea that national politics could serve as a means of individual and collective "moral regeneration" (Parry, 5, 28). It was God's intention that England should serve as the agency whereby the providential order of world history might unfold. "Self-improving working-men" (Parry, 436) were attracted to this view as a means of gaining dignity and respectability for themselves and other workers. From 1864 onward, Gladstone joined with working-class radicals in advocating this view as a basis for widening the franchise.[41] Gladstone was additionally influenced in this direction by discoveries in geology, biology, and anthropology that emphasized the production of large-scale effects through incremental change over long periods of time (Hilton, 45–46). Transferring this sense of change in time to politics, he argued that the "successive stages" of national development provide evidence for "the argument of [creation by] *design*" (46).

Gladstone had been an Anglican with strong Tractarian leanings in the 1830s. Although he later continued to share the interest of Tractarians in the sacraments and an elaborated church ritual, he came to reject the Tractarian view that the established church could function as an authoritative guide to the state in religious and moral matters. In later life, Gladstone professed moderate Anglican evangelical views, emphasizing justification by faith and the overwhelming importance for salvation of Christ's Atonement while playing down the Calvinist idea that nonbelievers are condemned to hell. In particular, he believed in the need for individuals to recognize the consequences of original sin and to experience conversion in order to be saved. In addition to faith, however, Gladstone believed in the necessity of individual agency both in the exercise of conscience and in action in the world.[42] This conviction matched his concurrent view that that the "vital principle of the Liberal party" was "*action*" (Parry, 431). In the concept of agency, individual and group effort, religion and secular politics met.

Gladstone's conviction, shared with Nonconformists generally, is important in three ways for Liberal politics after 1867. First, when transferred to the public realm, the belief in justification by faith demands an unconditional commitment to uphold the principles of the English constitution.[43] The force of this demand has a powerfully shaping impact on political subjectivities and, hence, on individual and collective identities. Second, the pattern of sin-conversion-conscience-atonement-salvation that, in Gladstone's view, structures Christian belief and individual religious experience serves as a paradigm for the political subjectivities of new voters enlisted as Liberals. Voters were called to intense moral reflection plus a commitment to political mobilization under the aegis of the Liberal party. Third, Gladstone's view of the religious character of political subjectivity helps explain the particular elements he brought to politics in the post-1867 situation: the mobilization of a coalition of middle-class with new working-class voters in moral crusades; the framing of these campaigns in religious terms; the invocation of a contest between the forces of good, on the one hand, and the forces of evil, on the other; and, consequently, the continual need for Others—Disraeli, Tories, aristocrats, financiers, Jews, and/or Ottoman Turks—against whom militancy could be directed (Hilton, 49–51; Parry 451–52).

As I mentioned earlier, Gladstone first learned how to mobilize the new voters by these means in the "Bulgarian Horrors" sensation of 1876.[44] Borrowing the melodramatic, narrative structure of articles that appeared in papers such as the *Daily News* and W. T. Stead's *Darlington Echo,* Gladstone's incendiary pamphlet became an immediate best-seller. In the subsequent campaign of 1879, he harnessed the popular agitation stirred by the press in the service of Liberal attacks on Prime Minister Disraeli, whom he accused of pursuing a pro-Ottoman foreign policy (Joyce, 195). Liberals contended that in doing so he sacrificed the Christian subjects of the Ottomans' European territories for the benefit of pro-Muslim, pro-Jewish interests, including those of Jewish financiers in the City. Disraeli's policy of noninterference made the English government an accomplice in crimes perpetrated against Christians in the Balkans, including sexual atrocities of sodomy and rape.[45]

Gladstone drew on the history of God's Covenant with Abraham and his seed in conceptualizing the character of English nationality. The most basic of these elements is a definition of the state that depends on the idea of a divine covenant. Another is the basis of national existence in the ownership of land and a literal genealogy, premised on a fiction of purity of blood. The story of Lot suggests that exclusionary violence is equally significant. This element requires that some individuals or groups should first be figured as external to the Covenant. Those so figured may then be subjected, in imagination or literally, to annihilation. Since the advent of gay historiography in texts such as Alan Bray's *Homosexuality in Renaissance England* (1982), critics and historians have frequently commented on how in early modern England those accused of practicing sodomy were also likely to be accused of blasphemy and treason. The theological term, sodomy, itself is a neologism based on the Greek word *blasphemia*.[46] What hasn't been argued is that Western concepts of the nation-state have been constituted in part in relation to the story of Sodom in Genesis. In other words, Judeo-Christian concepts of the state depend upon the imaginary projection of a condemned opposite, called Sodom in the Bible. Imaginary constructions of the national subject depend upon a shadowy, abjected Other, namely, the S/sodomite. For this reason, the figuration of sodomy has implications far beyond its immediate implications for men with sexual and emotional ties with other men. Sodomitic rhetoric has been a general feature of Western religio-political discourse.

Another feature of the biblical account is its reversibility. As Robert Alter demonstrates, the story of the destruction of Sodom in Genesis "becomes the great monitory model, the myth of a terrible collective destiny antithetical to Israel's. The biblical writers will rarely lose sight of the ghastly possibility that Israel can turn itself into Sodom."[47] The divine protection afforded Abraham and his kin is provisional, revocable, depending on the fidelity of the Jews. Accordingly, while the concept of covenant might seem to stabilize group history, it also provokes continual anxiety, lest faith be lost and infidelity be punished by divine judgment. Furthermore, divine covenant is transferable. While the biblical account of Sodom counters Abraham's kin to the men of Sodom, in the Christian period, Jews found themselves displaced across the binary divide to the place of Sodomites. Likewise, in early modern England, Roman Catholics and Irishmen found themselves shifted by Anglicans and other English Protestants into the position of the infidel and blasphemous men of Sodom. Sodom was getting crowded.

The drawing of linkages between national infidelity, Jewish conspiracy, and sexual perversity is usually associated with proto-fascist propaganda in England during and after World War I.[48] It is important to recognize, however, that this line of attack begins with Liberal and Radical politics after 1867. Liberal and Radical tactics in the period 1876–80 ushered in the era of mass electoral politics in England. This turn marked precisely the sort of vulgarization of national politics that many of those concerned about the effects of extension of the suffrage had feared in the first place (Parry, 30). Gladstone's strategy also contributed to the rise in importance of the politics of social purity in the 1880s (Joyce, 202). The "Bulgarian Horrors" agitation exemplified the sort of political party agency open for new voters. Writers such as Eliot, James, and Wilde quickly perceived the negative effects of this mode of democratization.[49]

As for women, Joyce observes that the pamphlet positioned them at the center of the moral campaign but in a way that had the effect of postponing their gaining of political rights. On the one hand, the rape and murder of women and children was the touchstone of Ottoman inhumanity (Joyce, 201). At the same time, the domestic values outraged by the Turks were embodied in the loving hearts of English wives and mothers. They personified what Gladstone termed "the great human heart of this country," which, in Joyce's words, "in all its moral certitude was now to dominate politics; 'the country' and 'the people' becoming moral principle incarnate" (195–96). For women, the way was opened to play leading roles in the social purity agitation of the mid-1880s. The agitation in turn exacerbated the tendency for scandal and sensation to become the medium of modern politics. There was, however, a price to be paid by women in forgoing other sorts of political agency. Both the portrayal of women in the Balkans as victims in need of male rescuers and the subsumption of female agency in post-1867 (male) party politics provided yet further ground for the continued deferral of voting rights for women at the national level.

Thus far, I have spoken of post-1867 politics with reference to "Eastern" issues that provoked Protestant antagonism against both Muslims and Jews. In the same years, however, religious issues related to Catholic Irish demands for autonomy likewise began to dominate national politics. According to J. P. Parry, these concerns accounted for Gladstone's loss to Disraeli in the parliamentary election of 1874. After 1867, Irish issues moved to the center of Liberal party politics, where they remained until the end of the century. In 1868, the Liberal party coalesced around the radical issue of disestablishing the Anglican Church of Ireland, an objective achieved in 1869. This success, however, sowed the seeds of a party split that led to overwhelming defeat at the hands of Disraeli. Unfortunately for Gladstone, disestablishment in Ireland prompted Radical and Nonconformist calls to disestablish the Anglican Church in Scotland and England as well, an enthusiasm that prompted Whig-liberal members of the party either to stay at home or to defect to the Conservatives in the election of 1874 (Parry, 430). Another trouble point was the Irish University Bill of 1873, which suggested to Whig-liberals that the government was prepared to support the role of the Catholic Church in education in Ireland, a role that they and many others envisaged as subversive of the state, anti-democratic, anti-Protestant, and anti-British.

Parry argues that religious concerns grounded opposition among Liberals after 1886 to Gladstone's policy of home rule for Ireland, which split the party and handed over the national government to the Conservatives for most of the remainder of the century. Irish home rule seems a natural issue for Liberals since it was consistent with their policy of supporting the principle of national self-government abroad in the 1860s and their emphasis on individual freedom and responsibility. But home rule clashed with the Whig-liberal view of providential history, according to which the state was responsible for shaping popular morality as well as for protecting individual freedoms, including freedom of religion. Presbyterians too, in Ireland and in England, feared, with good reason, that an autonomous Ireland would become a priest-ridden regime, unduly influenced by the Vatican to the detriment of the Protestant minorities. In contrast, Gladstone believed that it was the providential role of politicians to heed the truth of public opinion: *Vox populi, Vox Dei* (Parry, 451). The Liberal split over the religious character of governance resulted in permanent deadlock over the issue of home rule. This failure of Parliament in turn undermined confidence in democratic politics.

Friendship, Citizenship, and Democracy

The two instances of the sodomite that I have discussed, one classically based, the other biblically, exist in uneasy relation with another set of terms within Western political theory: namely, invocations of brotherhood and friendship that link personal intimacy with the ideal and practical worlds of governance. For example, during the "Bulgarian Horrors" agitation, male-male sexual assault was often referred to as Turkish "pederasty," a conflation of terms that could not but work to subvert the validation of pederastic tradition ongoing at the time in the work of writers such as Walter Pater, J. P. Mahaffy, and John Addington Symonds (Joyce, 202). Moreover, the classical and Jewish traditions are already interfused in the Christian Bible, most pointedly in John 13:21–30.[50] In this account of the Last Supper, the author associates Judas with the sins against faith and charity of which the men of Sodom are guilty. He is further associated with their sexual offenses through his betrayal of friendship-love for Christ (412). George Steiner argues that the phrase referring to John as the disciple "whom Jesus loved *('on' egapa)*" (413) is lodged within a Judaic-Hellenistic, Neoplatonic tradition that suggests that the love of this pair is both embodied and transcendent (419, 410). Steiner argues that this sublimating love is contrasted to Judas's sin against the love of one's friend, a sin that Steiner interprets as one of sexual jealousy (415). He further points out that Judas, "the son of Simon Iscariot," is the only disciple of Christ whose Jewishness is underscored. Steiner reads this emphasis as carrying horrific implications for the subsequent fate of Jews at the hands of Christians, including the Holocaust (416–17). In the figure of Judas, the violent exclusions of the Sodom story are carried to the heart both of Christianity and of modern political history.

In Greek and Roman philosophic and literary tradition, perfect friendship between two men is often taken as paradigmatic of the virtues that are necessary in a just polity.[51] For his part, Michel Foucault has drawn close connections between the formation of ancient Athenian citizens and the practice of friendship. Within the Athenian institution of pederasty, a citizen and an adolescent joined in a mentor-protégé relationship, motivated by erotic attraction, in particular on the part of the older participant, and directed toward education of the younger partner in the virtues required for participation in the government of the city.[52] Foucault argues that reflection on the "right use" of *ta aphrodisia*, "things" or "pleasures of love," was a focal point in the fashioning of the self, whose objective was the emergence of the younger member as citizen and equal of his older friend.[53]

These ideals gained currency in humanistic and court circles in the Renaissance, where they were formulated anew in the work of teachers and writers such as Roger Ascham and Montaigne.[54] But friendship was not merely a literary or philosophic ideal. In Renaissance and, earlier, medieval England, friendship was also a political mechanism of the first importance. It offered rulers, aristocrats, and members of the gentry a way to establish linkages with others outside the limits of the dominant form of affiliation, the "*deployment of alliance*: a system of marriage, of fixation and development of kinship ties, of transmission of names and possessions."[55] The practice of friendship provided an important means of organizing public responsibilities and patronage in ways not subsumed within the terms of alliance. Such friendships could be intense, romantic, and at times sexual, as, for example, in the friendship of James I of England with his de facto chief executive officer, George Villiers, duke of Buckingham.[56] Moreover, the political significance of friendship in early modern England required that such intimacy be publicly performed in words, gestures, and gifts. Both the function and the expression made it likely that such ties would be construed by political antagonists as sodomitic. In *Politics of Friendship*, Jacques Derrida argues that the institutional significance of friendship was problematic in principle. Within friendship writing, it was axiomatic that true friendship was disinterested in character. In politics, however, friendship had a basis in mutual interest and obligation. For this reason, writers on friendship argued that political friendship is always secondary in character (*PF*, 230). Moreover, both in friendship writing and in political polemic, subordination and the dependence of one man on another was seen as devirilizing.

While, as I have mentioned, Foucault emphasizes the relationship between the formation of citizens and emotional, and at times, sexual ties between males in Athenian society, Derrida approaches the issue of the relationship between citizenship, friendship, and male intimacy with a mixture of intensity and restraint. Addressing psychic aspects of friendship through the medium of Immanuel Kant's reflections on the relation, Derrida observes that "in its perfection, that is, as an unrealizable but practically necessary Idea, friendship supposes both love and respect. It must be equal and reciprocal. To seek it is a duty. . . . But one of the difficulties, in the very idea of friendship, comes from the contradictory character and thus the unstable equilibrium of the two feelings that are opposed in the mode of 'attraction' that tends towards fusion (love) and 'repulsion' that holds at a distance (respect)."[57] In this formulation, Derrida links a central democratic value—respect for the singularity of the other—together with romantic love and emotional and sexual restraint. According to this argument, fusion—both in the sense of psychological identification and in the sense of the loss of self in sexual union—needs to be foregone if male love, ego, and mutual respect are to survive.[58] Unchecked, fusion negates both selfhood and the respect for alterity that is a necessary condition of democracy. Love between friends animates the exercise of friendship in democratic governance, but fusion arising from this love threatens to undercut the respect for the singularity of one's friend that, in Derrida's view, is the basis of democratic idealism and practice.

At the outset, I observed that, because of limited suffrage, in the nineteenth century parliamentary government in England was a form of oligarchy. Parliamentary government was also oligarchic in the sense that it was composed of members of an elite linked by family, education, and association with members of other elite strata. Among members of these elites, friendship was highly prized. In the works that I examine, there appears to be widespread agreement that friendship "in its perfection" is "an unrealizable but practically necessary idea" in governance. For example, in Trollope's *The Prime Minister*, the prime minister, the duke of Omnium, seeks to realize a government of friends among the members of his cabinet. From

the start, however, he knows that the men he has appointed lack this reciprocal capability. And when events bear out the duke's initial assessment, he
falls into depression and loses the will to govern. Estranged as well from his
wife, he turns for support to his private secretaries.

One could pursue the conviction that true government is a government of friends by having recourse to biography. One might consider Alfred Tennyson's absorption in his young Cambridge friend Arthur Henry
Hallam, who, Tennyson believed, would in future become a leading figure
in British politics. Or one might reflect on Gladstone's romantic idealization of young scions of the political elite such as Arthur Balfour. Disraeli
himself became entangled in a series of friendships with young men with
political interests.[59] The study of Victorian political history would benefit
from better acknowledgment of the importance of friendship in parliamentary practice. This effort, however, is not the object of the present book.
Biographical reference can provide a sense of the motives and affects that
characterize elite politics in Victorian England. But none of the writers
whom I consider in the following pages, with the significant exceptions of
Beckford and Wilde, are known to have had sexual and emotional ties with
members of the same sex. Nor, even if others such as Henry James were
likewise entangled, is there a method available whereby sexual practices and
relationships may be posited convincingly as the cause of literary, theoretical, and political effects. Instead, my attention is directed toward aesthetic
contexts where mutual attraction in same-sex friendship, particularly in
mentor-protégé relationships, absorbs writers' attention.

These relationships usually exist between an older man and a younger
one. Often, the older one is experienced in the realities of politics, the other
a neophyte. The appeal of such friendships is pervasive, both in the attraction of fusion and in the notion that the perfect sympathy of a friend would
make the burden of political leadership tolerable, shared, and magically
transparent. Fusion, if it could be realized, would obviate both the work of
political tactics and strategy as well as the ethical project of self-reflexive
erotics—or *ascesis*—that characterized the institution of Greek pederasty.[60]
However, the dangers of fusion, discussed above, were well known to the
Victorians, who repeatedly traced them in their writing. This study covers
both tendencies within the dynamic.

Finally, on a personal note, readers are likely to sense the engagement
of the author in the pleasures and recoils of Victorian friendship traced in
the following pages. Since early in life, I have been fascinated both by the
possibilities of and the limitations of male friendship. Long before I read

Walt Whitman's celebration of the love of comrades in "Calamus" or learned the names of late Victorian homophiles such as Edward Carpenter and John Addington Symonds, I sensed as well an imperative to link friendship with the pursuit of social justice. It was only in university that I learned that this desire had been an important motive in cultural and sexual dissidence in the late nineteenth century. In an unmistakably Victorian register, for example, Symonds wrote in response to Whitman's ideal of amatory friendship:

> He expects Democracy, the new social and political medium, the new religious ideal of mankind, to develop and extend "that fervid comradeship," and by its means to counterbalance and to spiritualise what is vulgar and materialistic in the modern world. . . . If this be not a dream, if he is right in believing that "threads of manly friendship, fond and loving, pure and sweet, strong and life-long, carried to degrees hitherto unknown" will penetrate the organism of society, "not only giving tone to individual character, and making it unprecedentedly emotional, muscular, heroic, and refined, but having deepest relations to general politics"—then are we perhaps not justified in foreseeing here that advent of an enthusiasm which shall rehabilitate those outcast instincts, by giving them a spiritual atmosphere, an environment of recognised and healthy emotions, wherein to expand at liberty and purge away the grossness and the madness of their pariahdom? . . . Eliminating classical associations of corruption, ignoring the perplexing question of a guilty passion doomed by law and popular antipathy to failure, he begins anew with sound and primitive humanity.[61]

In the course of the Victorian period, an expressly sexual component of male friendship comes into view. This emergence proved influential in the development of the democratic politics of sexual dissidence in the twentieth century. For some readers, my commitment to this project will be seen to be something of a disqualification from the effort to understand friendship as it figures in Victorian culture. My concern, however, is not restricted to a sexualized male friendship. Rather, I engage numerous challenges to the concept of friendship that arise in a democratizing age. One of these, as Wilde points out and I argue in the Coda, is the challenge to revise the traditional view that holds that marriage and primary friendship are incompatible. Another is the question of friendship between women. Most centrally, another challenge, which this book attempts to begin to respond to, is that of imagining a conceptual space in which both the ideals and experience of a Whitman and a Symonds can be worked out while tenderness between members of the same sex and across lines of sex can be constituted in other ways as well. I have tried neither to foreclose nor to predetermine these possibilities since the work of activating them seems to me precisely to be part of the ongoing work of democracy in the twenty-first century.

Chapter 1

Pure Oliver, or Representation without Agency

In this chapter, I am concerned with the ways in which desire between men and boys is characterized by Charles Dickens in his early novel, *Oliver Twist*. How does Dickens configure the processes whereby younger males supposedly achieve parity with male adults? And how are these representations connected with issues of citizenship in the politically volatile opening decade of the Victorian period? In attempting to answer these questions, it is important to be aware of the dramatic shift from the production of books as petty commodities to the conditions of modern publishing that were taking place at the time that Dickens undertook the book. In 1837, Dickens the novelist was in the process of being born or, in a more apt figure, of being constituted through serial publication, publishers' contracts, and reviews that appeared in contemporary newspapers and journals with each succeeding installment. When Dickens began the part publication of *Oliver Twist* in 1837, it was not yet determined to what genre the new work would belong.[1] Only after the text was specifically contracted as a novel did Dickens begin to address questions of genre whose answers would determine how male relations were to be represented.

Traditionally, writers had retained ownership of their texts even when booksellers published them; but, in the 1830s, literary creativity was being converted into a form of surplus value for publishers through the alienation of ownership in copyright. In this way, a writer like Dickens came to be in the same sort of legal relationship to his publisher as any other worker contracted to an employer.[2] The new mode of production had other effects as well. Through serial publication, large new markets could be created. These markets had a particular class character, not popular or plebeian but bourgeois.[3] Factors such as these constitute, in turn, the possibilities of representation so that generic choices need to be construed within the context of the mode of production. For Dickens, these conditions were likewise implicated in the struggles over male suffrage that shaped English politics during the decade. The efforts of working-class Chartists for the legal reform of industrial relations and for securing universal male suffrage were based on concerns about the ownership of the product of one's labor that Dickens knew firsthand as a result of his complicated negotiations with publishers. The form in which these concerns could be addressed to a new public, which included Chartists and their supporters, was encoded within a new mode of production that shaped the radicalism that motivated Dickens's exploration of life among the underclass in *Oliver Twist.*

Michel Foucault has argued that Christianity demands of the subject an "austerity . . . linked to the necessity of renouncing the self and deciphering its truth."[4] In the second half of *Oliver Twist,* Dickens endorses such austerity by removing Oliver from the creatural satisfactions afforded by Fagin's den and insisting that the young orphan demonstrate his "true" self. This truth is, however, not religious but socioeconomic. For Oliver, what Foucault describes as "the problem of purification" focuses on his mysterious origin, out of wedlock.[5] From where, or more properly from what class does he come? The problem focuses likewise on his relation to the bodies of lower-class men and boys. The integrity of a *boy's* body can be affirmed only by removing him from the possibility of violation by these others. In the world of crime and poverty that Dickens portrays, the contamination of young male bodies is usually described in terms of eating and drinking. Within the novel, the sociable indulgence that once characterized lower-class life as festive and oppositional in character is relegated to the underworld of the *lumpenproletariat.* To cross over into this world or to be seized into it, as Oliver is, exposes the body to violent abuse and, ultimately, to annihilation.

While the character of Dickens's investment in Oliver's physical integrity requires attention, I have already indicated that this investment is constituted in relation both to the mode of production of the text and to contemporary political debates. Investments in Oliver are both psychological and sociological. As Jacqueline Rose has pointed out, these are usually removed from the field of inquiry by confining the analysis of desire in children's literature to a study of the author's intentions, avowed or implicit. This focus covers over the character of "the adult's desire for the child" represented or to whom a text is addressed. Rose emphasizes that this desire can be eroticized without necessarily being sexualized: "I am using desire to refer to a form of investment by the adult in the child, and

to the demand made by the adult on the child as the effect of that investment, a demand which fixes the child and then holds it in place."[6]

The phantasmatic body that needs to be defended, violated, and restored is metamorphic. Not only a child's body, it is the social body whose
integrity is threatened. The word "body" is especially pertinent because in
the early nineteenth century the island of Great Britain was a body of land
under threat of foreign invasion, literal and ideological. The constitution of
British subjects as a unified people, that is, as a national body, was one
consequence of efforts to ward off this danger. This incorporation joined
together ethnic and economic groups in ways that emphasized both unity
and a new and powerful sense of difference among particular groups. For a
generation after 1815, the regulation of this new body became a focus of
aggravated anxieties but likewise of democratic and egalitarian dissidence.
In the mid-1830s, as a disciplinary structure in its own right, the mass circulation of fiction in the form of serial publication over an extended period
of months helped bring into existence a cross-class readership.[7] But just as
patriotism simultaneously prompted an awareness of specific differences,
the creation of a reading public enabled not only dominant modes but also
a variety of oppositional modes of reading and writing.

Dickens parodies male mentorship at the opening of *Oliver Twist* in
the relation between the boys of the parish workhouse and the beadle, Mr.
Bumble.[8] George Cruikshank's illustrations, which accompanied the original publication of *Oliver Twist,* play on Dickens's treatment in a fashion
that borders on sexual grotesquery. In the first illustration, "Oliver Asking
for More" (Fig. 2), Cruikshank represents the relationship between man
and boy through the shocked gaze of Mr. Bumble as he stares at Oliver.
Dickens connotes gender inversion in the name of "Mrs. Mann," who manages the workhouse. Cruikshank supplements this suggestion with the connotation of sexual perversity. He draws an oversized spoon directed at a
forty-five degree angle from Oliver's crotch to the open mouth and popping
eyes of Bumble. Standing behind him, Mrs. Mann is a stick figure, open
mouth, and eyes. She "sees" the scandalous abuse of workhouse children
by those who are supposed to be their legal protectors. Michael Steig refers
to the illustrations to Dickens's novels as "an iconographic counter-text,"
but Cruikshank's text is counter only to the humanistic responses, appearing in contemporary reviews, that emphasize the humor, pathos, or satire
of the verbal text at the expense of covering over its expression of class
anger.[9]

Cruikshank's not very oblique reference to male fellatio in "Oliver

Fig. 2. George Cruikshank, *Oliver Asking for More,* in chapter 2 of Charles Dickens, *Oliver Twist.*

Asking for More" suggests sexual impurities implicit in the verbal text. Illustration permits the representation of a sexualized male gaze that remains literally unsayable. Bumble's splayed stance and bulging belly, covered with a big white apron, comment as well, in ironic fashion, on the representation of Mr. Pickwick in *The Pickwick Papers,* which was being published serially at the same time that the opening numbers of *Oliver Twist* appeared. "Phiz" (Hablôt K. Browne) plays with Dickens's portrayal of Pickwick as a genial sun of human contentment and benevolence by turning his large stomach into an orb of light at the center of illustrations. But the image can also signify excessive consumption when Pickwick's "legs are drawn almost as the naked lower body of an older man, the absence or almost total absence of visible indication of his sex serving to make him look somewhat grossly epicene."[10] Cruikshank, for his part, makes Bumble's obesity illustrate a hunger that threatens to more than swallow the boy looking up at him.

The opening chapters of the novel are full of ominous warnings about the sexual abuse of children. Oliver, for example, is consigned to Sowerberry "to do what he likes with."[11] These threats render less occluded the relations of desire between adults and children that Rose finds to be characteristic of children's writing. The usual negation of desire in these relationships determines what Rose calls "the impossibility of children's fiction," a phrase by which she means that it is impossible to address children in literature precisely because the constitution of "the child" either as a literary protagonist or as a reader is withdrawn from the field of inquiry. This withdrawal makes it possible to represent the child as pure while ignoring the impurities, sexual and otherwise, that attend it. Purity becomes an aspect of textuality in yet another way in the sense that in writing for children, "the child and the adult" become "one at the point of pure identity."[12] Identification depends on withholding from consideration the author's and other adults' investment in the representation.

Dickens's novel provides a more complicated example since there is little doubt about many of the impurities in which Oliver is implicated. The contrast between the degeneracy of his keepers and his purity puts that purity in question even more so because of the extraordinary lengths to which Dickens and Oliver's middle-class benefactors must go to prove him pure. The truth of purity, which the plot equivocally discloses, is impossible. Dickens stands on both side of this dilemma, proving Oliver's moral purity while confirming the illegitimacy of his birth. The same legal document, his father's will, makes both points.

Rose's argument helps explain a number of silences in *Oliver Twist*, including silence about male working-class agency. Because the threat of working-class insurgency in the 1830s was real, the character of such agency mattered. Dickens ushers Oliver on stage as a young representative of his class. This start implies a progress toward emancipation or, to use a Foucauldian term, "definitive status."[13] In the context of popular agitation, this status meant achieving civil status, which was denied at the time to children, women, and most men. Young Oliver's demand for "more" partakes in this effort since Chartists wanted the vote in order to correct economic abuses. Dickens characteristically resorts to the iconography of radical protest in the novel. For instance, the sale of Oliver to Mr. Sowerberry, the parochial undertaker, recalls the abuses condemned by Richard Oastler, "the fiery Yorkshire industrial reformer." His attack on working conditions for children employed in the Bradford textile mills "inaugurated the Ten Hours Movement and ignited a general controversy over factory labor in the 1830s and 1840s."[14] In 1832, Oastler condemned "Slavery at Home." Similarly, Chartist writers, disillusioned with the Reform Bill of 1832, declaimed ironically against their status as supposedly "FREE LABOURERS" under a "FREE GOVERNMENT."[15]

But, of course, Oliver does not grow up to become a *big* working-class hero. This outcome is excluded from the generic possibilities available to the novel in the 1830s. The English novel at this time included paradigms for protagonists from the *lumpen* but not for successful working-class spokesmen. A protagonist from the lower orders could be represented only if he were denied agency as a representative of popular reform or revolt. Dickens gains civil status for Oliver by plotting his rise out and away from the class among whom he is born. Doing so, however, promises to confirm the bourgeois (and generic) biases that diminish the humanity of the lower classes in the first place and which were used to justify their exclusion from the vote. The complicated plotting that Dickens resorts to in the second half of the novel has long been criticized for aligning moral integrity with class origin.[16] The ideological constraints of serial publication for a rapidly increasing readership limit his vision. But the constraints of political economy and aspects of ethnic, racial, and class bias likewise inhabit radical outlooks themselves. As Peter Stallybrass has shown, proponents of the working class such as Karl Marx and Friedrich Engels tend to bifurcate the lower classes between the proletariat, with whom they identify and whom they believe to be destined to become the subjects of history, and the contaminated riff-raff known as the *lumpenproletariat.* Dickens represents Oliver as a junior version of a working-class hero at the same time that his imaginary counterparts, Jack Dawkins, Bill Sikes, and Fagin, parody what John Forster, Dickens's biographer, refers to as "lower life."[17]

By insistently representing Fagin *as a Jew,* moreover, Cruikshank and Dickens participate in the tendency of writers like Marx and Engels to "use *lumpenproletariat* as a racial category."[18] Anxieties about purity in the novel find a major focus in Fagin's attempts to corrupt Oliver. This anxiety is at once extravagantly anti-Semitic and anti-bourgeois since to be deracinated is to be despeciated and thereby to confirm the conservative political view that the lower classes threatened the very survival of the human species. Dickens resists this view by taking as his protagonist a boy from the very bottom of the social order. Doing so, he challenges ethical and demographic distinctions drawn, on the one hand, between gentlemen and laborers, and, on the other, between the decent working poor and the criminal *lumpen*. He makes it clear that the representation of the poor as a nonhuman Other is an ideological construct of their class enemies. Further, in a blow at the pretenses of liberal reform following passage of the Reform Bill of 1832, he sets the novel within the reformed workhouses of the mid-1830s, an instrument of demographic regulation that reform had made possible. The New Poor Law of 1834 was a Whig measure, but it was motivated by a reactionary animus against the people that was lodged in Robert Malthus's widely held axioms about the dangers posed by excess population.

An alternative genre that was open to Dickens is that of the Newgate or criminal novel. Oliver's cognomen, "Twist," plays on this possibility by combining the associations of early, violent death with those of excessive consumption and what Malthus refers to as "unnatural passions."[19] "To twist is to hang, and represents an all-too-likely end for a parish boy." To twist also means "to eat heartily; . . . a twister is a very hearty eater." The word also connotes "perversion."[20] In representing Sikes, Dickens adopts the kind of narrative contained in books like the "history of the lives and trials of great criminals" (196) that Fagin gives Oliver to read. In this way, Dickens conforms to novelistic expectations. But by parodying them he invites readers to laugh at the rules of genre together with the moral and social assumptions that they encode. Conversely, Dickens refuses to plot for Oliver the route upward into the middle class that is signaled by the novel's subtitle, "The Parish Boy's Progress." Oliver is no Dick Whittington. The claim to Oliver's humanity rests elsewhere than in upward mobility.

Who is the purest boy in Victorian literature? One is likely to answer "Oliver," the little boy in *Oliver Twist*, who has the chutzpah to ask for "more." Doing so, he unwittingly confirms a principle of nineteenth-century political economy, namely the tendency of the poor to consume an excessive amount of resources. If someone does not say "no" to Oliver and the other poor boys who crowd Cruikshank's illustration, the population will grow unchecked with the results of "war, pestilence, plague, and famine" that Robert Malthus predicts in his study, *An Essay on the Principle of Population* (23). It needs to be remembered that this principle is scientific. "The causes of population and depopulation," as Malthus says, "have probably been as constant as any of the laws of nature with which we are acquainted."[21] Oliver's plea is consistent with natural law, but it also exceeds the natural order since it implies a threat to the survival of others.

The opening chapter of *Oliver Twist* both acknowledges and challenges this view of political economy. First, it recognizes Malthus's principle of "Necessity, that imperious all-pervading law of nature, [which] restrains . . . [population] within the prescribed grounds" (14). Second, Dickens represents an institution shaped in deliberate accordance with this principle: a workhouse reformed under the terms of the 1834 act. Malthus, who died in 1834, had long argued against the provisions of the old Poor Law on the grounds that the right of the poor to parish relief tended to promote "vice and misery" by encouraging population growth. In line with this view, the law of 1834 segregated workhouse residents by sex and mandated a "low diet to discourage paupers."[22] Dickens satirizes this operation.

In Cruikshank's illustration, the gaze that Bumble directs at Oliver's spoon belongs to him as representative of the bureaucratic oversight of poor relief. His gaze is the gaze of Enlightenment institutions as Foucault describes them in texts such as *The Birth of the Clinic*. "Clinical experience—that opening up of the concrete individual, for the first time in Western history, to the language of rationality, that major event in the relationship of man to himself, and of language to things—was soon taken as a simple unconceptualized confrontation of a gaze and a face, or a glance and a silent body; a sort of contract prior to all discourse, free of the burdens of language, by which two living individuals are 'trapped' in a common, but non-reciprocal situation."[23] This "confrontation," however unconceptualized, is beset with a political unconscious that fantasizes the lower-class penis as a huge spoon—a phallus that consumes as well as spends. It is excessively productive in contrast to the genuine productivity of manual labor.

In the language of Malthus, "man" is "impelled to the increase of his species" by a "powerful instinct" (14). Unchecked by "reason" (14), this instinct produces overconsumption. Humanity is threatened by cannibalism, at first metaphorical, later literal, as some eat the resources that are necessary to the survival of the species. Eighteenth- and nineteenth-century discourse about sexual perversity follows a homologous course. Spending/

taking semen outside the normal circuit of (re)production "threatens be-cause of its seeming *limitlessness.*"[24] These discussions are carried on in the midst of a continuous struggle over the allocation of resources. Malthus explains how the stresses that accompany demographic pressures result in increased concentrations of capital, higher productivity, and falling real wages (28).

Malthus first produced the *Essay* in 1798 as "a polemic against radical egalitarianism" in contemporary French and English thought.[25] Malthus, however, who had been educated in the very tradition against which he reacted, regarded his efforts as consistent with the Enlightenment project of improvement and with Christian theodicy since the need for prudence forced human beings to develop their moral and intellectual capacities.[26] Committed to educating the general population in the necessity of delayed marriage and reproductive prudence, he was "convinced that nothing would so powerfully contribute to the advancement of rational freedom as a thorough knowledge, generally circulated, of the principle cause of pov-erty" (243). This view was at odds with radical thinking in the 1830s, within which the difficulties faced by "the lower classes of society" were much more likely to be regarded as resulting from the denial of citizenship. The fact that most men and all women and children in Great Britain were de-nied the vote was a sign, at once practical and symbolic, of their lack of full civil status. The demand for "more" is a demand for citizenship—with all that implies in terms of empowerment and a share of resources.

Oliver is "the small rebel" (56) chosen by lot by the other boys to ask for more gruel. His innocence threatens Bumble just as it later threatens the police-magistrate, Mr. Fang, and as it threatens Fagin. Dickens drama-tizes the scene so as to parody Malthus's grim view of nature: "Oliver Twist and his companions suffered the tortures of slow starvation for three months: at last they got so voracious and wild with hunger, that one boy, who was tall for his age, and hadn't been used to that sort of thing . . . , hinted darkly to his companions, that unless he had another basin of gruel *per diem,* he was afraid he might some night happen to eat the boy who slept next him, who happened to be a weakly youth of tender age. He had a wild hungry eye; and they implicitly believed him" (56).

However much Dickens contests the political implications drawn by Malthus, he does accept a number of his principles. In the preface to the 1850 cheap edition of the novel, he calls for rebuilding London's slums because otherwise "those classes of the people which increase the fastest, must become so desperate and be made so miserable, as to bear within themselves the certain seeds of ruin to the whole community."[27] At times, he and Cruikshank carry over and exacerbate biases built into their representational models. In an engraving entitled *Gin Lane,* for instance, William Hogarth portrays the degeneracy of lower-class mores under the impact of the unregulated sale of gin in the mid-eighteenth century. "What traces of social, economic, and human identity remain, are being destroyed through intoxication, perverted into their opposites."[28] Many of Cruikshank's plates for *Oliver Twist* could be described in the same terms. Missing from Cruikshank and Dickens are representations that show the consumption of alcohol serving positive functions. For example, in *Beer Street,* a contrasting diptych, Hogarth shows the survival of "traditional plebeian sociability and solidarity" among workers in London.[29] In this plate, "the liberal sociability of Beer Street appears as a Utopia, built upon a harmonious balance of work, nourishment and pleasure."[30]

Elements of *Gin Lane* such as the parish overseer and the coffin maker's shop play a prominent role in *Oliver Twist,* but the celebration of consumption that appears in *Beer Street* has no correlative. Hogarth's allegory is replaced by the beer tavern that stands behind Bill Sikes in the engraving, "Oliver Claimed by His Affectionate Friends." In the transfer, what is denied are friendship, solidarity, and *fraternité.* In this respect, Malthus, Cruikshank, and the Dickens of *Oliver Twist* are at one. Consumption in Malthus's *Essay* and in the novel signifies social, moral, and economic disorder. The absence of a sense that aspects of plebeian culture continued to exist into the early Victorian period and that they had significant connections with the self-consciousness of the Chartists skews lower-class representation in the novel. This omission correlates with the absence of agency in the representation of Oliver. On both counts, the novel is contradictory, motivated by radical perspectives but excluding constructive oppositional practices and radical political agency.

The place of the people in British society changed forever as a result of the mass mobilization of men during the Napoleonic Wars. Motivated by fear of invasion, the landed elites, together with their allies in the government, press, and church, encouraged the development of a militant patriotism. This weapon, however, was double edged since "by summoning men from all classes, all political opinions, all parts of Great Britain and all religious denominations to its defense . . . , by treating them indiscriminately as patriots, the authorities ran an obvious risk of encouraging demands for political change in the future." Already during the Napoleonic period, officers learned that when they attempted to use militias in order to control local disturbances, soldiers balked. In May 1809, a private was rescued from a guardhouse by his fellows after he answered a roll call with the words, "Here, with an empty belly." "On several occasions, volunteers exhibited solidarity not just with one another, but with the local poor. In the north of Scotland, in the Midlands and in the south of England, volunteers joined and in some cases instigated food riots, or simply refused to suppress food riots when called upon to do so."[31]

By the early 1830s, many of the one-third of a million men demobilized during the economic depression of the decade after Waterloo had been radicalized, especially around the issue of universal male suffrage. The limits of the Reform Bill of 1832, which excluded 80 percent of adult males from the franchise, bitterly disappointed these men. The act belied the language of "patriotic union" that the Whigs had invoked in campaigning on its behalf. "Anger among the excluded was immense" (Colley, 349). These men possessed the numbers, the vigor, and the organizational skills to threaten the stability of the reformed Constitution. According to Linda Colley, this was the one generation of British men in the nineteenth century who could conceivably have led a mass insurrection (361–63).

The illustrators of patriotic prints during panics about French invasion register the ambivalence of the governing elites regarding the agency of workers newly mobilized in defense militias. In *Buonaparte 48 Hours after Landing!* (1803), the head of Napoleon mounted on a pitchfork is noticeably Roman. Even severed, the head remains that of "an officer and a gentleman." At the same time, "the artist has found it impossible to celebrate the ordinary volunteer soldier who is his fellow countryman without simultaneously demeaning him" (Colley, 283). Phallic dismemberment has more dignity than popular power. A reform print of 1831 inverts the tendency to deny humanity to the plebs by portraying them as John Bull's bull dog, toying with a parliamentary rat.

Dickens lodges middle-class anxieties about aggressive lower-class men in the figure of Sikes, thief and murderer, whose life ends in what is, in effect, the exemplary spectacle of public execution. When first introduced, he is accompanied by "a white shaggy dog, with his face scratched and torn in twenty different places" (136). But in Fig. 5, the dog becomes a mongrel bull dog. For his part, Bill acquires negroid features. Further on, after Fagin consigns Oliver into Sikes's hands for a break-and-entry, Sikes becomes drunk and falls into "most unmusical snatches of song, mingled with wild execrations" (193). This behavior parodies characters in the novels of Sir Walter Scott such as Madge Wildfire in *The Heart of Midlothian*

(1818), though an even more apt comparison might be with the Whistler, a young Highland brigand who is sold to a planter in Virginia, kills his master in an uprising, and is ultimately forced to take refuge among a tribe of "wild Indians" (chapter 52). Creating a nation of Britons to fight Napoleon meant downplaying ethnic differences, yet the string of associations that can be played on the word "savage" indicates the countertendency to project ethnic and class Others as racially inferior. Malthus, for example, contends that "if America continue increasing [in population] . . . , the Indians will be driven further and further back into the country, till the whole race is ultimately exterminated" (18). In making this observation, Malthus does not endorse the extermination of the Indians, but in describing it as a natural process rather than as a de facto result of national policies, he provides the grounds of an apology for annihilation.

Oliver's arrival in London adds the reminder of the additional threat posed by the cityscape of the "great towns" (23) criticized by Malthus. Oliver sees with a demographer's eyes: he

could not help bestowing a few hasty glances on either side of the way, as he passed along. A dirtier or more wretched place he had never seen. The street was very narrow and muddy, and the air was impregnated with filthy odours. There were a good many small shops; but the only stock in trade appeared to be heaps of children, who, even at that time of night, were crawling in and out at the doors, or screaming from the inside. The sole places that seemed to prosper amid the general blight of the place, were the public-houses; and in them, the lowest orders of Irish were wrangling with might and main. Covered ways and yards, which here and there diverged from the main street, disclosed little knots of houses, where drunken men and women were positively wallowing in filth; and from several of the doorways, great ill-looking fellows were cautiously emerging, bound, to all appearance, on no very well-disposed or harmless errands. (103)

But if Irish urban squalor, crime, excess reproduction, and intoxication represent one set of inhumanities, the Jew Fagin threatens Oliver's bodily integrity with racial contamination.

Here again traditional iconography intervenes since Cruikshank's representations of "the Jew" belong to a tradition of caricature by printmakers such as Hogarth and Thomas Rowlandson that dates to mid-eighteenth century parliamentary debates over the naturalization of Ashkenazic Jews.[32] These images indicate how alien to British nationality Jews were reckoned to be. The tradition continues in Phiz's representation of Ikey Solomon, Fagin's real-life prototype, in *The New Newgate Calendar* (1841).[33] Entitled

Doing a Jew (Fig. 3), the illustration shows Solomon having his beard pulled by a Bill Sikes look alike, who happens to be accompanied by a terrier ripping at the Jew's coat. These representations capitalize on contemporary ambivalence about Jews. Following passage of the Catholic Emancipation Act in 1829, a similar measure was proposed on behalf of Jews. Introduced a second time in 1833, the Jewish Emancipation Bill passed the House of

Fig. 3. Hablôt Browne ("Phiz"), *Doing a Jew,* in *The New Newgate Calendar* (1841).

Commons. Despite this fact and the admission of Jews to municipal offices, the bill "was consistently rejected by the Lords in one session after the other."[34]

Cruikshank's representation of Bumble staring at Oliver implicitly draws attention to the gaze that the novel's illustrations and text direct at the boy. Both Dickens and Cruikshank associate their judgments with the moral wisdom that Hogarth tries to capture in his engravings. This wisdom does not, however, exist in a universal moral discourse set apart from the Enlightenment project of general education. Rousseau and Bentham both imagine "a transparent society" in which virtue would be immediately evident. Dickens's journalistic scrutiny is in the service of this "universal visibility." However, such seeing is itself a mode of power, dominating the objects represented and the readers of the text. Significantly, Hogarth's friend and ally, John Fielding, whom Dickens emulated, was not only a novelist but also a London magistrate. In imitating Fielding's moral realism, Dickens makes himself the subject of a juridical gaze. Seeking to illuminate, he shows instead how resistant individuals and institutions are to rational benevolence. What remains most compelling are social and psychic "zones of disorder."[35]

Cruikshank's plate, *Oliver Introduced to the Respectable Old Gentleman* (Fig. 4) is a diptych to *Oliver Asking for More*. The workhouse boys have been replaced by four preternaturally aged boys smoking at a table. Fagin, grinning, looks at Oliver. In contrast to Mr. Bumble, he holds the handle of a pan of (pork?) sausages cooking over a fire. In his hand, he holds a toasting fork pointing upward to the broadside of a public execution, an image of Oliver's likely future under Fagin's care. As in the earlier illustration, Oliver carries an object at an angle, not a spoon this time but a walking stick acquired on the way to London.

Fagin provides the creatural satisfactions denied at the workhouse. But details of Dickens's description of Oliver's introduction to Fagin (the epithet, "the 'spectable old genelman," the toasting fork, Fagin's red hair) are drawn from the iconography of the devil.[36] Dawkins, who stands as intermediary, is "one of the queerest-looking boys that Oliver had ever seen. . . . He had about him all the airs and manners of a man" (100). What, apart from theft, smoking, and gin-drinking accounts for this liminal state of man/boy? What secret ties the boys so closely to Fagin that they dare not "peach" on him even after arrest? Why does he periodically arrange for them to be caught, tried, convicted, and sometimes hung? What motivates the extreme guilt he evinces before his own hanging? Why does

Fig. 4. George Cruikshank, *Oliver Introduced to the Respectable Old Gentleman*, in chapter 8 of Charles Dickens, *Oliver Twist*.

Oliver yearn for release from his bodily self while in a hypnagogic state the morning after he arrives at Fagin's?[37]

    Could the answer be sexual abuse? In a well-known essay, "Who Is Fagin?", Steven Marcus implies as much, beginning with a comment on "Alec Guinness's lisping, asthmatic, and vaguely homosexual Fagin," and later referring to Dickens's dependence on Bob Fagin, a fellow worker at the blacking warehouse where he worked as a boy while his father was in prison for debt. Marcus refers to Dickens's friendship with Fagin as "a companionship or affection which is at once needed and intolerable." The ambivalence suggests the "profound attraction of repulsion" that Dickens exhibits in the opening chapters of *Oliver Twist*. While these comments suggest the simultaneous existence of homosexual attraction/repulsion in writer and child, Marcus heterosexualizes Dickens's dis-ease by insisting that what Oliver sees after his first night at Fagin's "corresponds" with a primal fantasy of parental coitus.[38] Yet the Oedipal construction of the primal fantasy is only one possible construction among several.[39] Since Oliver, who has never met his parents, last remembers being given "a glass of hot gin and water" by Fagin, then being "gently lifted on to one of the sacks" (106), and falling asleep, other fantasies are more likely. An unmentionable act may be concealed in the darkness of Fagin's den. Whether sexual abuse literally occurs or not, Dickens's intense gaze prompts the thought. Modern surveillance is sexualized by the anxieties of its operators.

Cruikshank hints at perversity again later when Oliver, having briefly been rescued from the gang, is kidnapped and returned to Fagin. In both the text and the plate, *Oliver's Reception by Fagin and the Boys* (Fig. 5), the recaptured boy's new trousers receive a lot of attention. Fagin still grins, open armed while holding an open O of a cap. "Delighted to see you looking so well, my dear (163)," he says. The fantasy of introjection (Fagin's address recalls that of Grimm's wolf) is exacerbated by Dickens's suppression of the domestic side of Fagin/Solomon as reported in *The New Newgate Calendar*.[40] Solomon, whose criminal career ended in 1831, was a family man who made a good living first in London, then in New York City, and eventually in Hobart. His loyal wife once helped him escape legal custody. He also set up his son in business. By excluding relations of this sort from *Oliver Twist*, Dickens exacerbates the intensity of Fagin's relationship with the boys.

Oliver speaks in an idiom of stagey innocence that belies his environment. The contrast to the Cockney slang of characters like Jack Dawkins, "the Artful Dodger," could not be more marked. Oliver pretends to find thieves' cant incomprehensible. This refusal is a necessary ruse since, if he were to show that he does understand the grammar and syntax of the dangerous classes, he would be capable of choosing to act as they do. William Cohen points to a scene in the novel in which Dickens shows Oliver unable to understand either the language of theft or the language of boyish perversity. Cohen emphasizes the play on the name *Master Bates*, but the insertion

Fig. 5. George Cruikshank, *Oliver's Reception by Fagin and the Boys,* in chapter 16 of Charles Dickens, *Oliver Twist.*

of foreign objects into the boys' mouths during the scene suggests the act of fellatio:

[The Dodger] looked down on Oliver, with a thoughtful countenance, for a brief space; and then, raising his head, and heaving a gentle sigh, said, half in abstraction, and half to Master Bates:

"What a pity it is he isn't a prig!"

"Ah," said Master Charles Bates; "he don't know what's good for him."

The Dodger sighed again, and resumed his pipe: as did Charley Bates. They both smoked, for some seconds, in silence.

"I suppose you don't even know what a prig is?" said the Dodger mournfully.

"I think I know that," replied Oliver, looking up. "It's a th—; you're one, are you not?" inquired Oliver, checking himself.

"I am," replied the Dodger. "I'd scorn to be anything else." Mr. Dawkins gave his hat a ferocious cock, after delivering this sentiment, and looked at Master Bates, as if to denote that he would feel obliged by his saying anything to the contrary. (181)

Cohen comments: "The gloss on 'prig' that Oliver is incapable of uttering is presumably 'thief,' yet the persistence with which the term goes undenoted throws us deliberately back upon the signifier—where, with the alacrity of any English schoolboy, we might take the usual phonemic detour from a bilabial to a fricative and detect a 'frig' (Victorian slang for manual stimulation of the genitals)."[41] Oliver's silence has a confessional aspect. It is not that he *can't* say the word, it is that he won't because acknowledging what he knows might suggest that he knows too much. (The boys are lecturing him about how important it is not to "peach" on one's fellows.) Oliver's silence is complicitous but also (self-)resistant, a way of saying "not me" by saying "you are."

After Dickens's death, Cruikshank claimed that he had suggested to him the possibility of a more suitable collaboration upon a different Oliver. Cruikshank wanted to "make Oliver a nice pretty little boy" so that "the public—and particularly the ladies—would be sure to take a greater interest in him."[42] Disagreement on this point caused Dickens to reject a late plate, *Rose Maylie and Oliver* (Fig. 6). Cruikshank also wanted a different story.

I suggested to Mr. Dickens that he should write the life of a London boy, and strongly advised him to do this, assuring him that I would furnish him with the subject and supply him with all the characters, which my large experience of London life would enable me to do. My idea was to raise a boy from a most humble position up to a high and respectable one—in fact, to illustrate one of those cases of common occurrence, where men of humble origin by natural ability, industry, honest and honourable conduct, raise themselves to first-class positions in society. And as I wished particularly to bring the habits and manners of the thieves of London before the public . . . , I suggested that the poor boy should fall among thieves, but that his honesty and natural good disposition should enable him to pass through this ordeal without contamination, and after I had fully described the full-grown thieves (the "Bill Sikes") and their female companions, also the young thieves (the "Artful

Fig. 6. George Cruikshank, *Rose Maylie and Oliver*, rejected plate for *Oliver Twist*.

Dodgers") and the receivers of stolen goods, Mr. Dickens agreed to act on my suggestion, and the work was commenced, but we differed as to what sort of boy the hero should be. Mr. Dickens wanted rather a queer kind of chap. . . .[43]

Oliver is "queer" because he is not one of those "men of humble origin" who succeed in raising themselves into positions of respectability, affluence,

and influence. Lacking this class interest, the pure boy is suspect as a protagonist.

In its second half, the novel is overtaken by an awkward mystery, in
debt to the Gothic novel, that ultimately produces an Oliver whose parents
are gentle folk. This outcome is usually seen as craven compliance with the
expectations of middle-class readers.[44] Yet the one thing that Dickens does
not offer at the end of the novel is a representation of a conventional nu-
clear family. The fraternity of Brownlow, Mr. Grimwig, Mr. Losberne, and
Oliver with which the novel ends is too obviously an inverse image of Fagin's fraternity not to have something odd about it. Cruikshank conveys the
sense of something askew in the illustrations—as Henry James remembered
from his experience of reading the novel as a youngster. In *A Small Boy and
Others,* James writes that *Oliver Twist* "seemed to me more Cruikshank's
than Dickens's; it was a thing of such vividly terrible images, and all marked
with that peculiarity of Cruikshank that the offered flowers of goodnesses,
the scenes and figures intended to comfort and cheer, present themselves
under his hand as but more subtly sinister, or more suggestively queer, than
the frank badnesses and horrors. The nice people and the happy moments,
in the plates, frightened me almost as much as the low and the awkward."[45]
James experienced attraction-repulsion not only to the dangerous world of
the boys but to the "solution" of Oliver's problems through his adoption
by a ring of bachelors.

When Cruikshank refers to Oliver as "a queer kind of chap," he uses
the word in its primary signification of "strange, odd, peculiar, eccentric,
in appearance or character." James supplements these meanings with the
further sense of "uncanny." The word also signifies sexually perverse, including homosexual though without the full panoply of medical and juridical meaning that the term acquired during James's lifetime. The
significations overlap just as they do in a sentence that the *OED* cites from
Dr. Jekyll and Mr. Hyde (1885): "The more it looks like Queer Street, the
less I ask." The *OED* locates the quotation from Stevenson in the context
of "cant" or thieves' argot, citing writers of the 1820s with whose work
Dickens was thoroughly familiar. In cant, the word signifies "bad" or
"worthless," especially with reference to counterfeit or forged coinage and
currency. Dickens exploits the range of significations in order to provoke
anxieties by uttering the unspeakable.[46]

Brownlow and Co. fill the role of good fairies that Jacqueline Rose
associates with an especially pernicious aspect of Thatcherite Tory ideology
in England in the 1980s: the elevation of "the principle of the good fairy—

'little people who grant wishes and do good deeds around the world'—into a social law" that excuses government in abdicating its responsibilities.[47] Rose argues that this form of benevolence subjectifies its practitioners as well as their objects.[48] She quizzes the meaning both of agency and of good intentions. Describing similar operations at work in the guise of nineteenth-century, bourgeois benevolence, Dickens shows the instability of the innocence that the "good fairy" model projects onto both benefactors and child. The word "gentleman" provokes similar disturbances in the text. Dickens plays up the analogy, present in *The New Newgate Calendar,* between commerce and crime. The redundant use of the term "gentleman" to refer to Fagin works similarly to suggest the possibility of comparing respectable male relations with Fagin's travesty. In the overworld of bourgeois gentlemen like Brownlow, who eventually adopts Oliver as his son, the perverse suggestiveness of Fagin's relationship with the boys is effaced. But how can the spirit of Oliver's deceased aunt adequately account for and contain the desires that bind Brownlow, the boy, and Edward Leeford, Oliver's dead father, who was at one time Brownlow's closest friend?

Once disclosed, the mystery about Oliver's origins negates his innocence. Though he is renamed, it is not as Leeford. His illegitimacy likewise mars the memory of his sainted mother. Nor can a father be exonerated who permitted himself to be forced into a "wretched marriage" motivated by "family pride, and the most sordid and narrowest of all ambition" (435). The face of Oliver's half-brother, Monks, is disfigured by a "hideous [read venereal] disease" (439). This barbarous history turns against the upper classes the complaint that Malthus had charged against the lower ones. The Gothic plot demystifies the allegedly superior values of the "country gentlemen" to whom Malthus (247) appealed against popular unrest as "the appointed guardians of British liberty" (245).

Instead, Oliver's birth demonstrates Malthusian principle against the grain:

When a general corruption of morals, with regard to the sex, pervades all the classes of society, its effects must necessarily be to poison the springs of domestic happiness, to weaken conjugal and parental affection, and to lessen the united exertions and ardour of parents in the care and education of their children; effects which cannot take place without a decided diminution of the general happiness and virtue of the society; particularly as the necessity of art in the accomplishment and conduct of intrigues, and in the concealment of their consequences, necessarily leads to many other vices. (23)

Together with the absence of the plot of upward mobility envisaged by Cruikshank, the Gothic narrative of *Oliver Twist* shows how strongly disidentified with middle-class certification Dickens was in 1837.

And yet the transformation of *Oliver Twist* from a series of sketches into a novel was a crucial incident in the production of "Charles Dickens" as a household name and professional writer. The upward mobility ratified by *Oliver Twist* is Dickens's. At the same time, he was involved in a continuing struggle to claim his name and career. Serial publication of the novel had begun under the pseudonym of "Boz," author of the *Sketches* of Cockney and criminal life that first brought Dickens to notice as a writer of "serial-fiction." *Oliver Twist* became a novel definitively only after Dickens proposed it to fulfill the terms of a contract signed a year earlier to provide Richard Bentley with two (unnamed) novels. By September, his new friend and legal adviser, John Forster, was puffing the serial as promising "to take its place among the higher prose fictions of the language."[49] Bentley retained copyright to the magazine serial of *Oliver Twist* as well as, for three years, the book version. In the meantime, Dickens continued to struggle with Cruikshank over who should determine the general shape and specific details of the text. This dispute originated again in the commodity-character of Dickens's early fiction. *The Pickwick Papers* had begun with a publisher's proposal that Dickens write "a new publication . . . to be published monthly and each number to contain four wood cuts."[50]

Dickens's first contracted "novel" focuses on a legal document that seeks to establish an equivalence between the monetary and moral worth of an individual. In making his name as an author, Dickens was doing the same. Within this context, purity—of form, of motive—can exist only on an ever receding horizon of expectations. While writing the novel, Dickens established agency—as a husband, a father, a moneymaker, and a professional writer. But he had no way at hand of turning "the orphan of a workhouse" into a man who could convert purity into respectability while continuing to represent the classes among whom he had been born.

Chapter 2

Constituting the National Subject: Benjamin Disraeli, Judaism, and the Legacy of William Beckford

Shortly after the passage of the first Reform Bill in 1832, Benjamin Disraeli began to write a romance about a legendary Jewish hero named David Alroy.[1] Why did he do so at a time when he was attempting to launch a political career in England, a country where Jews were not permitted to hold seats in Parliament? Why, moreover, did the book, when published, bring Disraeli to the attention of William Beckford, a wealthy amateur musician and author of Oriental romance whose main claim to fame had been his involvement in a notorious sexual scandal? And why did Richard Harris Barham, a noted humorist and Anglican divine, immediately pen a parody of Disraeli's text, in which Barham identifies Jewish literary aspiration with theft and Jewish heroism with an assault on the established church? Barham in a poisonous sketch identifies Alroy and Disraeli with Isaac Solomon, the best-known Jewish criminal of the 1830s (and the model of Fagin in *Oliver Twist*, 1838).

In publishing *Alroy* (1833), Disraeli attempted to constitute himself as a national subject, affirming his identity simultaneously as a *minority* and as an *imperial* subject. As a young man, he wrote: "My mind is a continental mind. It is a revolutionary mind."[2] Nor did a single continent suffice. Disraeli's mind and travels included not only Europe but also the Middle East, where he traveled in 1830 and 1831, and extended as far afield as India. Because his personal and political ambitions were bound up from the outset with an identification with the British empire,[3] he might well be described as an imperial Briton. In Disraeli, this outlook does not merely extend the survey of the nation-state; it changes self-concept as well as the meaning of being a national subject. Commentators today are generally agreed that Disraeli's ability to speak as an "I" on the political stage depended upon his finding a way to affirm the fact that he was of Jewish descent.[4] Regarding himself as an imperial subject enabled him to develop a public persona capacious enough to include Jewish difference, but it was being Jewish that enabled him to make the claim in the first place.

Since both suffrage and membership in Parliament were restricted to men, the work of gender involved in becoming a national subject was necessarily masculine. In this light, the connotations of effeminacy that Barham and reviewers of *Alroy* lodged against Disraeli functioned so as implicitly to deny him the status he sought.[5] By affecting the dandy in his personal and prose style, Disraeli attempted to turn such criticism back upon itself.[6] Even more troubling for some contemporaries, through his investment in the literary heritage summed in the name "Beckford," Disraeli signaled the central place of desire between men in British politics, whether religious or parliamentary. This desire threatens to become as explicitly sexual in *Alroy* as it does in Beckford's *Episodes of Vathek.*[7]

In his earlier romance, *Vathek* (written in 1782 and published in 1786), Beckford is preoccupied with pederastic desire, the innocence of which he attempts to affirm by dissociating it from property, dynastic power, and family.[8] He focuses on the figure of Gulchenrouz, the thirteen-year-old boy with whom the beautiful young Nouronihar is in love—at least until she falls under the erotic sway of the Caliph Vathek. Vathek's first great crime is to sacrifice fifty of "the most beautiful sons" (42) of his viziers and great men to the monstrous Giaour, who promises to bring him to "the Palace of Subterranean Fire" (41). Gulchenrouz, however, is protected from a similar fate by the intervention of a "good old genius" (84), who transports him to safety in a Rocs' nest above the clouds. There Gulchenrouz finds his fifty youthful companions, whom the genius has likewise saved. The boys live happily ever after in a hypererotic, desexualized paradise:

Gulchenrouz . . . admitted without fear the congratulations of his little friends, who were all assembled in the nest of the venerable genius, and vied with each other in kissing his serene forehead and beautiful eyelids.—Remote from the inquietudes of the world; the impertinence of harems, the brutality of eunuchs, and the inconstancy of women; there he found a place truly congenial to the delights of his soul. In this peaceable society his days, months, and years glided on; nor was he less happy than the rest of his companions: for the genius, instead of burthening his pupils with perishable riches and vain sciences, conferred upon them the boon of perpetual childhood. (85)

At the end of the tale, Beckford contrasts "the pure happiness of childhood" to Vathek's pursuit of "empty pomp and forbidden power" (97).

Beckford, however, purchases this purity at the price of mystifying his own romantic obsession, at the time, with William Courtenay, a young aristocrat the same age as Gulchenrouz. Beckford saves Gulchenrouz, William, himself, and his fictive creations from the tensions of actual friendship and the sexual implications of pederastic desire by relegating these objects of desire to a sensuous but presexual paradise.

Given what I say in the Introduction about the sexual politics of male friendship in elite English society, Beckford's fantasy is "Oriental" also in the sense that it is removed from the actualities of English life, to which he himself would soon fall victim. The work is also in the tradition of the genre of the Oriental tale in France and England in the eighteenth century, whereby Oriental alterity provided, through exaggeration or contrast, a moral commentary on the corruption of European existence. In this context, Beckford's tale is harshly critical of domestic norms, especially in male-female relations. Vathek's mother, Carathis, is even more depraved than Vathek; and Nouronihar, after rejecting the boy, hastens with Vathek to the depths of hell. In contrast, Beckford affirms the innocence and seductive attraction of a boy. But this polemical affirmation is compromised by the need to withdraw it to an exotic never-never land.

In the first of *The Episodes of Vathek,* written one year later, in 1783, Beckford turns to the subject of the desire of a beautiful and powerful young man for a boy. Beckford intended to incorporate these short fictions within the longer text in the manner of inserted tales in the *Arabian Nights.* The *Episodes of Vathek,* however, were so unconventional that they remained unpublished until the twentieth century. In the opening lines of the first of these, "The Story of Prince Alasi and the Princess Firouzkah," Beckford, on the verge of his own scandal, introduces the problematic of friendship between a young man and a boy. Speaking in the voice of Prince Alasi, Beckford writes: "I reigned in Kharezme, and would not have exchanged my kingdom, however small, for the Calif Vathek's immense empire. No, it is not ambition that has brought me to this fatal place. My heart . . . was armed against every unruly passion; only the calm and equable feelings of friendship could have found entrance there; but Love, which in its own shape would have been repelled, took Friendship's shape, and in that shape effected my ruin."[9] As in *Vathek,* Beckford instates a binary opposition between "Love," which here means love of a man for a woman particularly in marriage, and "Friendship," which, by sanitary cordon, Alasi defines as excluding "passion." At the very outset, however, Beckford uses the episode to put in question this structural feature of the longer narrative. Alasi acknowledges his sexual aversion to women, by whom he is "repelled." But he is also forced to acknowledge that his desire for his friend—the young stranger, Firouz—is neither "calm" nor "equable."[10]

Beckford pursues this novel situation in two ways. One is by immediately engaging Alasi in the sort of internal examination and confession that Michel Foucault associates with the development of a post-Enlightenment view that identifies the truth of the self with the secrets of one's sexuality.[11] The other is by rehearsing Alasi's discovery within the classical rhetoric of male friendship as the proper medium of governance. In this respect the date of Beckford's fiction—written in the years immediately preceding the French Revolution—is crucial for, after 1789, it would have been impossible in England, the self-styled land of "liberty," to regard friends active in politics as constituting political representation in the state.

Alasi says:

I felt the need of introspection. This was not at first easy: all my thoughts were in confusion! I could not account to my own self for the agitation of feeling I had experienced. "At last," said I, "heaven has hearkened to my dearest wish. It has sent me the true heart's-friend I should never have found in my court; it has sent him to me adorned with all the charms of innocence—charms that will be followed, at a maturer age, by those good qualities that make of friendship man's highest blessing—and, above all, the highest blessing of a prince, since disinterested friendship is a blessing that a prince can scarcely hope to enjoy." (Beckford, *Episodes of Vathek*, 24)

Alasi's confused efforts at self-analysis indicate Beckford's unease with his growing awareness of sexual implications in the relationship with William. Moreover, Beckford was already growing disillusioned with his beloved, who would grow from angelic boy into an effeminate young man with an excessive interest in fancy dress.[12] Beckford's changing attitude suggests that it is a mistake to identify him exclusively with pederastic interests, as Adam Potkay does, for example.[13] Beckford thinks of intimacy between an adult male and a boy, ardent, embodied, even sexual, as directed toward what will become proper friendship between two grown men active in public life. In other words, as in Foucault's account of Athenian culture, such friendships are envisaged as part of the process whereby the younger male enters into the privileges and responsibilities of citizenship.[14] Alasi's idyll suggests the importance of ideal friendship within aristocratic circles; the irony of the passage suggests how far short of the ideal reality could fall. Beckford's later connection with his agent, George Clarke, and his long, intimate relationship with Gregorio Franchi, a young musician sarcastically dubbed the "Portuguese orange" after he followed Beckford from Portugal to Madrid, provide evidence that he enjoyed close relations with men of various ages who were subjects of same-sex desire.[15] His eventual choice of a condition approaching celibacy indicates as well the near impossibility that attended the complex set of demands that inhabited his ideal of erotic friendship.

Alasi's remarks place in doubt the possibility of a transparent relationship between friendship and the exercise of political responsibility. As he falls under the influence of Firouz, moreover, other men at court grow angry, seeing the prince's favor for the boy as a sign of disorder: Alasi's infatuation disrupts the proper relations of male hierarchy in governance. The resulting tensions closely resemble those between Edward II, the Barons, and Gaveston, the king's "minion," in Christopher Marlowe's play, *Edward II* (1.4.87). Alasi rejects the dynastic need for marriage and embarks with Firouz on a course of ever wilder crime that leads both, literally, to hell.

Although Disraeli's *Alroy* is also an Oriental romance, the text is much more overtly political than Beckford's since Disraeli deals with the Jewish question—namely, with the question of the place of Jews in a predominantly gentile society. This society is, moreover, both multi-ethnic and imperial, and, in these respects, modern despite the medieval setting. *Alroy* focuses on the career of young David Alroy, a latterday Jewish Alexander, who leads the oppressed Jewry of the Middle East against the rule of the caliph of Bagdad. Alroy's progress, however, is measured less in terms of plot and action than in the form of intrigues involving his relations with three older men. The first is Bostenay, the uncle who raised him. Bostenay's success as a merchant is outweighed by his acquiescence to routine humiliation at the hands of his Muslim fellows. The second is a Jewish rabbi named Jabaster, who urges the young commander to establish a Jewish state in Jerusalem; the third is Jabaster's brother, Honain, a medical doctor and "Marrano," or disguised Jew, who has abandoned his faith and concealed his identity in order to achieve wealth, acceptance, and influence.[16]

In *Alroy*, Disraeli attempts to validate friendship as a means of achieving religious and cultural freedom along with political agency. He also validates friendship in politics insofar as it meets the demands and pleasures of government in a multi-ethnic state. As in Beckford's fiction, however, the purity of the male ephebe cannot be preserved. The compromises, revulsions, and contaminations of mentorship capture Alroy in a double bind for they make possible his success only at the price of lost innocence and guarantee his ultimate failure. At the end of *Alroy,* Alroy, now become caliph, is betrayed by his Muslim wife, Schirene, and decapitated at the order of a king of Karasmé who is very different from the elegant young Prince Alasi. In the terms of a reductive Freudian psychology, Alroy is deprived of his masculinity; he is castrated. In the terms of Jewish nationalism as they were to develop in the course of the nineteenth century, the Jewish seed is dispersed as the seductive possibility of a renewed national center glimmers, then fails.[17]

In view of arguments put forward by Sander Gilman, Daniel Boyarin, and Marc A. Weiner, one could conflate Jewish aspects of Disraeli's text with male homoeroticism through the mediating term of "effeminacy," which, in Gilman's and Boyarin's arguments, is understood to render Jews improperly masculine and, in that respect, reducible to the figure of what, by the end of the nineteenth century, is referred to as the sexual invert—the man whose body is inhabited by the "soul" of a woman.[18] To do so, however, would be to telescope a set of stereotypical identifications that become fully elaborated only later on. Moreover, one would emphasize sexological contexts to the neglect of others. Effeminacy in *Alroy* connotes more the danger of the contamination of men by uxoriousness, an excessive desire for women. Anxieties about sexual contamination by another man focus on the institution of male mentorship. Concerning the latter, my claim is that erotic and sexual aspects should be construed at times within religious or political terms; at other times, sexual aspects dominate political ones. Depending on context, the two terms are reversible.

In 1833, the most salient other context was that of successful passage of the Reform Bill one year earlier. Although the exclusion of working-class men from the vote led to intensified political unrest among workers,[19] the victory of the Whigs in the subsequent national election ushered in a period of legal reform that seemed to promise the possibility that at least some excluded others might be able to improve their position. Men with sexual and emotional ties to other men hoped that the death penalty for sodomy might be lifted.[20] Following the achievement of Catholic Emancipation in 1829, Jews hoped that they too might gain full civil rights. And, in 1833, the Jewish Emancipation Bill successfully passed the House of Commons only to be rejected by the House of Lords.

The genre of the Oriental tale entailed commentary on contemporary political and moral conditions (*Vathek,* xvii–xxii). In *Alroy,* Disraeli shifts attention from class issues to others: in personal terms, to the proper function of friendship in a time of political upheaval; in social terms, to the need to diversify the bases of citizenship. The claim to purity that Alroy puts forward at the end of the romance is made in the name of fidelity to a reclaimed Jewish tradition. He can do so, however, only in revolt against Bostenay and both his mentors.

"I am pure."[21] With these words, Alroy in contrast rejects the demand that he become an apostate. His integrity depends upon being true to his faith—and his "sacred race" (261). But it is also true that earlier in the novel, at the height of his military success against the caliph, Alroy refuses to comply with Jabaster's demand that he establish Judaic law in his new kingdom. Instead, recognizing the status of Jews as a minority in the midst of an Islamic world, Alroy declares that "we must conciliate": "Universal empire must not be founded on sectarian prejudices and exclusive rights" (149, 148). Alroy/Disraeli points to a double moral about the need to reconcile minority existence with imperial citizenship. The necessity and sanity of this theme, which Daniel Boyarin has argued, in another context, to be a central one in Jewish culture, should not blind us to some of its implications.[22] For example, as Gauri Viswanathan has argued, the conciliation of British rule with local practices was a prime means used to maintain British hegemony within the empire.[23] Later, as prime minister, Disraeli would sponsor initiatives whose net effect was to increase homogeneity at home while contributing to the consolidation of imperial power. Furthermore, Disraeli the politician was not averse to exploiting the maltreatment of members of one minority group as an argument to defend the subordination of other minorities within Great Britain.[24]

Disraeli's emphasis on the need to avoid ethnic and religious fanaticism in constituting governments is very much in the spirit of the Enlightenment. Considered together, the double face of his moral is both rationalistic and universalizing, on the one hand, and, on the other, romantic, emphasizing the necessity of affirming Jewish custom and ritual, the *body*, so to speak, of Jewish existence. Disraeli defends this heritage at the same time that he rejects sectarian exclusivity, as does his father, Isaac, who published his treatment of the Jewish question, *The Genius of Judaism*, in the same year in which *Alroy* appeared.

Disraeli's affirmation of Jewish faith corrects Beckford on this point. In Beckford's tale, Vathek's long descent into hell has the architectonic structure of an opium-induced reverie that one finds in romantic texts by Beckford, Coleridge, and De Quincey. At the end of his progress, Vathek arrives at the tomb of Solomon, an undead creature who is represented, as he is presumably in Muslim tradition, as a fire-worshipping infidel.[25] Solomon tells Vathek:

In my life-time, I filled a magnificent throne; having, on my right hand, twelve thousand seats of gold, where the patriarchs and the prophets heard my doctrines; on my left, the sages and doctors, upon as many thrones of silver, were present at all my decisions. Whilst I thus administered justice to innumerable multitudes, the birds of the air, hovering over me, served as a canopy against the rays of the sun. My people flourished; and my palace rose to the clouds. I erected a temple to the Most High, which was the wonder of the universe: but, I basely suffered myself to be seduced by the love of women, and a curiosity that could not be restrained by sublunary things. I listened to the counsels of Aherman, and the daughter of Pharaoh; and adored fire, and the hosts of heaven. I forsook the holy city, and commanded the Genii to rear the stupendous palace of Istakhar. (*Vathek*, 93–94)

Until he is rescued by the angelic love of his sister, Miriam, Alroy follows a similarly idolatrous path: marrying Schirene, daughter of the caliph whom he has supplanted, and agreeing to attend Muslim services.

But the dream of Solomon figures very differently in Disraeli's text. There, through a standard quest narrative, Disraeli appears to solve the problem of the potentially degenerate effects of male friendship by presenting Alroy's maturation into a conventional masculine subject. His illumination is conjured not by intoxication but occurs in a dream-vision that climaxes his pilgrimage to Jerusalem. As his Cabalistic mentor, Jabaster, has predicted, Alroy there receives the sceptre of Solomon that confirms him in his role as the long-awaited Jewish Messiah: "Further on, and far above the rest, upon a throne that stretched across the hall, a most imperial presence straightway flashed upon the startled vision of Alroy. Fifty steps of ivory, and each step guarded by golden lions, led to a throne of jasper. A dazzling light blazed forth from the glittering diadem and radiant countenance of him who sat upon the throne, one beautiful as a woman, but with the majesty of a god. And in one hand he held a seal, and in the other a sceptre (95–96)." Alroy approaches and mounts the steps to the throne: "Pale as a spectre, the pilgrim, whose pilgrimage seemed now on the point of completion, stood cold and trembling before the object of all his desires and all his labours. But he thought of his country, his people, and his God; and, while his noiseless lips breathed the name of Jehovah, solemnly he put forth his arm, and with a gentle firmness grasped the unresisting sceptre of his great ancestor. And as he seized it, the whole scene vanished from his sight!" (96).

Alroy is empowered as the result of thinking "of his country, his people, and his God." His act offers a rebuke to the secular position taken by Disraeli's father, who, in his book, argues that Jewish heritage is spiritual not material and that Jews can be admitted to full citizenship only when they are prepared to relinquish the detailed observances prescribed by Judaic law.[26] This moment in Alroy's adventures likewise offers a rebuke to the author, who was also a "Marrano." Baptism into the Church of England had been forced upon Disraeli at the age of twelve upon the advice of a friend of his father named Sharon Turner. This influence was determining for, had Turner not intervened, Disraeli would have been ineligible to take part as a candidate, albeit unsuccessful, for Parliament in 1832. Turner played the role of a latterday Honain to Disraeli.[27]

The main erotic dramas in *Alroy* occur between men, usually between David Alroy and an older man: Bostenay, Jabaster, Honain. Although essential to David's fulfillment of the task of regaining the rod of Solomon, all three relationships are destructive. Bostenay attempts to corrupt David with the luxury of Jewish commercial success. Later, when Honain first meets David and declares his affection, he offers him the luxury of high office at the court of the caliph. Jabaster deprives Alroy of the counsel he needs to create a multi-ethnic administration and state. In his role as interpreter of the law, he intends to dominate Alroy's kingdom. David's disillusionment with all three relationships suggests how guarded Disraeli himself found it necessary to be in searching out the path toward an "embodification" that would enable him to link "character" with "career" (*DL* 1:447).

Shortly after the passage of the Reform Bill in 1832, Disraeli himself became an agent in defining the modern British state by outlining his political philosophy in a series of articles in the *Morning Post*. Earlier, his career had begun in typical nationalist fashion with an effort to establish a national newspaper (Ridley, 34–41). Later, in the 1850s, he owned his own journal, *The Press*.[28] In major aspects of his mature career—the extension of the suffrage to one million adult males in 1867, the attempt during the 1870s to make the Conservatives the "national party" by espousing a populist imperialism, the declaration of Queen Victoria as empress of India in 1876—he abetted the process of conventional nation-building that Ernest Gellner defines as "the principle of homogenous [sic] cultural units as the foundations of political life, and of the obligatory cultural unity of rulers and ruled."[29] Yet, as I have said, the very possibility of Disraeli's political career depended on the assertion of Jewish difference. Moreover, in the *Morning Post* essays and elsewhere, he identified himself against processes that Gellner identifies with nationalism but that Disraeli associated with the perfidy of political opponents: Whigs, Utilitarians, and, later, the Liberals. Commentators such as Simon During point out that in the eighteenth century, Tories, defining nationalism in terms of "patriotism," had emphasized "love of country" in contrast to the use of politics to pursue "personal ambition." Likewise, they affirmed traditional affiliations as opposed to the exercise of "state power . . . by the Whigs to make room for the free play of the market."[30] In the *Morning Post,* Disraeli writes against Whig reform from within Burkean tradition:

The King of England is the avowed leader of the Conservative party. . . . We have upon our side also the Peers of England; we have upon our side the Gentlemen of England; we have upon our side the yeomanry of England; we have upon our side their armed and gallant brethren; we have upon our side the universal peasantry of England; we have upon our side the army and navy, the Church, the learned professions to a man, the Universities, the Judges, the Magistrates, the merchants, the corporate bodies of all descriptions, and a large party in every town, agricultural, commercial, and even manufacturing. What constitutes a people if these do not afford the elements of a great and glorious nation?[31]

Just as the emphasis on Jewish particularity is at odds with the drive toward homogeneity, likewise this historically oriented, contingent view of what constitutes the nation cuts across what Gellner sees to be the main trend line identifying processes of industrial development and modernization with the formation of the imperial nation-state.

The passage also offers a good example of how individual subjectivity, in this case Disraeli's, can be constituted in relation to identification with a particular political party, a major function, as Joseph Childers points out, of Disraeli's later novel, *Coningsby* (1844).[32] Disraeli's Ciceronian period organizes differences into a "we" that is a multiple corporate body: "we" the Conservative party and "we" the people, embodied, in atavistic fashion, in "the King of England." The passage constitutes the continuum of a body at once real and local (the writer's body, the king's body) and simultaneously social and symbolic (the body of the Conservative party, the body of the people). Particular bodies (Alroy's in the romance; the king's body here) provide switch points at which these different sorts of embodiment coincide.

Disraeli's best-known reflections on the course that his self-fashioning would take occur in an entry in the so-called "Mutilated Diary" that survives in the Hughenden papers at Oxford. Writing at age twenty-nine, Disraeli weaves together his aspirations, recognizes the prejudice he must overcome, and indexes the narrative of Jewish self-affirmation in *Alroy*. In the passage, the particular word that he uses to refer to the process is one of becoming-body, or, to use his word, "embodification":

The world calls me "*conceited.*" The world is in error. . . . My mind is a continental mind. It is a revolutionary mind. I am only truly great in action. If ever I am placed in a truly eminent position I shall prove this. I c[ou]ld rule the House of Commons, although there w[ou]ld be a great prejudice against me at first. It is the most jealous assembly in the world. The fixed character of our English society, the consequence of our aristocratic institutions, renders a career difficult. Poetry is the safety valve of my passions, but I wish to act what I write. My works are the embodification [sic] of my feelings. In Vivian Grey I pourtrayed [sic] my active and real ambition. In Alroy, my ideal ambition. The P. R.[33] is a developmt. of my poetic character. This Trilogy is the secret history of my feelings. I shall write no more about myself. (*DL* 1:447)

Disraeli bases the passage upon a binary distinction between "action" and "writing" that tends to corroborate During's argument that while nineteenth-century nationalism tends to be associated with a militant, masculine ideal, aesthetic production, in particular in the realist novel, focuses increasingly on creating a world parallel to but removed from the "ethical" demands of modern nation-building.[34] During instances Sir Walter Scott's *Waverly* and Jane Austen's novels as examples of this shift in generic development. But he does not mention that what he sees to be an ethical retreat occurs in parallel with the destruction of imperial/republican aspirations at the time of the defeat of Napoleon on the continent. In Disraeli (as in Shelley and Byron), romantic narrative operates so as to keep the ethical demand for political possibilities alive. Disraeli terms the demand a "wish," but this wish really *is* a demand and not the wish fulfillment in terms of which Freud characterizes aesthetic creation.[35] Moreover, by insisting not upon transcending material existence but on achieving fulfillment in and through it, the wish tends to break down the binary structure upon which the diary entry is based.

The elements of the entry may be diagrammed as follows:

$$
\left.\begin{array}{l} \text{"action"} \\ \text{"rule"} \\ \text{"career"} \end{array}\right\} \text{EMBODIFICATION} \left\{\begin{array}{l} \text{"poetry"} \\ \text{"my feelings"} \\ \text{"my passions"} \\ \text{"ambition"} \\ \text{"character"} \end{array}\right.
$$

Mediating between these sets is the unusual word "embodification." The term construes the body as a place of active political, personal, and aesthetic formation. Disraeli uses the word as a synonym for his autobiographical fictions. But it also refers to the work that he needs to do to transfer his wishes into the "rule" of others in a political "career."

In *Alroy*, the project is twofold. It occurs in the narrative of a medieval Jewish warrior, DAvId ALRoY. But, as the partial anagram of Disraeli's name suggests, the text also provides a site for coming to terms with the problems that concerned its young politician/novelist/journalist/dandy/author. Alroy's "ideal ambition" is to redeem his people from their subjection to Muslim rule. In the course of the novel, he comes to believe that this aim can be achieved only by taking the power of the caliph of Bagdad to himself in order to establish a new regime based on mutual tolerance among peoples.

Unlike Iskander, the successful military commander of the short story of the same title that was published together with *Alroy* in order to fill out the requisite length of the three-decker book (Ridley, 127), David does not look the part of the conquering hero. At the outset, he is an androgynous youth of eighteen years, who lives comfortably with his sister, Miriam, and uncle, Bostenay. Despite his ostensible good fortune, however, he and his fellow Jews exist in abjection variously marked. For example, in the preface to the novel, Disraeli remarks that "the natural effects of luxury and indulgence" (x) have rendered the sultanate of Bagdad vulnerable to invasion at the hands of the kings of Karasmé. In turn, the novel begins on the day of the annual procession when Bostenay, as Prince of the Captivity (1), must bear tribute to the caliph. Upon his return, Bostenay suffers "the audible curses and the threatened missiles of the unbelieving mob" (1) of Muslims outside his door. Even Bostenay's success as a trader signifies inferiority. "Dreams, dreams!" he says. "We have fallen on evil days, and yet we prosper. I have lived long enough to feel that a rich caravan, laden with the shawls of India and the stuffs of Samarcand, if not exactly like dancing before the ark, is still a goodly sight" (4). The wealth of the Jewish community is a sign of its decadence and yet one more aspect of a general corrupting "luxury." In a statement of his own "Marrano" mentality, Bostenay says: "The age of power has passed; it is by prudence now that we must flourish. The gibe and jest, the curse, perchance the blow, Israel now must bear, and with a calm or even smiling visage" (4).

Bostenay's nephew, David, who is in line to succeed him as prince, chafes. As he says, his "pedigree is pure" (6), by which he means openly resistant to Muslim dominance. After he leads a successful revolt, however, he refuses to follow his advisor Jabaster's lead in establishing a "Theocracy" (166, 184): "The Hebrew legislator requires but little musing to shape his order. He has a model which time cannot destroy, nor thought improve" (157). Jabaster demands that the Jews leave Bagdad, drive the Crusaders out of Jerusalem, and reestablish the Temple:

"I wish . . . a national existence, which we have not. You ask me what I wish: my answer is, the Land of Promise. You ask me what I wish: my answer is, Jerusalem. You ask me what I wish: my answer is, the Temple, all we have forfeited, all we have yearned after, all for which we have fought, our beauteous country, our holy creed, our simple manners, and our ancient customs. . . . We must exist alone. To preserve that loneliness is the great end and essence of our law. . . . Sire, you may be King of Bagdad, but you cannot, at the same time, be a Jew. (162, 164)

Yielding to conspirators, Jabaster lends the authority of his wisdom and office to a palace revolt. Endorsing it, he uses the rhetoric of purification that Mary Douglas finds in Leviticus and that Julia Kristeva argues is directed against a pollution associated with menstrual blood, female sexuality, and the mother's body:[36] "Who would have the ark polluted, and Jehovah's altar stained with a Gentile sacrifice?" (191–92).

The opposites posed by Jabaster can be construed as a (masculine-identified) logocentrism versus a (feminine-identified) abjection. Jabaster's nationalism, however, requires not the expulsion of femininity but what he regards as the proper subordination of subject populations, including women, to Judaic law. The order that he seeks, including both masculine and feminine efficacy, can be signified, in psychoanalytic terms, as the maternal phallus.[37] The association of Jewish existence with an originary "womb" characterizes Jewish nationalism during the nineteenth century.[38] David Kaufmann, the Jewish nationalist who wrote a commentary on George Eliot's *Daniel Deronda*, refers to the Jewish "species" as "a wild luxuriance of unceasing growth" with an "inherent prolific power of propagation," a force of "unceasing fecundity."[39] But how is this force to be directed?

The work of the Jewish subject is to subordinate this power within a newly created nation-state. In psychological terms, it means disciplining feminized aspects of the male subject through the regulating concept of effeminacy. The ideal formulation of this order occurs in the relationship between Alroy, his Jewish mentor, and the law, whose minister Jabaster claims to be:

the Law

Alroy   Jabaster

In this formulation, Alroy's subjection to his mentor is mystified in the form of the dedication of both to the Law.[40] In the story, however, Alroy negates both in order to constitute himself as an imperial subject ruling a multi-ethnic state.

Women are implicated in the triangle in three ways. First, Esther, the female Jewish prophet, who attempts to stab Alroy to death after he marries Schirene, embodies the view uttered by David in the first chapter that it would be preferable to die rather than to remain the slave of infidels. She represents a gendered, ethnically identified aspect of Alroy's interiority that threatens him with destruction if his subordination to the rabbi should be put in question. She also figures a danger in the Jewish body politic: namely, its capacity to rise up and destroy an unfaithful leader. The other implicated female presence is that of "the Daughter of the Voice," a legendary oracle that warns Jewish leaders of impending danger. Jabaster introduces Alroy to this oracle.

the Law

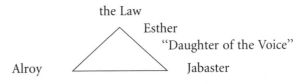

Esther
"Daughter of the Voice"

Alroy   Jabaster

In a note to the text in the manner of Beckford's annotations to *Vathek,* Disraeli quotes a source that reports: "Both the Talmudick and the latter Rabbins . . . make frequent mention of *Bath Kol,* or *Filia Vocis,* or an echoing voice which served under the second temple for their utmost refuge of revelation. For when [the original] oracle was ceased, and prophecy was decayed and gone, they had, as they say, certain strange and extraordinary voices upon certain extraordinary occasions, which were their warnings and advertisements in some special matters." Equivocally, Disraeli cites another source that contends that while the voice "was used for a testimony from heaven, [it] was indeed performed by magic art" (271). Mysteriously, however, after Jabaster's death, the voice is heard one more time at the scene of Alroy's execution (265). Jabaster's access to the voice offers Alroy access to his own messianic future. The dubeity of the oracle, however, implies the abuse by the rabbis of secret knowledge in order to secure their objectives.

The allegation, a commonplace of modern anti-Semitism, recurs at the end of the novel when, after yet one more turn of the political wheel, Schirene denounces Alroy to the King of Karasmé as a black magician. Predictably, Honain transfers his loyalties to the new conqueror.

While Alroy waits in prison, the forces unleashed by his betrayal of Judaism are brought back into alignment by a rearticulated triangulation in a third term. Alroy's devoted, "pure" sister, Miriam, serves as the term that restores Alroy to Jabaster.

The reconciliation of the pair enables David to be reunited with Jabaster, who returns to him in a vision "full of love" (254). The relation of the trio seems to correspond with Eve Kosofsky Sedgwick's model of male homosocial triangulation, in which the intensities of male-male attraction/repulsion are mediated through a single female figure. But Miriam's function may better be staged in binary terms that emphasize the reliance of this relationship on the Byronic/Shelleyan ideal of twinning affection between a young man and woman, usually brother and sister. In this context, Miriam's unsullied faith in her brother mirrors to him the broken covenant of his relationship with Jabaster as mediated by devotion to Judaic law. The female Other is the male self's imaginary Other. Moreover, this binary relation connotes perversity since brother-sister love, in Byron's biography and in texts such as *Manfred,* has incestuous overtones.[41] Disraeli does not exploit the inversion of this ideal, but it cannot be altogether dismissed from mind in view of the book's emphasis both on infidelity and perversity in closely related contexts.

In the imperial context of the multi-ethnic state, Schirene, to whom Honain introduces Alroy and whom he has selected as the vehicle of his continuing influence at court, provides the familiar Sedgwickian figure of the woman who mediates desire between two men. She mirrors David's androgyny, at first playfully, then with increasing perversity: "If I were only a man!" she exclaims. "What a hero you would be!" Honain rejoins. Schirene continues:"I should like to live in endless confusion." Honain comments: "I have not the least doubt of it" (70). Female gender transgression results in personal and social disorder, ultimately in the execution of Alroy;

but Schirene's delight in "confusion" suggests as well Alroy's confusion about his status as a masculine subject.

If the relation to femininity is unruly, Disraeli is even more anxious about the dangers of intimacy in mentor-protégé relations, which seem to put in question the very existence of both the masculine subject and the identification of masculinity with proper authority. This point is suggested at the end of Alroy's dream-vision of Solomon, when "the unresisting sceptre" that he has seized vanishes "from his sight." Alroy then wakens, with a start, to find himself, inexplicably, in the arms of Jabaster. "He faintly moved his limbs; he would have raised his hand to his bewildered brain, but found that it grasped a sceptre. The memory of the past returned to him. He tried to rise, and found that he was reposing in the arms of a human being. He turned his head; he met the anxious gaze of Jabaster!" (97). The sceptre authenticates the experience Alroy has just had. But is it, like the voice of the daughter of the people, just another toy in Jabaster's bag of tricks? Is the dream just ended Alroy's or a hallucination induced by his mentor? And since Alroy is traveling without Jabaster, how does it happen that the latter appears in Jerusalem at this moment? Or is Alroy's entire pilgrimage to Israel yet one more of Jabaster's mirages? There is good reason for Jabaster to be "anxious" about the young man under his "gaze" at this moment. Alroy too has reason to direct an anxious gaze towards the rabbi, whose very name threatens to disintegrate into a series of words with troubling meanings—jabber, jabster, jokester . . .

In Beckford's, "The Story of Prince Alasi and the Princess Firouzkah," skepticism about the governance of friends quickly degenerates into cynicism; in *Alroy,* cynicism becomes nihilism. Mentorship threatens to dispel as illusory the very knowledge-power that it promises to communicate and instate. The same paradox haunts Alroy's relationship with Jabaster's brother, Honain, the renegade Jew. Honain confesses his love to Alroy shortly before introducing him to Schirene. The "moral" to be derived from the example of Honain, however, is that the one constant of the politician's life is the pursuit and exercise of power—stripped of any group or individual allegiance. Within this context, to become an imperial ruler becomes an act devoid of human significance.

By focusing on Alroy's betrayal by his wife and male mentors or by insisting on Alroy's beheading as the moment of narrative closure, one could find the text to be dominated by sexual panic in the face of any desire directed toward a male. To do so, however, would be to miss the delight in young men that also motivates Disraeli's writing. It's important to recognize the worldliness that welcomed this pleasure and made it possible for Beckford and Disraeli to meet. In addition to the lure of Alroy's androgynous male beauty, the interchange between the two men reinscribes, in an Oriental setting, the neoclassic myth of artistic genius, one of whose cardinal signs is attraction (emotional, aesthetic, and often sexual) to youths. In the scholarly annotation that he appends to *Vathek*, Beckford links "these supposed intermediate creatures between God and man" in Islamic mythology with the Ωντες and Εωντες of Platonic tradition (99).

In the eighteenth century, in contrast to other aestheticians such as Edmund Burke and Immanuel Kant, Johann Winckelmann finds the norm of beauty to exist in the sculpture of a desirable male.[42] Of figures such as the winged ephebe of the Borghese Genius or Eros (Louvre), brought back to Paris by Napoleon after the conquest of Italy,[43] Winckelmann writes: "What human conception of divinity in sensuous form could be worthier and more enchanting to the imagination than the state of an eternal youth and spring-time of life, whose recollection even in our later years can gladden us? This corresponded to the idea of the immutability of divine being, and a beautiful godly physique awakens tenderness and love, that can transport the soul into a sweet dream of ecstasy, the state of bliss that is sought in all religions, whether they understand it correctly or not."[44] Winckelmann's transposition of religious idealism into an erotic and aesthetic ideal suffuses both the representation of Alroy and the term "genius," which was variously ascribed to Disraeli by Beckford, by reviewers, and himself.[45] This particular embodification helps explain both the response of the reviewer for *The Athenaeum,* who recognized "genius . . . stamped on every page" as well as the complaint in the *American Monthly Review* that the style showed the want of gentlemanly "pure taste."[46] In contrast to the pure bliss of Winckelmann's response, the reviewer uses the term in the opposed, Kantian sense of being free from an excessive attraction to Apollonian beauty.

Genius is not confined to the realm of taste. As the connection between the Borghese Genius and Napoleon suggests, this figure and others such as the *Apollo Belvedere* that Winckelmann celebrates (and the King Solomon, "beautiful as a woman," whom Disraeli describes) are associated with an aristocratic ideal of heroic action. The conjunction of seductive beauty, aesthetic idealism, and "a true heroic loftiness of soul" throws into relief Alroy's description of himself as a young Alexander.[47] Praising "the heroism of the youthful and still lovely Alroy" (Oliver, 300), Beckford responds to the combination of youthful beauty and adult valor and accomplishment in Disraeli's presentation. This neoclassic amalgam subtends the erotic tenor of his concept of imagination, which refers to a genius both aesthetic and political. The heady combination informs, in turn, his investment in Alroy's relationships with Jabaster and Honain.

In the 1830s, Beckford, now in old age, was about to enjoy renewed literary celebrity as a result of the publication of his travel writing, *Italy: With Sketches of Spain and Portugal* (1834). After having been forced into exile in 1785 as a result of his imaginatively productive but personally disastrous and unfortunate infatuation with Courtenay, later Earl of Devon, Beckford eventually returned to a life of retirement in England.[48] I say "unfortunate" because Lord Loughborough, Courtenay's uncle by marriage, was a bitter rival and political enemy of Beckford's guardian, the lord chancellor, Lord Thurlow. Add to this Loughborough's envy and dislike for the witty, effeminate, very wealthy young man; Beckford's irritating show of interest in Courtenay; and the fact that the newspapers were reporting that he was about to be named Lord Beckford of Fonthill, and Loughborough had more than sufficient motive to attempt to entrap Beckford in a sexual indiscretion with his wife's nephew. Even though Loughborough failed in this objective, he used gossip and the press in order to force Beckford to flee the country. The point of these details is not merely anecdotal. The wealth of Beckford and Courtenay, their parliamentary connections and aristocratic ties, far from shielding their friendship, exposed it to the politics of scandal. Minus these elite entanglements, Beckford is unlikely to have faced disgrace. As for Courtenay himself, years later, he would be forced into exile in order to avoid prosecution for sodomy.[49]

Beckford was implicated in Disraeli's expression of the "secret history of my feelings." Immediately following the passage in the "Mutilated Diary" that I analyzed earlier in this chapter, he writes:

Beckford was so enraptured when he read "the Psychological" that he sent Clarke, his confidential agent and publisher with whom alone he corresponds to call upon me on some pretence, or other, and give him a description of the person, converse etc. of the author of what he was pleased to style "that transcendant work." Clarke called accordingly and wrote back to Beckford that Disraeli was the most conceited person he had ever met in the whole course of his life. B. answered and rated C. roundly for his opinion, telling him that what "appeared conceit in D. was only the irrepressible consciousness of Superior power." Some time after this when Clarke knew me better, he very candidly told me the whole story and gave me a copy of B's letter. (*DL* 1:447)

In the trio of Beckford, Clarke, and Disraeli, we find the sort of informal social grouping of privileged men, bound in part by desire for other men, that existed before words like "homosexual" or "subculture" had as yet been invented. For Disraeli, such relations included other persons, often with connections to Lord Byron, such as Edward Bulwer-Lytton, Thomas Moore, and John Cam Hobhouse, who were familiar with Byron's sexual divagations. In the early 1830s there was an effort under way in similar groups, for the most part among Disraeli's Whig and Utilitarian antagonists, to relieve the legal sanctions against sodomy.[50] Renewed interest in Beckford as a writer in these years was symptomatic of efforts to alleviate the position of men with sexual and emotional ties to other men. As in the case of Jewish emancipation, in *Alroy* Disraeli intervened on behalf of legal reform by generating an atmosphere sympathetic to difference.

Beckford met Disraeli on only one occasion, a performance of Rossini's opera, *Semiramide* on June 12, 1834.[51] To his delight, he discovered that, along with a taste for opera, he and Disraeli shared many other interests. After the performance, they conversed for three hours. Enthusiastic about Disraeli's writing, Beckford was eager to learn, with Clarke's assistance, just how sympathetic or, to use Beckford's term, how "partial . . . to French" the young author might be (Oliver, 298).[52] He considered letting Disraeli read the unpublished manuscript (in French) of *The Episodes of Vathek* (Oliver, 298). Beckford eventually decided that Disraeli's "french accent" was not good enough to merit sharing the *Episodes*; but Beckford continued to believe that Disraeli's Oriental aesthetic closely resembled his own: "He is so strongly imbued with Vathek—the images it presents haunt him continually—the halls of Eblis, the thrones of the Sulimans are for ever present to his mind's eye, tinted with somewhat different hues from those of the original, but partaking of the same awful and dire solemnity" (Oliver, 299, 300). Beckford provides a guide to a sexually dissident reading of *Alroy*, noting not only the attractions of its young protagonist but also the negativity toward women that accompanies Disraeli's investment in relationships between Alroy and older men. Beckford also recognizes the importance of Honain, which later commentators overlook: "What can be truer to Nature or more admirable than the delineation and development of the character of Honain?" (Oliver, 299–300).

Beckford also enjoyed Disraeli's sodomitical play with the threat of impalement that impends over Alroy at the end of the novel as a punishment for supposedly having engaged in "intercourse with the infernal powers" (244), an allegation traditionally lodged in Christian culture against both Jews and sodomites. Disraeli archly withholds this fate while dangling it before the reader. In a note, he writes: "A friend of mine witnessed this horrible punishment in Upper Egypt. The victim was a man who had secretly murdered nine persons. He held an official post, and invited travellers and pilgrims to his house, whom he regularly disposed of and plundered. I regret that I have mislaid his MS. account of the ceremony" (281). In the 1835 account of his visits to two Portuguese monasteries, Beckford includes a similar sly reference to the mode of execution of Edward II. At the high point of the book, an account of Beckford's introduction to the Portuguese regent in the royal palace at Queluz, Beckford reports: "At this moment, the most terrible, the most agonising shrieks—shrieks such as I hardly conceived possible—shrieks more piercing than those which rung through the Castle of Berkeley, when Edward the Second was put to the most cruel and torturing death—inflicted upon me a sensation of horror such as I never felt before. The [mad] Queen herself, whose apartment was only two rooms off from the chamber in which we were sitting, uttered those dreadful sounds: 'Ai Jesous! Ai Jesous!' did she exclaim again and again in the bitterness of agony."[53]

Because Disraeli associated *Alroy* with his "ideal ambition," commentators assume that he identified with the young protagonist. They ignore his similarly intense engagement with Honain and the sympathies that bind the latter to Alroy. The word "sympathy" is tricky. On the one hand, Alroy's success depends upon "the strong national sympathy" (124) of the Jews. In this light, Honain is chastised for want of sympathy with his brother, Jabaster. Jabaster notes that, when the two men met after having been separated for twenty years, Honain "shrank from my embrace." Someone replies: "Honain is a philosopher, and believes in sympathy. 'Twould appear there was none between you. His system, then, absolves you from all ties" (182). In this context, sympathy based in blood ties is contrasted to a "philosophy" whose concept of sympathy is put in question insofar as it validates ignoring such links. At the same time, Alroy is right in refusing to identify Jewish identity either with blood relationship, subjection to Judaic law, or the refounding of the kingdom at Jerusalem. His imperial identity is based on coexistence with others and a model of Jewish identity whose emphasis is temporal not spatial, based in shared memory, responsibilities, and aspirations.[54]

Honain is susceptible to another kind of sympathy, which holds open the possibility of developing sociality on a basis of what Edward Said once referred to, in another context, as affiliation in distinction from and in contrast to filiation.[55] When Honain meets Alroy, he lays claim to a "pro-phetic sympathy": "I loved thee from the first" (59). "Our affections are not under our own control; and mine are yours. The sympathy between us is entire" (62). The mutual dedication of the pair leads Alroy, as conqueror of Bagdad, to make Honain his chief vizir (181). Of course, Honain has developed their sympathy exactly for such a purpose; his relationship to affiliation is altogether "wicked" (250). He plays the role of mentor much as, in the *Episodes*, Firouz plays the role of junior partner. In retrospect, Alasi writes: "Firouz knew me better than I knew myself. He played upon me as he wished. Besides, he had himself well in hand, knew how to act so as to excite my sympathy, and to seem yielding and amenable, as it served his purpose."[56]

As the novel unfolds, the full extent of Honain's cynicism becomes evident. This is the "realism" of the portrayal that Beckford finds so persua-sive. From the outset, however, Disraeli has made it clear that Honain is a Jew who is prepared to efface his identity in order to rise to the top. As David remarks when they first meet: "Thou has quitted our antique ark; why; no matter. We'll not discuss it" (61). Honain responds with a sort of Shakespearian soliloquy:

You see me, you see what I am; a Hebrew, though unknown; one of that despised, rejected, persecuted people, of whom you are the chief. I too would be free and honoured. Freedom and honour are mine, but I was my own messiah. I quitted in good time our desperate cause, but I gave it a trial. Ask Jabaster how I fought. Youth could be my only excuse for such indiscretion. I left this country; I studied and resided among the Greeks. I returned from Constantinople, with all their learn-ing, some of their craft. No one knew me. I assumed their turban, and I am, the Lord Honain. Take my experience, child, and save yourself much sorrow. Turn your late adventure to good account. No one can recognise you here. I will introduce you amongst the highest as my child by some fair Greek. The world is before you. You may fight, you may love, you may revel. War, and women, and luxury are all at your command. With your person and talents you may be grand vizir. (62)

Honain's apologia is likewise Disraeli's confession. He too reached for the highest honors and influence. Acquiescing in becoming a Protestant En-glishman, he had relinquished the antique ark. And like Honain, he knew that the byways to power led not only through women's boudoirs but also by way of the ineffable sympathies of male intimacy. It is important to recognize Disraeli's ambivalent engagement on Honain's side of the men-tor-protégé dyad; it is just as significant as his cathexis with David Alroy.

Disraeli's partial self-portrait as Honain anticipates the antagonistic, anti-Semitic reaction that he had every reason to expect proper Englishmen to have against this book. Just as the accident of the survival of Beckford's letters indicates one important context of *Alroy*, the existence of an unpublished manuscript, written immediately after publication of the novel, provides another. The Berg Collection of the New York Public Library holds the manuscript of the draft outline of a satiric parody of *Alroy* entitled "The Wondrous Tale of Ikey Solomons," which, to the best of my knowledge, has hitherto escaped critical comment. Although corrections indicate the manuscript to be a working draft not to be read by others, the text does convey the anti-Semitic attitudes of the English elite among whom its author, Richard Harris Barham, a well-known clergyman and comic author, circulated. Barham's parody is based on the idea of substituting Isaac Solomon for Alroy as hero of the narrative. Solomon had been in the news in 1831, when, at the end of a long, highly successful career in business and crime on three continents, he was transported to Hobart Town for receiving stolen goods. The life of Solomon in *The New Newgate Calendar* (1841) parodies the typically English story of the poor boy who manages to parlay a "small capital" into a large fortune.[57] Solomon was well known for his extraordinary effrontery and success (at the time of his arrest he was reported to be in possession of £20,000 in stolen goods).

Barham also includes a parody of Jabaster in the figure of the High Priest, who looks upon Alroy/Ikey with "large luminous eyes." Further details of the description (the "beard" that hangs "down to his waist-band, red plush breeches with yellow buttons," and "greasy hat") indicate that Barham's principal interest is in conflating Jabaster, Honain, and Alroy with popular representations of Jewish immigrants and criminals.[58] Barham's "Wondrous Tale" conflates anti-Jewish stereotypes with popular attacks on members of the lower classes, who contaminate the body politic through crime and grossly excessive consumption of food, drink, and intoxicants. To these charges are added the further allegations that Jews, being foreigners, can speak or write in English only on the basis of fraud. To Disraeli's affectations of genius, Barham responds that such "genius" can only be "a Literary Larceny."[59]

Anglo-Saxon, Protestant, middle-class prejudice against Disraeli was to characterize later representations of Disraeli the politician. In political cartoons in publications such as *Punch*, he was represented in the guise of a Jewish pedlar. And, after being elected prime minister in the mid-1870s, he became the target of English nationalism in other ways. In the mid-1870s, Liberals, Radicals, Nonconformists, and a number of Anglicans led a campaign against Disraeli's foreign policy in which it, he, and English Jews generally were attacked on the ground of what William Gladstone referred to as their "Judaic sympathies."[60] After Disraeli returned from the Congress of Berlin in July 1878, having checked Russian influence in the Balkans, gained the island of Cyprus as a British outpost in the Aegean, and guaranteed the integrity of the Ottoman Empire in Asia, one commentator wrote: "That day represented the triumph, not of England, not of an English policy, not of an Englishman. It was the triumph of Judea, a Jewish policy, a Jew. The Hebrew, who drove through these crowds to Downing Street, was dragging the whole of Christendom behind the juggernaut car over the rights of Turkish Christians, of which he was the charioteer."[61]

In the face of the unembarrassed directness of this assault, the radicalism of Disraeli's early Oriental romance is yet more evident. Disraeli defended Jewish cultural practices, religious belief, and historical identity at a time when they were under attack even by his own father. In contrast, Disraeli endorsed the concept of a futurity for Jewish collectivity at the same time that he dissociated the state from a singular religious ideology, ethnic, or racial identity. This double view demanded courage, subtlety, and intellectual toughness. And it is cognate with what Daniel Boyarin has described as the double tendency within Jewish cultural tradition to validate both Jewish practices and a vision of universal emancipation. The suppleness of Disraeli's thought and commitment help account for George Eliot's turn to the rhetoric of Jewish emancipation in expressing her own resistance to a unitary national subject in *Daniel Deronda* (1876), which she wrote at a time of both belated vindication and continuing vilification of England's Jewish prime minister.

Chapter 3

Tancred *and the Character of Influence*

In 1847, Disraeli published *Tancred,* the third and final novel of his trilogy on the condition of England.[1] After two opening books set in contemporary England, the novel's course shifts to the Holy Land, where the remainder of the action takes place. In making this excursion, Disraeli changes genres, abandoning the proto-Wildean tone and topical targets of the English sections for the moonlit landscapes of Oriental romance.[2] In so doing, he returns to aspects of his own earlier effort in this genre, *The Wondrous Tale of Alroy.* Key elements of that text such as the integral but potentially destructive character of friendship in politics and the place of Judaism within European geopolitics, receive something approaching definitive treatment in *Tancred.*[3]

In the years in which he published the trilogy, Disraeli established himself at the head of Young England, a small but well-known group of young Tory parliamentarians.[4] Tancred recalls one of these, Lord John Manners, a devout, thoroughly conservative young graduate of Eton and Cambridge. Tancred's friend Fakredeen recalls another, George Smythe, to whom Manners was devoted and Disraeli was strongly attracted. Smythe was a witty, indiscreet young man, continually involved in sexual escapades.[5] Despite the pleasure that Disraeli took in the mutual flattery of this circle, during the years of the Peel administration his career hung in the balance. Disraeli had begun on the wrong foot by asking Peel for office in the new government, a position for which he was not in line. As time went on, Disraeli began to criticize the prime minister in Parliament. Eventually, he broke with Peel and led an effort, ultimately successful, to split the party and bring down the government. It was a Pyrrhic victory. The Conservatives would not win a majority government again until they did so under Disraeli's leadership in 1874. Moreover, although Disraeli was left standing as the only highly competent politician in the new Protectionist party that he and Lord George Bentinck led in the House of Commons, party members were wary of entrusting leadership to the hands of this foreign-seeming politician.

At this juncture, the perennial question of political rights for Jews reemerged. In the elections of 1847, Disraeli's friend, Baron Lionel de Roth- schild was returned as Liberal member for the City of London. Since only Christians could subscribe to the parliamentary oath, Lord John Russell, the prime minister, introduced a motion calling for the removal of civil disabilities against Jews. On previous occasions in 1837, 1841, and 1845, Dis- raeli had voted—silently—on behalf of similar bills. Now, coming out in support of the motion, Disraeli repeated arguments in favor of Jewish spe- cialty that he had recently published in *Tancred*. The speech was met with disapproving silence from both sides of the House. Bentinck, who spoke in support of Disraeli, resigned as party leader when members voted against the motion.

What is the proper exercise of the influence of office? What role does friendship have among parliamentary politicians? Disraeli struggled with the first of these questions during the 1840s (Blake, 237–39). Among parlia- mentarians, debates over who was or was not a friend mixed with argu- ments about the propriety of excluding individuals and groups from Parliament on religious and ethnic grounds. Peel was vulnerable to charges on this score. Responding to one of Disraeli's attacks, Peel made the mis- take of quoting a line of verse written by an earlier Tory prime minister, George Canning: "Save, save, O save me from the candid friend" (Blake, 185). In 1827, Peel had refused to support Canning's move to remove civil disabilities against Roman Catholics, a move with implications particularly for Catholic Irishmen. The dispute that followed destroyed Canning, yet only two years later Peel supported passage of the Catholic Emancipation Act. In response, Disraeli promptly asked whether Peel had been Canning's friend. This question returned in the final stages of the effort to topple Peel when Bentinck, who as a young man had served as Canning's private secretary, attacked Peel for having "chased and hunted an illustrious rela- tive of mine to death" (Blake, 240). The dumping of Peel and the split among Tories over the Jewish question foregrounded questions about loy- alty and betrayal among gentlemen and fellow party members. Nor was it self-evident whether friendships could exist between Gentiles and Jews. The pressures of these concerns make themselves felt in Disraeli's novel.

Tancred leaves England because he is disillusioned with modern life. He is a devout Christian but finds no faith in contemporary England, no principle upon which individual duty might be based. While this disorder is expressed in terms of a personal crisis, he also sees it, politically, in terms of the disintegration of the British Constitution. The monarchy has been deprived of its prerogatives. The aristocracy may lose theirs. And as for democracy, on the one hand, no one believes in it. On the other, the people don't think and therefore are incapable of governing themselves. Tancred hopes, by going to the Holy Land, to find a principle of public and private conduct. Once there, he appears to find it—in the prophetic utterances of Eva, a beautiful young Jewish woman, with whom he falls in love, and in the flattery and scheming of Fakredeen, a young Maronite Christian emir, who becomes both an intimate friend and a political ally. Tancred and Fakredeen agree to lead an armed struggle to free Syria from Turkish domination.[6] At the end of the novel, however, Tancred learns that Eva will not be his. He also learns that, as a result of Fakredeen's betrayal, he has become the "unconscious agent" of a "great mystification."[7] At this point, it is time to return home.

Tancred in its final two books focuses on the romance and failures of male friendship. In these final sections, Disraeli likewise becomes outspoken about the contempt and violence faced by Jews. It's as though he could sense the open resistance he was about to meet on the Jewish question from his colleagues in Parliament. In Book 5, this animosity is expressed both by Gentiles, including Anglo-Saxons, and by fellow Semites in Syria. Neither in the West nor in Asia are Jews safe. In *Coningsby* (1844) and *Sybil* (1845), earlier novels in the trilogy, Disraeli's leading political concern appears to be anxiety about the possible outbreak of class warfare in England. In *Tancred,* the threat to Jewish survival, both in Europe and the Ottoman Empire, is of foremost concern.

The novel is preoccupied with the effects of friendship and of race. In Syria, Tancred is kidnapped for ransom. Once prisoner, he meets Fakredeen. Unbeknownst to Tancred, who finds himself "attracted to the young stranger" (248), Fakredeen (that is, fakir, faker) is responsible for his abduction by the Jewish Bedouin leader, "Amalek, great Sheikh of the Rechabite Bedoueen" (243). Fakredeen is likewise attracted, and the two men become fast friends. What is one to make of the language that the narrator uses to describe Fakredeen's infatuation? "His mind and his heart were so absorbed at this moment by the image of Tancred, and he was so entirely under the influence of his own idealised conceptions of his new and latest friend, that, according to his custom, no other being could interest him" (296).

Disraeli describes the connection in terms of "influence," a word whose force is characterized in the speculative terms of magnetic attraction.[8] These terms are romantic, invoking the concept of elective affinities between soul mates, often a man and a woman, and scientific, depending on notions of mesmeric influence.[9] In this light, while influence is experienced between persons, influence is not simply a question of physical attractiveness, personality, et cetera. Influence is a mode of physics. And it is bipolar not unipolar. It works in both directions. For example, although in Book 5 the narrator frequently speaks of Tancred's influence on Fakredeen, when they first meet the flow of energy is in the opposite direction. Tancred himself, however, and English character more generally, are to a degree reserved from the homoerotic charge of the connection by the narrator's emphasis on the young Arab's emotional volatility.

Magnetic attraction is an aspect of natural science; but in the passage, the narrator understands it in psychological terms. Influence is reflexive, the effect of one's "idealised" projections onto another. Although the mesmeric influence is often described in terms of a man's power over a woman, in the novel the screen of projection is interchangeably male or female. And the connection lacks durability. Tancred is not Fakredeen's last friend, only the newest and "latest," an adjective that suggests that Tancred too will be superseded. This is precisely what happens in Book 5, where Fakredeen finds himself as violently repelled by Tancred as he was forcibly attracted earlier. At the same time, Fakredeen shifts his focus to a new object, Astarte, the mountain queen. Similarly, just before Fakredeen becomes entangled with Tancred, he has sworn devotion to his foster-sister, the wealthy Eva. Given Fakredeen's oscillation between male and female objects of fascination,[10] it should be kept in mind that Disraeli describes Fakredeen's "love" of women as distinctly unfamilial. Indeed, Fakredeen is "totally insensible to domestic joys." Rather, his wish to marry Eva is based on the positive fact of Jewish money: "He wished to connect himself with great capitalists, and hoped to gain the Lebanon loan for a dower" (218).

In these fixations, what matters is not the gender of the object but the relation of the subject to itself. The ego is attracted to another on whom it has projected its ideals. In the most untechnical sense of the term, personal influence is an expression of narcissism. These terms of analysis call to mind the thesis of Richard Sennett's book, *The Fall of Public Man* (1977), namely, that since the end of the eighteenth century, politics has become increasingly psychologized. This change has occurred at the expense of "public matters which properly can be dealt with only through codes of impersonal meaning."[11] Instead, the tendency has been for the public sphere to be turned into an arena for the formation and affirmation of personal and collective identity. According to Sennett, masculine existence has been diminished by the loss of a psychological sense of the subject as existing in part through its performance of a repertory of public roles. Sennett describes this change in terms of a loss of virility, including the sense that masculinity is a civic virtue. Instead, men are effeminated, both as charismatic political leaders, who owe their success to their seductive capability, and as subjects, members of the fraternity or brotherhood who are the objects of seduction in mass politics.

The passage from *Tancred* that I cited earlier can be used to exemplify this tendency. Fakredeen is preoccupied with politics, but in the passage political concerns take the form of a personal relationship, intense male bonding. And friendship, in turn, is a mode of narcissism. The passage exemplifies a retreat from public to private concerns or, alternatively, the overwriting of personal needs, affects, and so on, upon public ones. Insofar as Fakredeen is able to bend men like Tancred and Amalek to his purposes, he may also be seen as exemplifying political charisma in action. It is precisely these reductions, however, that I wish to resist. Sennett's thesis suffers from the fact that it is reversible. In any situation where both personal and public elements overlap, the personal can be read as motivating the public and vice versa. Fakredeen's political objectives make marriage to Eva highly desirable. Likewise, when Sennett describes friendship as a private relation (17), he begs the question of the public role that it has played in governance since the time of the ancient Athenians.

To repeat, then, how is one to read the passage? While observing the aspects that I mention above, for me the answer is that the passage's intensities, including those that may be sexual, should be allowed to register. At the same time, I don't think that readers should be at pains to label affects, acts, and/or desires as homosexual, heterosexual, or homosocial. Such efforts simply impose present-day terms on fictional subjects who lived in other circumstances. It is better to attempt to understand how experience may have been different for the writer and his contemporaries. The reader should be no more surprised at Fakredeen's ardor vis-à-vis Tancred (and vice versa) than at his attraction to Astarte or his semi-incestuous desire to marry Eva.[12] Seemingly contradictory energies continually reconfigure the field of desire. At the same time, the question of how to read—and how to write—friendship, both in its intimate and in its public aspects, needs to be recognized as central. The narrator makes this point at the beginning of Book 5:

We sadly lack a new stock of public images. The current similes, if not absolutely counterfeit, are quite worn out. They have no intrinsic value, and serve only as counters to represent the absence of ideas. The critics should really call them in. In the good old days, when the superscription was fresh, and the mint mark bright upon the metal, we should have compared the friendship of the two young men to that of Damon and Pythias. These were individuals then still well known in polite society. If their examples have ceased to influence it, it cannot be pretended that the extinction of their authority has been the consequence of competition. Our enlightened age has not produced them any rivals.

Of all the differences between the ancients and ourselves, none are more striking than our respective ideas of friendship. Graecian friendship was indeed so ethereal, that it is difficult to define its essential qualities. (341)

The passage contextualizes friendship in terms of rhetoric. To represent friendship is not to describe it but to convey a sense of it by developing a set of analogies, whether positive or negative. In the paragraph, there are three of these. First, there is the friendship between Fakredeen and Tancred, which is the elusive object of representation. Second, there is the possibility of comparing their connection with the legendary friendship of Damon and Pythias. The latter represents an ideal standard in relation to which Fakredeen's and Trancred's friendship can be assessed. The third point of comparison is with the friendships of young aristocratic men in contemporary London, which Disraeli has already satirized in chapter 3 of the opening book of the novel. In terms of the traditional rhetoric of friendship, such friendships exist partly for the pleasure of shared luxuries and pastimes but mainly for use. Such friendships are relations of exchange between young men in which either or both parties try to obtain material advantage from the other.

This set of analogies in turn contextualizes the narrator's discussion in terms of a particular rhetorical, even philosophic, tradition.[13] That tradition is centrally concerned with both the character of friendship (it is male, it is reciprocal, it occurs between equals, etc.) and with its relation to the polis. Articulated in key texts by Plato and Aristotle, it is, quite literally, *Greek* friendship. And, in this sense, a bit of an interloper in *Tancred*, which, in Book 5, suddenly turns to Greek topics after having earlier elaborated a Christian/English/European versus Jewish/Muslim/Arabian/Asiatic polarity. Friendship implies the existence of a democratic constitution. Aristotle and later writers argue that there is an analogy between the virtues (love and respect) that constitute friendship in its primary signification and the virtues that will be actualized in a democracy.[14] Of course, in the Middle

East there is neither polis nor state. Instead, there is territorial conquest, foreign interference, the slow disarticulation of the Ottoman Empire, and remnants of feudal/patriarchal social organization. All of these political factors can be described in terms of a continual jar of adversarial influences.

Thus far I have described the passage as foregrounding rhetoric insofar as the narrator attempts not description but the use of analogies and insofar as he signals the place of his discussion within the philosophic tradition of the politics of friendship. But the passage is rhetorical in a yet more evident way. It challenges one of the grounding assumptions of Aristotelian philosophy by denying that language is able to provide "an epistemologically accurate" way of rendering "the world's facticity intelligible."[15] Language is unable to "define . . . essential qualities" because language itself has "no intrinsic value" (341). Rather, it is a system of similitudes that have lost any ability they may once have had to represent actualities. If, in the terms of the narrator, "similes" are "counterfeit" coinage, he has set himself an impossible task. The friendship of Fakredeen and Tancred eludes representation not only because friendship as a categorial term does so but also because there is no such thing as adequate representation. Their tie is an absent hyphen, space around which the text can weave its "worn out" figures of speech. Finally, readers should remember that Jews too have been vilified with the rhetoric of forgery. Jewish identity counterfeits the identity of a true Christian subject.

"Worn out" suggests wasted, used up, decadent. The narrator's summary phrase, "Graecian friendship" constitutes a decline into Latinate embellishment from properly Greek heights. Disraeli writes before the official advent of the Decadence within French nineteenth-century literature. But he instates a rhetoric of literary decadence in English literature at a time usually characterized by critics as the high water mark of Victorian realism. Like posing or imposture, counterfeiting is a central figure of decadence. In *Degeneration,* for example, Max Nordau characterizes decadent writers as "unscrupulous copyists and plagiarists," who "crowd round every original phenomenon, be it healthy or unhealthy, and without loss of time set about disseminating counterfeit copies of it."[16] Decadence in Disraeli carries biological connotations (the tradition of primary friendship faces "extinction") plus political overtones. In contrast to the influence and "authority" of philosophic friendship, contemporary English "polite society" lacks "ideas." "Our age" is "enlightened" within the lens of sarcasm. Nothing escapes social and linguistic contamination.

To appeal to the "essential qualities" of Greek friendship is ambiguous since they are not sayable. What remains is an enigmatic hermeneutic of friendship and a testamentary idea. The classic texts of friendship present "friendship *par excellence,* the friendship of virtue" as having existed in the past—in heroic models such as Damon and Pythias or in the perfect friend whom the writer has already lost to mortality.[17] The narrator doesn't deny the actuality of the friendship of virtue although he is not exactly in a position where he can affirm it either. What he is confident of is the inability to realize it in language. The phrase, Damon and Pythias, is an enigmatic key.[18] The evocation of friendship is based on an appeal to an experience, a legend, a regulative norm that is severed from himself and his readers by time. The work of friendship involves a continual effort to remember such possibilities. The work of politics is to actualize them in an as yet unrealized democracy.

"O my friends, there is no friend." In the following paragraph, the narrator paraphrases the tag attributed to Aristotle.[19] Ideas of friendship, writes Disraeli:

must be sought in the pages of Plato, or the moral essays of Plutarch perhaps, and in some other books not quite as well known, but not less interesting and curious. As for modern friendship, it will be found in clubs. It is violent at a house dinner, fervent in a cigar shop, full of devotion at a cricket or a pigeon match, or in the gathering of a steeple chase. The nineteenth century is not entirely skeptical on the head of friendship, but fears 'tis rare. A man may have friends, but then, are they sincere ones? (341–42)

"Friends" yes, but no "friend," except in antique pages.

Faced with this dilemma, the narrator assesses the friendship as follows. In doing so, he makes a reservation common in the discourse of nineteenth- and twentieth-century friendship. The friendship that does exist is attributed to the secondary party rather than to the protagonist. Tancred is thereby reserved from the full intensities but also from the ideal reaches of friendship. The friendship is still exceptional, offering no more and no less than "happiness"; but this happiness is not reflective. "As we must not compare Tancred and Fakredeen to Damon and Pythias, and as we cannot easily find in Pall Mall or Park Lane a parallel more modish, we must be content to say, that youth, sympathy, and occasion combined to create between them that intimacy which each was prompt to recognize as one of the principal sources of his happiness, and which the young Emir, at any rate, was persuaded must be as lasting as it was fervent and profound" (342)

If, as the authors of the tradition of friendship contend, the virtues of friendship parallel the qualities necessary in an ideal polity, one way to understand the friendship between these two young men is to understand their politics. The errancy of friendship and love in Fakredeen, bouncing from Eva to Tancred to Astarte and back to Eva, the push-pull of excessive attraction and repulsion that he feels for Tancred are paralleled by Fakredeen's passionate involvement in politics. More than anything else, his politics is characterized by a lack of aim or of what Tancred, in the opening English section of the novel, calls "principle" (49) and later, in the Oriental section, "faith" (259). Precisely these lacks in modern England have led Tancred to embark on his Eastern journey. To the contrary, however, what his new friend Fakredeen likes about politics is "intrigue" (259), which may be glossed as the pursuit of political maneuvering for its own sake. In this respect, friendship and politics are akin, twin careenings, enjoyed more for the excitement than because one is actually going somewhere.

As one might expect, Fakredeen's excess in this regard provides Disraeli with the opportunity for comment, by exaggerated analogy, on the current state of the British constitution, especially in a government led by his fellow Tory and political nemesis, Sir Robert Peel. In Disraeli's repeated charge, Peel and the Tories lack political principle. As a result, parliamentary politics has lost its authority. The same allegation can be made against Protestant denominations, including the established church. In the opening books, the point is made by the failure of the local bishop to persuade his distinguished young parishioner to listen to his parents and put off his planned trip. In the mountains of Lebanon, the decadence of Christian belief and the loss of religious authority are summed up in the figure of the mountain prelate, Bishop Nicodemus. Nicodemus has the makings of a successful international politician, but like Fakredeen he fails because of his absorption in intrigue: "He wasted his genius in mountain squabbles, and in regulating the discipline of his little church; suspending priests, interdicting monks, and inflicting public penance on the laity. He rather resembled De Retz than Talleyrand, for he was naturally turbulent and intriguing. He could under no circumstances let well alone. He was a thorough Syrian, at once subtle and imaginative. Attached to the house of Shehaab by policy, he was devoted to Fakredeen as much by sympathy as interest" (351–52). "Sympathy," affinity, interest, desire—the word returns. This is not surprising, because in the Orient of this novel personal and public desires are modes of one another or rather there is no distinction to be drawn between the two. This contention on Disraeli's part is important since it presents character as continually shifting and without depth. The character of influence depends upon character, but character is no single thing. It evades representation as much as does friendship—or a viable policy of state-formation in the Middle East. Likewise, the result of influence is or should be the formation of character. But character in this sense likewise is elusive and influence liable to continual changes in direction and object.

At one point in the novel, the narrator says that the proper constitution is that of a Protestant church in a country with a representative government (379). This assertion is ungrounded in reason or argument. Instead, it is a sleight of hand, the fusion of the narrator's point of view with the presumed opinions of English readers. These axioms are basic and unquestioned simply because they are shared. They require no thought. This absence suggests that Disraeli is skeptical as to the existence of any founding political principles. Insofar as such principles do have merit, the merit is historical. Disraeli's skepticism may be called cynical; it may also be called materialist. The meaning of political influence tends to be similarly without metaphysical mooring. Fakredeen exerts influence in the mountains in part because of his charm but mainly because of his position as head of the house of Shehaab. As he tells Tancred, the sole basis of political power in the mountains is "personal influence: ancient family, vast possessions, and traditionary power; mere personal influence can only be maintained by management, by what you stigmatise as intrigue; and the most dexterous member of the Shehaab family will be, in the long run, Prince of Lebanon" (259).

Until the passage of the Catholic Emancipation Act of 1829, England had been a confessional state. Removal of civil disabilities against Roman Catholics posed implicit questions about the relationship between religion and nationality. The constitution was, de facto, no longer Protestant. Tancred sees this unmooring as catastrophic. In his view, nation-building depends upon "popular sympathies" (258), and popular sympathies depend upon a shared religious commitment. The dysfunctions of a fractioned faith, so to speak, are amplified in the Middle Eastern sections of the novel, where Fakredeen, for example, takes the plurality of creeds to signify that state-formation cannot be based on any one in particular. That said, if faith is necessary to popular mobilization, in Fakredeen's view, *any* faith will do. This position is cynical in a second sense of the word, one that Disraeli does not endorse. Fakredeen responds to Tancred:

You forget the religions. I have so many religions to deal with. If my fellows were all Christians, or all Moslemin, or all Jews, or all Pagans, I grant you, something might be effected: the cross, the crescent, the ark, or an old stone, anything would do: I would plant it on the highest range in the centre of the country, and I would carry Damascus and Aleppo both in one campaign; but I am debarred from this immense support; I could only preach nationality, and as they all hate each other worse almost than they do the Turks, that would not be very inviting; nationality, without race as a plea, is like the smoke of this nargilly, a fragrant puff. (258)[20]

This is the point at which the category of race, distinct from nationality, enters as a possible ground of faith.

In *Tancred*, Disraeli continues the work, begun in *Coningsby* and subsequently continued in his 1852 biography of Lord George Bentinck, of developing a racial basis for European geopolitics. Fakredeen's comment is situated within the terms of Disraeli's racial theorizing. Disraeli argues that Muslim Arabs and Jews are both members of a single category, "the Bedoueen race." This race originated in the Caucasus, where the races of western Europe likewise originated. Not only do Arabs and Jews belong to the same category; Jews also belong with Anglo-Saxons among the highest human varieties, the Caucasian races. In the second quarter of the nineteenth century, it became fashionable to write of the Teutons and their descendants as the foremost race.[21] Demystifying such claims at the same time that he spins mystifications of his own, Disraeli contends that the Arabians are the most highly developed of human types. Their superiority to other Caucasians, "the Teutonic, Sclavonian, and Celtic races," is indicated by the fact that the latter groups "have adopted most of the laws and many of the customs of these Arabian tribes, all their literature and all their religion."[22] He never tires of making this point, especially in the face of continual European persecution of the Jews. Other races, "the Mongolian, the Malayan, the American, the Ethiopian" are less highly evolved types of human being.[23] In his biography of Disraeli, Stanley Weintraub asserts that Disraeli's concept of race is not based in the physical sciences (216), but Disraeli set great store on the relative degree of purity of racial types. In *Coningsby*, he asserts: "An unmixed race of a first-rate organization are the aristocracy of Nature." Moreover, as an expropriated and exiled people living in accordance with Mosaic law, "The Hebrew is an unmixed race." For Disraeli, race is biological, "a positive fact" though the evidence of racial superiority is primarily cultural.[24] Races are to be assessed on the basis of the degree of their "influence" over other races.[25]

Tancred's emphasis on the need for "faith" as an element of nation-state formation echoes the view of Jewish influence that Disraeli puts forward in the biography of Bentinck: "The Jewish race connects the modern populations with the early ages of the world, when the relations of the Creator with the created were more intimate than in these days, when angels visited the earth, and God himself even spoke with man. The Jews represent the Semitic principle; all that is spiritual is in our nature."[26] Disraeli poses this principle in opposition to those of "Celtic" cultures, in which he includes French culture with its revolutionary and cosmopolitan tendencies. The Jews "are a living and the most striking evidence of the falsity of that pernicious doctrine of modern times—the natural equality of man. The political equality of a particular race is a matter of municipal arrangement, and depends entirely on political considerations and circumstances; but the natural equality of man now in vogue, and taking the form of cosmopolitan fraternity, is a principle which, were it possible to act on it, would deteriorate the great races and destroy all the genius of the world."[27] Tancred argues that the emancipation of Syria depends upon the emergence of a great national leader, who can muster "popular sympathies" (258) and a shared faith in order to overthrow the Turks. By Book 5, Tancred has found the answer to the disintegration of contemporary Western civilization in a scheme to lead the Arabians (Muslim, Christian, and Jewish) in an armed uprising against the Turks. Utility enters his friendship for Fakredeen insofar as he needs an Arabian prince to head this uprising. While this project may readily be seen to be both foolhardy and yet one more turn of the screw of European influence upon the Muslim Middle East, one needs to take in its full grandiosity.

Tancred announces the program when he and Fakredeeen seek the assistance of Astarte, queen of the Ansarey, a mysterious mountain people who have successfully resisted the incursions of the Ottomans. Tancred says:

The world, that, since its creation, has owned the spiritual supremacy of Asia, which is but natural, since Asia is the only portion of the world which the Creator of that world has deigned to visit, and in which he has ever conferred with man, is unhappily losing its faith in those ideas and convictions that hitherto have governed the human race. We think, therefore, the time has arrived when Asia should make one of its periodical and appointed efforts to reassert that supremacy. But though we are acting, we believe, under a divine impulse, it is our duty to select the most fitting human agents to accomplish a celestial mission. We have thought, therefore, that it should devolve on Syria and Arabia, countries in which our God has even dwelt, and with which he has been from the earliest days in direct and regular communication, to undertake the solemn task. Two races of men alike free, one inhabiting the Desert, the other the mountains, untainted by any of the vices of the plains,[28] and the virgin vigour of their intelligence not dwarfed by the conventional superstitions of towns and cities, one prepared at once to supply an unrivalled cavalry, the other an army ready equipped of intrepid foot-soldiers, appear to us to be indicated as the natural and united conquerors of the world. We wish to conquer that world, with angels at our head, in order that we may establish the happiness of man by a divine dominion, and, crushing the political atheism that is now desolating existence, utterly extinguish the grovelling tyranny of self-government. (421–22)

If Fakredeen's behavior exemplifies unregulated desire, Tancred is at the opposite pole. In his self-presentation, behavior is directed toward a singular "dominion" governed by the principle of what Disraeli refers to as "the great Asian mystery" (166), namely, the monotheistic principle. In terms of character, where Fakredeen is unfixed and mobile, Tancred is fixed and rigid, dominated by dogmatic views that justify a scarcely concealed desire for violent action.[29]

Tancred's telos is Eurocentric. The "world" that he refers to at the beginning of the passage is the world of western Europe and its colonial extensions. It is the loss of "faith" there, resulting in "political atheism" (a dig at the Whigs and the Tories under Peel) and representative government, that motivates Tancred's mission to regenerate the East, which he sees as the source of the best ideas and values within Western culture. The faith he refers to is monotheism, a principle shared by Muslims, Jews, and Christians. It makes possible the grounding of the promised nation-state of Syria in "theocratic equality" (367)—a state based in a theology that acknowledges a measure of truth in all three major faiths.[30]

In these comments, one sees how a singular principle becomes hybrid for Tancred even though he continues to think within terms of binary opposites—the opposite of monotheism being idolatry, the worship of graven images. Ironically, he makes this speech to Astarte, whose people turn out to be a remnant of the Greek population of ancient Antioch. The people of Ansarey continue to worship statues of the Greek gods and goddesses, transported from the wrack of the city to a mountain temple. The narrator sees such investments as operating on the cultural level in much the same way as Fakredeen's function on the personal. The worship of images is a narcissistic projection onto material objects of the wishes and needs of human subjects. The narrator recognizes the delusional character of such entanglements, but he also recognizes their cultural productivity. He observes in the statues: "all that the wit and heart of man can devise and create, to represent his genius and his passion, all that the myriad developments of a beautiful nature can require for their personification" (424).[31] Moving back toward psychology, the narrator reads opposite-sex attraction in the same way. After Astarte, for example, falls in love with Tancred, she fuses her image of him with the form of the statue of Apollo before which she prays.[32] Logically, Tancred should abjure political alliance with a nation of idolaters. But, as Fakredeen has already pointed out to him, in the mountains of Lebanon, the exigencies of nation-building do not permit such discriminations. When it comes to political need, both Fakredeen and Tancred are prepared to overlook ideological abysses in order to secure the "human agents" necessary to act under "a divine impulse."

Tancred sees the united Arabians as the "natural and united conquerors of the world." Nature is another term used in the singular but actually comprised of variations. Analogous with nature is race, a term that refers in the singular to "the human race," in whose name war is to be waged. But races also exist in the plural, even when saying so is a bit of a stretch. For example, Tancred describes the Arabians of the mountains and those of the desert as "two races" when what he means is two variations. Use of the word "race" brings us back to Fakredeen's earlier use of the term, when he argues paradoxically that nationality (by which he means what today might be referred to as ethnicity or even "tribalism") is an insufficient basis on which to lead a national revolt. There needs to be another and different amalgamating term. Fakredeen suggests "race"; Tancred suggests "faith" and "sympathies." Although the terms have different referents, their meanings interlace.

Tancred's words are those of a putative virgin-warrior. As I have suggested, they are also couched within the terms of the biblical narrative of Sodom.[33] On the one side are the enemy, the Ottoman Turks, who suffer the "vices" of the "cities" "of the plains," the biblical term for Sodom and Gomorrah. (The associative links are familiar: Southern/Mediterranean/Ottoman/Turkish/Oriental/Eastern/Jewish/infidel/blasphemer/S[s]odomite). Opposed to them is the "virgin vigour" of Arabian mountain- and desert-dwellers. Tancred means literally what he says when he says that "angels" will be "at our head." The angels he has in mind are those of Lot. Early in the novel, he announces to his father that he awaits the visit of "an angel . . . as he visited the house of Lot" (51). By this phrase, Tancred means a heavenly messenger, armed with a message of social justice.[34] Tancred decides to go to the Holy Land in the belief that he may there experience the visitation he seeks.

His oracular quest becomes ambivalently overlaid with the quest of the medieval Jewish emancipator, David Alroy, about whom Disraeli had written in the romance of the same title published a decade earlier. In *Alroy,*

the key vision is that which occurs to David after he has been sent to Jerusalem by the rabbi Jabaster. In the vision, David mounts the steps, flanked
with golden lions, to the throne of Solomon, from whom he takes the
sceptre of a regenerate Israel. As a result of the vision, David is convinced
that he is destined to restore the kingdom of Israel. He goes on to become
a great warrior and leader. Disraeli refers to that earlier vision in *Tancred*
but in the mode of a materialist reduction. Before Tancred's departure, the
Jewish financier Sidonia gives him letters of introduction to two men in
Jerusalem. One is a Marrano, the Sephardic prior of a monastery there. The
other is to Adam Besso, the leading Jewish banker in Jerusalem. In the
letter, Sidonia says: "If the youth who bears this require advances, let him
have as much gold as would make the right-hand lion on the first step of
the throne of Solomon the king; and if he want more, let him have as much
as would form the lion that is on the left; and so on, through every stair of
the royal seat" (166). As I have said, this reference is marked by ambivalence. On the one hand, Sidonia is the leading Jewish figure in the novel,
an international banker, a type of modern hero unrecognized by Carlyle
but essential to Jewish self-esteem at a time when Jews remained under civil
disabilities in England and a number of other Western countries. Sidonia's
financial influence is able to turn high ideals into realities. At the same
time, a lion literally of gold is not the same as the golden lion of a dream-
vision. And this difference between dream and reality haunts Tancred as it
haunts Disraeli's hopes for the renewal of Jewish life in Europe and the
Middle East.

Once in the Holy Land, Tancred is disappointed to discover that the
oracle eludes him. When it finally does manifest itself, it does so in extreme
circumstances. After Tancred is wounded, captured, and survives a severe
illness, he is permitted to complete his pilgrimage to Mount Sinai. At night,
on the spot where God is said to have given his law to Moses, "the solitary
pilgrim" (289) receives an angelic visit: "'Child of Christendom,'" said the
mighty form, as he seemed slowly to wave a sceptre fashioned like a palm
tree, 'I am the angel of Arabia, the guardian spirit of that land which gov-
erns the world; for power is neither the sword nor the shield, for these pass
away, but ideas, which are divine. The thoughts of all lands come from a
higher source than man, but the intellect of Arabia comes from the Most
High. Therefore it is that from this spot issue the principles which regulate
the human destiny'" (290). In order to remedy the loss of faith and duty
in contemporary Europe, Tancred is advised to "announce the sublime and
solacing doctrine of theocratic equality" (291).

The vision declares two concepts that are central to Disraeli's politics. The first, as I have already termed it, is the monotheistic principle.[35] This principle aligns Judaism with Protestant thought in opposition to the cult of the saints and the veneration of images in Roman Catholicism, an opposition which, translated into the terms of British politics of the 1840s, puts Disraeli in alliance with Tory aristocrats such as the Bentincks.[36] It also puts him in opposition to the marshaling of Irish Roman Catholics in the 1840s under the leadership of Daniel O'Connell.[37] As the publication of Pope Pius IX's anti-liberal manifesto, *Syllabus Errorum* (1864) would underscore later, Roman Catholicism was committed to the concept of the theocratic state, that is, one antagonistic to both Protestant and Jewish inhabitants.[38] In *Tancred,* the Ansarey, with their belief in the Greek gods, indicate the barbarism, as Disraeli sees it, of European civilization. In this light, they stand in for the modern Irish with their religion-based politics and worship of Mary and the Crucified Christ. A theocratic exclusivist, Astarte turns out to be an extreme anti-Semite as well as anti-Christian and anti-Muslim.

In contrast both to Roman Catholic bigotry and to the generally negative Christian stance toward the Muslim East, Disraeli's position affords an opening onto the sort of Muslim thinking that afforded Jewish populations a measure of protection in the Ottoman Empire.[39] Muslims share the principle of monotheism. The Shari'ha,

the Sacred Law of Islam, conceived of the world as being divided into two parts, the Domain of Islam and the Domain of War. The duty of true believers was to expand the first at the expense of the second. The Domain of War itself comprised two groups, the Idolaters and the People of Scripture; the 'scriptural' peoples, consisting of Zoroastrians, Jews and Christians, found themselves ranked more highly than the Idolaters and were to be tolerated, because Zoroaster, Moses and Christ were regarded as prophets akin to Muhammad. The People of Scripture retained their own respective religions and became subjects of the Sultan.[40]

The principle of theocratic equality reciprocally affords the promise of civil status to Muslim populations.

In addition to this principle, Disraeli shares Judaism's belief that human history has shape and an objective. Both he and his fictional protagonist reject the idea of progress (though not its ancillary term, decadence), but Disraeli's concept of "destiny" shares with Jewish tradition the idea that history has a telos, an end or goal, that is immanent in one's actions in the present. Culture and politics are prophetically linked in calling for and achieving this end. Commentators on the work of Karl Marx have long

regarded his call for revolution as a secular translation of Jewish messianism. Derrida argues that this metaphysical structure, along with its translation into Christian terms, is likewise central to the ongoing project of
democratic transformation (*PF,* 306). While the content of the two calls is
different, Derrida argues that philosophic friendship includes the rhetorical
structure of promise. The absent friend of Greek philosophy ("Oh my
friends, there is no friend. . . .") offers both a benchmark and a rhetorical
destination of the continual work necessary to actualize friendship. In his
argument, Derrida contrasts this notion to the norm of fraternity, meaning
blood-community, as a democratic principle. Given both the political conservatism and the racial ideology of Disraeli, it is important to recognize
how, at the level of principle, his politics moves beyond the politics of
literal genealogy. True, Tancred's vision is patriarchal. The angel says: "The
equality of man can only be accomplished by the sovereignty of God. The
longing for fraternity can never be satisfied but under the sway of a common father" (291). But both in its cultural specificity, in its willingness, so
to speak, to listen to the complexities of Muslim culture, and in defining
equality beyond the terms of consanguinity (*PF,* 306), Disraeli opened conservative (and Conservative) politics to the very principle of "cosmopolitan
fraternity" that he vilifies within republican tradition. The parallel between
the prophetic character of the institution of friendship and the prophetic
character of democratic practice underscores the intricating, if I may coin
a verb, of friendship with politics. Fraternity, in this sense, is both a principle and a practice.

Disraeli's democratic opening is not only theoretical. In May 1844,
Disraeli opposed Peel's efforts to water down an attempt by Parliament to
reduce maximum hours of work for boys in factories. A few weeks later,
Disraeli joined with others in successfully opposing Peel's attempt to reduce
tariffs on sugar grown by slaves to the same level as the tariff on "free"
sugar produced in the British West Indies. And, when famine struck in
Ireland that same year, he said in Parliament:

Consider Ireland as you would any other country similarly situated. You will see a
teeming population which, with reference to the cultivated soil, is denser to the
square mile than that of China; created solely by agriculture, with none of the
resources of wealth which develop with civilisation; and sustained, consequently,
upon the lowest conceivable diet, so that in the case of failure they have no other
means of subsistence upon which they can fall back. That dense population in
extreme distress inhabits an island where there is an established Church which is
not their Church and a territorial aristocracy the richest of whom live in distant

capitals. Thus you have a starving population, an absentee aristocracy, and an alien Church, and in addition the weakest executive in the world. That is the Irish question.[41]

Finally, the measure on which Bentinck and Disraeli brought down Peel was the Irish Coercion Bill of 1846, a response to civil unrest in Ireland that, if passed, would have suspended *habeas corpus* while introducing a curfew and military tribunals (Blake, 235).

In Tancred's vision, destiny seems to be drained of conventional religious content. Rather, its dogmatic content is racial: the angel is not the angel of God but "the angel of Arabia." "The intellect of Arabia" guides humanity forward. Given the emphasis on individualism in nineteenth-century thought, especially English, and the exponential growth in anthropological awareness of human populations, one might expect that a theory of history based on a biological principle would encounter resistance on both individual and cultural grounds. As a racial theorist, Disraeli attempts to deal with these factors by subsuming them within the notion of race. As Sidonia asks Tancred: "What is individual character but the personification of race, its perfection and choice exemplar" (149). Likewise, because Jewish law, ideas, and religious belief dominate the formerly barbarian cultures of western Europe, the superiority of Jewish stock to Anglo-Saxon is obvious. These arguments are both invidious and circular. The linkage between racial heredity and individual achievement is nonfalsifiable and, therefore, to use Disraeli's phrase, not "positive fact." Signs of individual genius are, ipso facto, evidence of Jewish heritage, hence the logic of Disraeli's contention that Kant, Mozart, and Napoleon are Jewish.[42] In actuality, Disraeli's racial typology is cultural, aesthetic, and individual in emphasis. This emphasis doesn't cancel its silliness, in one register, or, in another, its pernicious biologism.[43] But it does shift the ground of the debate over the character of influence.

How seriously is one intended to take the angel's racial message? Since it is consistent with Disraeli's arguments elsewhere, it seems to be clear that Disraeli would like it to be authoritative. As a vision, however, the apparition of the angel is of limited worth. First, the message is secularized, neither Jewish nor Christian nor Muslim but racial. Second, its authority derives less from the authenticity of experience than from iteration. Eva's articulation of the same view to Tancred when they first meet at Bethany is its most persuasive presentation in the novel. Even at that time, Tancred has already heard it in England from Sidonia. And there are moments when this view, Tancred's, and the narrator's merge. At such times, the "we" of the narrator appears to include in consensus the author and readers as well (266). Iteration, however, can also imply redundance. The repetition of tendentious arguments does not make them true; rather, it tends to expose their wishful or dogmatic status. Disraeli's tendency to refer to "pure" racial "organization" operates in the same way, implicitly putting in question the very truth that he is at effort to have "us" share with him. This tendency may also exist in the fact, as I have mentioned, that Eva most persuasively poses these views. Rhetorically, she is positioned as what Disraeli in *Alroy* refers to as the "Daughter of the Voice," "an echoing voice which served [the Rabbins] under the second temple for the utmost refuge of revelation" but whose subsequent manifestations were exposed as fabrications.[44] Eva is the most intellectual character in the novel as well as a gifted physician. But she remains dependent, having agreed to marry an unprepossessing young Jewish cousin selected by her father. During the novel, she becomes romantically attached to Tancred, but when, in the final chapter, he urges that she defy custom and marry him, she falls into a swoon. As reciprocal of Tancred, Eva fulfills the role familiar in romantic literature of the opposite-sex friend as a literal or figurative sister whose desires mirror those of a man.[45] In *Alroy,* David's sister Miriam serves this function. And, in life, Disraeli had a comparable relationship with his sister, Sarah.[46] Eva is prevented by gender from achieving full friendship, namely, that of an equal. Her subordination to men qualifies in turn her position in the novel as a spokesperson of "Semitic principle."

While the truths of racial superiority begin to sound like words, words, words, there is little doubt that the novel expresses with increasing vehemence Disraeli's anger against intolerance for Jews both in England and on the Continent. For example, in one of the passages in which Disraeli melds the views of Gentiles and Jews, he writes:

Why do these Saxon and Celtic societies persecute an Arabian race, from whom they have adopted laws of sublime benevolence, and in the pages of whose literature they have found perpetual delight, instruction, and consolation? . . . Independently of their admirable laws which have elevated our condition, and of their exquisite poetry which has charmed it; independently of their heroic history which has animated us to the pursuit of public liberty, we are indebted to the Hebrew people for our knowledge of the true God and for the redemption from our sins. (266)

If the tone of the novel is bracingly philosemitic, it can be withering about the philistinism of Anglo-Saxon culture. The most familiar example occurs in Book 5, where a highly romantic description of how the Feast of Tabernacles is kept by Besso's family in Damascus is contrasted to the meager approximation of the same ritual by Ashkenazi immigrants in the East End of London. Passersby mock their fellow-subjects:

A party of Anglo-Saxons, very respectable men, ten-pounders, a little elevated it may be, though certainly not in honour of the vintage, pass the house, and words like these are heard:

"I say, Buggins, what's that row?"

"Oh! it's those cursed Jews! we've a lot of 'em here. It is one of their horrible feasts. The Lord Mayor ought to interfere. However, things are not as bad as they used to be: they used always to crucify little boys at these hullabaloos, but now they only eat sausages made of stinking pork."

"To be sure," replies his companion, "we all make progress." (390)

In the passage in which Disraeli asks why "Saxon and Celtic societies" persecute Jews, he makes use of the privilege that is his as a Christianized Jew to speak both as one of the Protestant majority and on behalf of minority objects of prejudice. In the second passage, he could not be at a further remove from the modern citizens whom he satirizes, men newly armed with the vote as ten-pound householders, a right available to no non-Christian Jew in England, not even a Rothschild. Disraeli challenges these actualities, not on a rational, Enlightenment (to his mind, Celtic and French) basis of the equal rights due to all human beings, but on a cultural basis, the shared belief of Jews and Christians that one should love one's neighbor as oneself.

Disraeli's contempt brings to mind one further question. In the tradition of Athenian pederasty, the best kind of friendship was reserved for present and future male citizens. Was friendship between Gentile and Jew possible in modern England, where Jews were still struggling to gain the vote and admission to the older universities? It is important to bear in mind that the question of civil disabilities is not simply a question of individual or group rights. It is even more a question of the measure of toleration that a given society has achieved and of the tolerance of which it is capable.[47] As a political leader, Disraeli was obliged to answer the question in the affirmative. And in the years in which *Tancred* was written and published, he formed close alliances with the Bentincks and other aristocrats as part of the strategy of becoming leader of the Conservative party. Bentinck resigned the leadership of the Protectionist party in Parliament in order to vote in favor of extending the vote to non-Christian Jews. And in 1847, the Bentinck family provided Disraeli with funds to purchase Hughenden Manor, the gentleman's estate requisite if he was to qualify as party leader. But just as marriage between the Anglo-Norman Tancred and the Jewish Eva is not possible, so also there is strong evidence that the kind of friendship that is based on love and respect could scarcely exist between a Jewish politician and his Christian allies.

This fact comes through most clearly in Disraeli's discussion of relations between Gentiles and Jews in the biography of Bentinck. Disraeli presents a bifurcated view of both groups. On the one hand, he sees Christianity as an idealized development and completion of the most positive aspects of Judaism. Both creeds are united in the primary maxim: "Thou shalt love thy neighbour as thyself. I am the Lord" (Lev. 19:18; quoted in *Bentinck*, 350n.). Disraeli, however, repeatedly condemns Europeans for their hatred of Jews: In eastern Europe, the Jewish population "was to be plundered, massacred, hewn to pieces, and burnt alive in the name of Christ and for the sake of Christianity" (362). Likewise in Spain. Disraeli's view of Jewry speaks of both attraction and repulsion. On the one hand, the Jewish race is idealized as the soul, so to speak, of the human species: "The Jews represent the Semitic principle; all that is spiritual in our nature" (356). In context in the biography of a leading conservative political leader, they also represent the soul of the Conservative party: "All the tendencies of the Jewish race are conservative. Their bias is to religion, property, and natural aristocracy" (356–57). At the same time, Disraeli identifies some Jews as his (and conservatives') chief enemy. Just as Marx directs animosity against a Judaism that he identifies with the worst aspects of capitalism, so also Disraeli expresses hatred for the Jewish "atheists" and "communists" who, he says, led the uprisings of 1848 (357). He further argues that, as a result of Christian persecution, many Jews have been degraded, with the result that they hate both themselves and Christians. The point is comparable with Eva's observation that Jewish children lose their good looks after they recognize how much they are despised by others. Kant argued that friends need to restrain the impulse to fuse with the beloved friend in order to control the revulsion that accompanies an excessive attachment.[48] Disraeli's presentation of Jewish-gentile relations is characterized by the affects of both fusion and hatred, including what Sander Gilman refers to as Jewish self-hatred. Unrestrained in argument, animosity needed to be quelled in the field of political activity. This necessity, both on Disraeli's side and on that of his Christian supporters, is perhaps yet one more aspect of democracy as a politics, so to speak, of the future.

At the end of the novel, Tancred is disabused of his ambition to play a leading role in the regeneration of the East. His parents arrive in Jerusalem to call him back to an arranged marriage and a safe seat in the House of Commons. Since Disraeli was highly sympathetic to the impulse among young upper-class Englishmen to resist the lives preordained for them by status and family, what is one to make of this downbeat ending? The will to become other than oneself is characteristic of the English world that Disraeli satirizes at the beginning of the novel. The first chapter begins with the adventures of Leander, an intensely competitive, gifted young chef of Cockney background. In ch. 2, his ambition is mirrored at the upper end of the social hierarchy in the history of Tancred's family, which is one of long effort to reclaim lost wealth, privileges, and titles. In ch. 3, young aristocratic idlers contemplate how they can fleece Tancred. All of these individuals, including Mrs. Guy Flouncey, a social climber whose success is traced in a later chapter, share in the urge to play, to perform, to change into something that they are not. Disraeli presents this drive as constitutive of modern existence.

He also criticizes self-fashioning both at home in England and, later, in a character such as Fakredeen. Philosophically and politically, Disraeli identifies the will to self-transformation with philistinism, capitalist excess, and liberal hypocrisy and indifference. Nonetheless, he recognizes the impulse to be crucial to democracy. In Books 1 and 2, he resituates the aspiration in frames of satire, wit, cynicism, and sheer joy in physical existence. In the Orient, he calls upon aesthetics, philosophy, and fantasy in order to complicate and enrich it. About its goal or objects, he is reserved. But, then, for Disraeli democracy is not a program. In a world dominated by self-absorbed individual and group competitiveness, democracy is or will be a competition in improvement.[49] Justice demands that we become better than ourselves and our neighbors and vice versa in a continuing, reciprocal effort. In that world, citizenship is possible for members of different races. Individual friendship can exist between Jews and Gentiles. Eva can marry Tancred if that is her choice. And Tancred will have found a principle of existence.

Excursus
The Economic Judaism of Karl Marx

In the works of fiction that I discuss in the following chapters, Jews are represented in two contrasting ways. In Anthony Trollope's *The Prime Minister,* Trollope uses the crypto-Jewish figure of Ferdinand Lopez as an allegorical figure of the acquisitive principle of modern finance capitalism itself. In this way, Trollope updates the traditional Christian identification of Jews with the sin of greed and the occupations of merchant and usurer. Albeit sentimentally, George Eliot also works within the terms of this moral-sociological typology in her portrait of the pawnbroker Ezra Cohen in *Daniel Deronda.* In Henry James's *The Tragic Muse,* the young painter, Nick Dormer, identifies Miriam Rooth's mother with the qualities of an appraiser "in a crammed backshop," features that he grounds in turn in a newly discovered sense of her being of "the Hebrew strain."[1] In Oscar Wilde's *An Ideal Husband,* the illegal act around which the plot revolves is the sale of privileged information by Robert Chiltern, private secretary to a member of Cabinet. Chiltern is seduced into crime as a result of the glamorous wiles of Baron Arnheim, an implicitly Jewish speculator from Vienna, who makes a great deal of money as a result. Although commentators on the play usually ignore the fact, Wilde's choice of this type echoes its prominence in left- and right-wing political polemic of the decades before and after he wrote: for example, in the rhetoric of Liberal and Radical attacks made on Disraeli in the 1870s and attacks on Prime Minister H. H. Asquith and other leading Liberals made by proto-fascist political activists during and after World War I. Among the latter group figured Wilde's former lover, Lord Alfred Douglas.[2]

These same writers, however, also portray Jews in a contrasting, idealizing light as figures of a post-Christian, post-nationalist cosmopolitanism. This tendency is most obvious in James's association of Rooth, a charismatic actress, with the hope that, in post-1867 England, the development of a national theater might contribute to creating a sense of community capable of overriding differences of class, religion, and race. The tendency likewise shows in the argument of the zealot, Mordecai, in *Daniel Deronda* that a reconstituted nation of Israel will join in "a covenant of reconciliation . . . with the nations of the Gentiles."[3] Eliot's position on the Jewish question shares with Disraeli's a sense of the importance of conserving specific cultural differences. Disraeli does so in the context of seeing such survival as a necessary condition of the stability of modern imperial nation-states with their diverse populations. Eliot in *Daniel Deronda* is strongly disidentified from the British Empire.[4] Instead, she turns to the example of nascent Zionism in order to conjure the possibility of creating a Jewish nation-state in the Middle East that would be ardently national and deeply religious while nonetheless cosmopolitan in its intellectual character and open to gentile cultures, both Eastern and Western. This position is in self-conscious distinction from a more liberal one, which welcomed the advent of the civic-minded, cosmopolitan Jew, free of the signs of Judaic religious and cultural practice.

Both the liberal and the conservative positions share the assumption that a sense of rivalry between members of the two groups is compatible with personal and civic friendship. I attempted to argue in the preceding chapter that, despite his skepticism as to whether friendship was indeed possible between Jews and Gentiles, Disraeli perceived the principle of individual and group competitiveness to be a necessary element in the creation of a democratic state. In *Tancred,* Disraeli sees the capability of individual self-transformation to be both a cause and an effect of social transformation, including the achievement of social justice. For its part, the liberal position is symptomatic of a more general shift, evident by mid-century, from understanding Jewishness in relation to religious belief, ritual, and customary practices to attempts to attach it to secular concepts. Karl Marx, for example, assimilates his comments on Judaism to his general humanist project of the 1840s, namely to arrive at a new definition of the human subject—of what he called species-being. For Marx, as in other secular attempts to define Jewishness, including Disraeli's, this effort leads to a recategorization of Jewishness in terms of newly defined, scientific definitions of race. As I will show in my discussion of Marx's essay, "On the Jewish Question" (1844), Marx unfortunately identifies Judaism (or what he refers to as *Judentum*) with the negation of human species-being. For him, the Jews are a species—or race—defined by their inhumanity.

Marx sees the defining trait of this species to be its economic activity, a framing that permits him to attack the competitive spirit as destructive of both oneself and others. This moral critique further permits him to attack both the principle of finance capital and, implicitly, its German Protestant practitioners. In both ways, the critique moves from its focus on *Judentum* to targets that Marx regarded as larger and more important. Moving in this direction, he also implicitly projects himself as the ideal embodiment of Jewish cosmopolitanism, namely, as the man who, in repudiating *Judentum,* has confirmed his position as a humanist philosopher. Oddly enough, however, this most modern and up-to-date philosophical position proved to be utterly atavistic. Marx's attack on *Judentum* in the essay relies for its polemical power upon bringing once more to the surface some of the oldest allegations leveled by Christians against Jews. George Steiner finds them already set out in the Gospel of John, which identifies greed, sexual jealousy, and the betrayal of friendship with Jewishness in the person of Judas Iscariot, he who "held the purse" (John 13:29) among Jesus' followers. In Steiner's words, John's account of the Last Supper "enmeshes the person and destiny of the Jew with that of money." At the end of his discussion, Steiner concludes: "Judas goes into a never-ending night of collective guilt. It is sober truth to say that his exit is the door of the Shoah."[5] Earlier, Sigmund Freud observed in *Civilization and Its Discontents* how the invention of the concept of the devil served to exonerate religious believers from holding the deities whom they revered accountable for the existence of evil. Evil could simply be pawned off onto the devil as God's nemesis. Writing in 1929–30 on the cusp of the Nazi takeover in Germany, Freud drew a further analogy concerning the place occupied by the Jew within Aryan mythology. "The Jew," he suggests, "can play the analogous role of economic relief or exoneration" in "the world of the Aryan ideal."[6] Marx, for his part, capitalizes on the alleged sins of the Jew in putting forward his own philosophy of humanity.

In his essay, "On the Jewish Question," Marx represents *Judentum* as the very antithesis of the utopian transformation that he looked forward to in the advent of socialism. Despite an attempt to couch his argument within humanist terms, the essay marks a significant moment within a specifically German culture war and in this way can serve as an example of how discussions about Jewishness functioned as part of nationalist discourses in the nineteenth century. Moreover, Marx's identification of Jewish culture with capitalism is, as I have already suggested, by no means confined either to him or to Germany.

Marx wrote "On the Jewish Question" at a time when the issue of Jewish emancipation was the focus of debate among left intellectuals in Germany. In his view, the debate implied the need first to resolve another

question: namely, whether the emancipation of Germany should be discussed in terms of expanding civil, political, and social rights or whether
the more proper focus was on issues of economic justice. Marx believed the
latter to be the case since, in the absence of such an emphasis, new legal
rights would merely serve as an alibi for those with economic power in the
continuing exploitation of others. For proponents of Jewish emancipation,
however, the extension of legal rights was a crucial step toward the creation
of a secular nation-state. Marx believed in German unification as a necessary first step toward creating the conditions for a socialist revolution.[7] But
his immediate objective in this essay is to win assent to universal principles
validating social transformation. Particularities of nationality and ethnicity
appear to be set aside. He argues that he uses the term *Judentum* or Judaism
to mark the limit between human and inhuman activity. Marx's insistence
on using *Judentum* to describe the values of the market economy, however,
reinscribes his humanist rhetoric within a national discourse whose binary
terms are Germany and Judaism.

German writers in the eighteenth and nineteenth centuries, whether
political radicals, devout Lutherans, or philosophers such as Kant and
Hegel, were united in seeing Jews as constituting a nation whose founding
documents are the Genesis stories of Abraham and his descendants. In writing against *Judentum,* Marx writes against the concept of the Jewish nation.
In doing so, he also writes against the related views that the divine promise
had been transferred first from Jews to Christians and, at the time of the
Reformation, to Protestants in Germany. Like friends and fellow left intellectuals such as Bruno Bauer, Marx attempts to dissociate the nascent German nation-state from the Lutheran church. In the effort to do so, however,
he falls into the trap of defining Jews as an anti-(German) nation. At the
same time, by identifying *Judentum* with bourgeois values, he negates the
difference between Christians and Jews. The term refers to both Christian
and Jewish members of the bourgeoisie.

It is no accident that the relationship between Judaism and citizenship
makes itself felt in the writing of Marx and Disraeli in the 1840s. The two
men have in common the fact that both belonged to something new: the
first generation of people of Jewish descent who came of age in western
Europe as the children of parents who were secular Jews. For men and
women of this generation, the relationship between individual, familial, and
group identity, on the one hand, and identity as subjects and citizens of a
modern state, on the other, inflected the most intimate traces of personal
existence. Disraeli's writing and Marx's essay both testify to this fact.[8] Be-

coming a consciously conservative politician, Disraeli contributed to the democratic refashioning of England through the conscious articulation of a set of particularities: British nationality, membership of the established church, *and* a continuing affirmation of Jewish existence. Marx's path proved to be more difficult since he believed that he could become himself—and a world thinker—only through a double negation. On the one hand, he had to deny Jewish existence, his own and that of others. On the other hand, he had to refuse to identify himself with Germany, the country of his birth. These denials might seem to offer a way in which Marx could avoid situating himself with reference to the binary opposition between being German and being Jewish. But Marx was in fact both Jewish *and* German, and the attempt to negate both identifications resulted in some unintended discursive effects. When Marx wrote "On the Jewish Question," he chose to write within the terms of an anthropological approach familiar in German philosophy[9] and within a genre—the philosophic essay in the form of a critical review—that both enabled and required these negations.[10] In other words, he is as much written by genre as he writes it. Within this situation, the essay is triply prophetic. Marx sets out the economic basis of philosophic thinking that would become his life work, but he also issues a patent for Jewish intellectual anti-Semitism and he sets the tone of future anti-Semitic, left-wing polemic.[11]

In part, Marx's dilemma arises from his status as a Marrano or baptized Jew. Conversion is a transformation into something or someone other, a psychic process that, in individual terms, is just as total as is the holocaust that overtakes Sodom in Genesis. Moreover, within the terms of Genesis narratives of the Covenant, of which the story of Lot is one part, conversion is not merely a personal matter. Fidelity to one's faith makes it possible for one's descendants also to be saved. In Marx's case, however, the test that he must pass is to remain faithful not to Abraham's kindred nor to German Protestantism but to Hegel's philosophic progeny.[12] Marx's (self-)inscription shows his determination to be faithful to his vow of philosophic conversion as a Young Hegelian. In the essay, he calls for the end of Jewish existence. This negation is the price he is willing to pay for entry into German philosophic tradition. Not surprisingly, a number of negative assumptions about Jews expressed in the essay echo this tradition. For example, Marx's portrayal of *Judentum* coincides with Immanuel Kant's representation of Jews in the *Anthropologie* as "a whole nation of pure merchants as non-productive members of society." So does Marx's eschatological call for the conversion of the Jews (Poliakov, 3:79). Similarly, the claim that Jews are characterized above all by egoism and that this fact makes them the enemies of humanity repeats allegations made by Fichte, Hegel, and Feuerbach. Fichte, for example, writes that "the Jew became an *egoist* and . . . the enemy of mankind, or more accurately, the despiser of mankind" (Poliakov, 3:194).

Belief in Jewish hostility toward Gentiles had often entailed a literal belief in ritual murder and cannibalism. This view was revived in the romantic period by Georg Daumer, who finds evidence for it both in traditional accounts of the murder of Christians by Jews and in the Gospel accounts of the Last Supper (Poliakov, 3:410–13). Marx for his part accepts Daumer's account of Christian cannibalism as a survival of Jewish practices and argues that the demystification of Christian ritual and the sacrament of the Holy Eucharist in particular presages in turn the dawn of a post-revolutionary society in which humans will no longer consume one another, either literally or metaphorically: "This history, as Daumer expounds it in his work, gives the final blow to Christianity. This makes us certain that the old society is approaching its end and that the structure of falsehood and prejudice is collapsing."[13] Léon Poliakov believes that Daumer's close friend, Ludwig Feuerbach, unconsciously echoes the belief in Jewish cannibalism in his analysis of Jewish "egoism" (3:415). A further echo can be heard in the ferocity of Marx's allegation that Judaism threatens the very survival of the human species.

Unlike the genres in which Disraeli wrote, the genres of Marx's essay efface personal contingencies. Nonetheless, changes occurring in Marx's life make themselves felt. Marx made three mutually constitutive commitments at this time: to communism (against *Judentum*); to marriage and heteronormative genealogy;[14] and to identification with male workers. Marx wrote the essay in Germany and Paris in 1843 and 1844 at a moment when, despite his efforts to inhabit German philosophic tradition, he was forced to leave the land of his birth and to enter upon a life that would eventually become one of permanent exile in England. The universality of the essay, its rejection of nationality as the basis of existence, expresses the loss and gain of Marx's removal. Likewise, this was the year of Marx's marriage; it was also the year in which for the first time "there emerged his preoccupation with that class which he called "*la plus labourieuse et la plus miserable,* the proletariat."[15] Michel Foucault has remarked that "to ally oneself with the proletariat is to accept its positions, its ideology, and its motives for combat. This means total identification."[16] Since the French word "classe" is feminine, the proletariat need not be automatically construed as masculine.

And, of course, the class includes many female workers. Nonetheless, the word proletariat usually brings to mind the working man; and the mode of affiliation between workers and vanguard intellectuals is conceived in terms of fraternity. Since identification is a mode of transference, it implies the existence of desire. This desire may be naturalized as brotherhood or it may be transgressive. In other words, the brotherhood of working men and intellectual leaders can be construed as democratic and egalitarian, on the one hand, or as an abuse of normal gender and sexual relations on the other.[17]

The fact that Jews could be socialists (not to mention political rivals of Marx) and that socialists could also be *Urning*s (Karl Ulrichs's term for men with sexual and emotional ties to other men), provoked considerable anxiety for Marx in his identification with workers. For example, of the successful German Jewish Socialist leader Ferdinand Lasalle, Marx in his correspondence writes that "the shape of his head and his hair show that he is descended from the Negroes who joined Moses' flock at the time of the exodus from Egypt."[18] And when Johann Baptist von Schweitzer, who had been arrested on a morals charge, succeeded Lasalle as leader of the General Association of German Workers, Engels mocked his sexual preferences in a letter to Marx. Citing a pamphlet by Ulrichs that Marx had sent Engels, Engels applies to *Urning*s the allegation of secret conspiracy more often applied against Jews: "The paederasts are beginning to count themselves, and discover that they are a power in the state. Only organisation was lacking, but according to this source it apparently already exists in secret."[19] Despite the self-conscious parody of these lines, they include a note of paranoia. Even more telling, Engels labels Schweitzer as a sodomite at the same time that he repudiates both the open role played by *Urning*s in socialist politics and the part played by female political leaders. Against these perversions, Engels affiliates himself with Marx as a fellow hetero male, "poor frontside people like us, with our childish penchant for females."[20] For Marx and Engels, left politics belongs to straight boys.[21]

The model of human relationship in "On the Jewish Question" is not friendship, whether between members of the same sex or the opposite, but heterosexual intercourse, which Marx refers to in the essay as the defining "species-relation itself, the relation between man and woman, etc."[22] Marx defines Jews against this norm. They belong to neither the productive nor the reproductive order. They are the undead, if not vampires, then parasites on the body of humanity. The general perversion is echoed in the perversity of their sexual relation to women: "What is present in an abstract form in the Jewish religion—contempt for theory, for art, for history, for man as an end in himself—is the *actual* and *conscious* standpoint, the virtue, of the man of money. The species-relation itself, the relation between man and woman, etc., becomes a commercial object! Woman is put on the market" (239).[23] Marx argues not only against the powers of the church and the remnants of feudalism but also against what Hegel refers to as civil society (230). According to Marx, the bourgeois liberal state creates citizens who are defined socially in terms of property and psychologically in terms of "egoism" (238). Hence, civil society must be destroyed in the name of creating an eschatological new kingdom of humanity. Because of the anthropological terms in which Marx writes, without eschewing a universal rhetoric, he is able to locate this moral/social condition in particular classes and in a particular religious and/or ethnic and racial minority: namely Jews, both financial leaders such as the Rothschilds (237) and, at the other end of the social spectrum, recent migrants from eastern Europe, visible as peddlers on the streets of Trier, Marx's native town:[24]

> Relations of sex and gender will be placed on a proper, i. e., a natural basis, only when the financier and the peddler are things of the past:
> What is the secular basis of Judaism? *Practical* need, self-interest.
> What is the secular cult of the Jew? *Haggling.* What is his secular god? *Money.*
> Well then? Emancipation from *haggling* and from *money,* i. e., from practical, real Judaism, would be the same as the self-emancipation of our age. . . .
> We . . . recognize in Judaism the presence of a universal and *contemporary anti-social* element whose historical evolution—eagerly nurtured by the Jews in its harmful aspects—has arrived at its present peak, a peak at which it will inevitably disintegrate.
> The *emancipation of the Jews* is, in the last analysis, the emancipation of mankind from *Judaism.* (236–37)

In defense of Marx, one may say that he is speaking allegorically here: "Judaism" is a metaphor of "egoism," the leading characteristic of all human beings, Christian or Jewish, in a market economy. Nonetheless, a progressive historical dialectic structures the passage: Jews, as Disraeli also claimed, have progressed to the forefront of commerce and finance in the ascendant market economy. This triumph, however, signals their subsumption in a new social order. Despite the qualifying adjective, "universal," the phrase "*contemporary anti-social* element" chills. The leap to the conclusion that removing this "element" will also remove the key human vice from society and thereby make socialism possible is obvious, even if Marx does not make it himself. Moreover, the apocalyptic character of the prophecy implies the necessity of violence. The individual and group conversion demanded is so total that it is difficult to imagine that any living human being could actually achieve it. This difficulty looms even larger in view of the fact that Marx, as I have argued, makes Jews the synecdoche of contemporary degeneration. How can a Jew exist, once egoism is excised?

Marx contrasts a truly human genealogy to *Judentum,* a German word that refers to Jews as an aggregate; to their traditions, beliefs, and practices; and to the commercial values informing modern finance, commerce, and industry.[25] Like other young revolutionaries such as Richard Wagner, who uses the term in the same way in *Das Judentum in der Musik* (1850),[26] Marx exploits the ambiguous usage in order to contrast his revolutionary call for a new humanity to the values and the persons that stand in its way. In order to bring the former into being, the latter must cease to exist.

Marx's call for the end of Jewish existence gives the essay an especially troubling place in the history of Western adaptations of biblical covenant narratives. In Marx's secularized narrative of human redemption, the Jews face a fate similar to that encountered by the citizens of Sodom in Genesis: namely, their literal effacement from the globe. "As soon as society succeeds in abolishing the *empirical* essence of Judaism—the market and the conditions which give rise to it—the Jew will have become *impossible.* . . . His species-existence will have been superseded" (241). Although writing as a self-conscious atheist, Marx also writes with a consciousness shaped by his experience as a Christianized Jew.[27] His narrative includes not only the sort of apocalyptic structure that one finds in the biblical account of the destruction of Sodom but also the displacement of privileged genealogy from one group to another that Steiner finds to be performed in John 13. In the Reformation and later, the Jews are superseded as the Chosen People by Protestant Christians of a specific nationality. Marx secularizes this narrative by arguing that the promise of collective salvation belongs to mankind in virtue of its humanity, which will come into existence as a result of the transformation of the existing order. Although the point becomes clear only later in Marx and Engels's writing, this conversion demands revolutionary terror.[28] In the imminence of apocalypse, Jews will no longer be Jews; instead, they will have become human beings: "The subjective basis of Judaism—practical need—will have become humanized and the conflict between man's individual sensuous existence and his species-existence will have been superseded" (241).

What Sander Gilman describes as the self-hatred motivating "On the Jewish Question" shows in Marx's positioning of himself as the post-emancipation, post-Jew.[29] The work of the essay in enabling his identification of himself as subject of the revolutionary vanguard demands an equally powerful disidentification from Jewish existence. The Jewish subject who is emancipated from *money* and *haggling* is none other than the secular, Westernized, communist Jew: that is, Marx himself, author of the passage. The passage enacts his dialectical capacity to cancel his present identity by rising from the embodied existence of a Jew to a new existence as a latter-day John the Baptist, so to speak, announcing the arrival of the kingdom of man.

And yet, as so often happens when the objects of prejudice attempt to dissociate themselves from the allegations stereotypically lodged against them, Marx symbolically acts out vices charged against Jews. What can be more egoistic than Marx's implicit interpellation of himself as revolutionary subject in place of the Jesus of Christian humanist tradition? And how might Marx more dramatically fulfill the allegation made by Fichte and others against Jews that they did not even defend each other? Notwithstanding this overreaching, Marx's expression of utopian hope in the essay draws on aspects of the very Jewish culture that he repudiated. Despite his negative use of aspects of covenant narrative in Genesis, the moral imperatives of "On the Jewish Question" are informed by the same book of the Hebrew Bible. There God affirms his promise to Abraham and his seed on the condition that they "do righteousness and justice" (Gen. 18:19). In the gloss of Robert Alter, "survival and propagation depend on the creation of a just society."[30] It is unfortunate that in his zeal for justice, Marx was prepared to sacrifice *Judentum*.

Chapter 4

The Lesser Holocausts of William Gladstone and Anthony Trollope

In this chapter, I focus on two texts. The first is *Bulgarian Horrors and the Question of the East* (1876), a pamphlet by William Gladstone in which he attacks Benjamin Disraeli for his government's implication in Turkish atrocities in the Balkans. The second is *The Prime Minister,* a novel by Anthony Trollope whose central incident is the suicide of Ferdinand Lopez, a young, ambiguously Jewish interloper into English society. Both texts involve what I refer to as lesser holocausts: in Trollope's novel, a suicide that is invested with fantasies of complete obliteration; and, in Gladstone's pamphlet, massacres of Christians by Muslims that Gladstone refers to, in a sodomitic pun, as "Bulgarian horrors." Both texts register what may be the decisive moment in the history of British democracy after the successful passage of the Reform Bill of 1867. On the one side stands a phantasmatic militant Christian national subject.[1] On the other stands an elderly man, a Jewish convert to Christianity, the Tory Prime Minister, Benjamin Disraeli, successful novelist and former dandy.

Before 1867, parliamentary politics had been regulated by the so-called Tory-liberal consensus, a set of accommodations between the traditional, landed ruling class and new commercial and industrial interests. Trollope describes this consensus in an 1865 article in which he defends the public schools from demands for radical reform: "It is the same with us Englishmen in all matters. At last, after long internal debate and painful struggle, reason within us gets the better of feeling. In almost every bosom, there sits a parliament in which a conservative party is ever combating to maintain things old, while the liberal side of the house is striving to build things new. In this parliament, as in the other, the liberal side is always conquering, but its adversary is never conquered."[2] When Trollope refers to "Englishmen," he is being precise. Even after passage of the Reform Bill enrollment in the voting list was limited to a minority of male adults; and only males could sit in Parliament. This gendered exclusivity is important for Trollope's novel, which registers the existence of individuals and groups demanding entry into public life: namely, women, Jews, immigrants, and upper-working-class male voters. In terms of the novel, the contemporary crisis of democracy in England is created by the demands for participation made by these players. The result, in terms of the novel, is a demonstration of the failure of the existing consensus.[3] This outcome leaves the country in a state of stasis. It leaves Trollope and his novel somewhere else, though. In the wake of the extension of the suffrage to many upper-working-class men, Trollope positions himself in alignment with the railway pundit who witnesses Lopez's suicide at the Tenway Junction.

In 1868, the Liberals won the first general election following passage of the Reform Bill, and Gladstone became prime minister. Trollope, who ran as a Liberal in his first and only bid for a seat in Parliament, was defeated in the notoriously corrupt riding of Beverley in the East Riding of Yorkshire. Following the election, a commission of inquiry was held and the borough was disfranchised.[4] Although Gladstone subsequently retired from politics after the defeat of his government by the Tories under Disraeli in 1874, he continued to be preoccupied with the question of how the new voters were to be politically organized. For Gladstone, the question meant, in effect, how were they to be won as permanent adherents to the Liberal party. The massacre of Christian Slavs by troops allied with the Turks in Bulgaria provided an excellent opportunity for organizing and consolidating working-class voters under the Liberal banner. Doing so, however, required workers to rise above their interest in legislation designed to ameliorate their economic condition and to see themselves, instead, as individuals enlisted in a religious and patriotic army dedicated to international moral reform. This was the form that "reason" was to take in post-Reform politics.

In the Introduction, I explore the nexus of different sorts of sins—against faith, charity, and the natural order of procreation—that commentaries in Victorian family Bibles identify in discussing the story of Lot. In his pamphlet, Gladstone pursues the same connections in condemning the Turks and their allies, among whom Disraeli especially is singled out. Conveniently for Gladstone, Disraeli's presence permitted a fierce attack against an infidel, idolatrous, and implicitly sodomitic political premier, allegedly in conspiracy with Jewish financiers in the City to subvert British interests. Against this phantom, Gladstone calls into existence a unified national subject, Protestant, militant, and male, who will defend innocent Christian victims against murder and sexual assault by heathen Orientals.

When I use terms such as idolatry and infidelity, I do so aware of the fact that the rhetoric of sodomy, both in Genesis and in Christian theology, includes connotations of these sins along with a wide range of sexual offenses against male property rights in marriage.[5] By linking these terms in his attack, Gladstone blackens Disraeli while investing national identity and moral imperialism with religious fervor and significance.[6] Because democratic society appears to be secular, it is easy to fail to recognize the religious character of many solicitations to political solidarity. The force, direct or subliminal, of such associations strengthens prejudice against the participation of new players in social life, even more so when these prejudices are racial and/or sexual and gendered. Within Gladstone's terms, moreover, something else is also at stake; namely, the proper character of Judaism. Paradoxically, for Gladstone, true Judaism exists in the form of modern liberal democracy.

In his view, the identification of Englishmen with the affirmation of freedom and justice abroad is a proper expression of Christian faith. This fidelity is based in turn on adherence to God's injunctions to the Chosen People in the Hebrew Bible. In accordance with the doctrine of "Christian supercession,"[7] the force of God's promises to the people of ancient Israel was subsumed in Christ's charge to his disciples and, at the time of the Reformation, transferred to Protestant Christians, in particular, to the Protestant subjects of the English crown. As a boy, Disraeli had been baptized as an Anglican. Far from operating in his favor, however, in Gladstone's diatribe, Disraeli's status as a converted Jew actually works against him. In Gladstone's eyes, Disraeli is a false convert, a traitor to Judaism's primary axiom of monotheistic faith. Instead, he is an infidel in masquerade; his particular representation of the national interest raises a false idol for the worship of the people. And, like the Turks, Disraeli is sexually corrupt.

Gladstone's views of democratic consensus are at odds with another view of the character of democratic change that exists in many different forms in nineteenth-century writing. In Trollope's writing, this alternative view exists as the expression of what one literary critic refers to as social desire. Social desire is the typically middle-class aspiration to improve one's status and material well-being. For Trollope, this means success in terms of marriage and career. At the same time, Trollope maintains that individual behavior should be disinterested in character. The two mandates are discontinuous. John Kucich argues that the tension, at times the contradiction between the two norms, is reflected in the lies, often implicit, of some of Trollope's morally good characters.[8] Lies contradict fidelity to the truth, a term guaranteed both by reason and, ultimately, by the authority of the God who, in Genesis, creates the world by his word.

In light of the discussion in the preceding paragraph, Trollope's commitment to progress can be seen as requiring both fidelity and infidelity. In other words, his position and that of his novel are compromised. Within *The Prime Minister*, moreover, expressions of social desire are harshly dealt with, especially in the behavior of members of two of the three groups whom I have mentioned—namely, women and Jews. Since social desire is a bourgeois phenomenon, however, its representation cannot be restricted to the behavior of those on the margins. Figured in the ill-informed and disastrous political interference of the prime minister's wealthy wife, Lady Glencora, social desire is also at work in the personal maneuvering of members of the Cabinet. Both elite Anglo-Saxon men and an upper-class woman are chastised for worshipping at the altar of influence and advantage. Within marriage itself, social desire fares little better. For example, when young Emily Wharton rejects her family's choice of husband in order to choose Ferdinand, her sexual attraction to the young man and her more diffuse desire to change her life are reduced to an example of fetish worship. Emily subjects herself to the assemblage of signs of gentlemanliness called Lopez.[9]

Lopez too acts like a Converso or infidel. In portraying him, Trollope takes a stance at once anti-dandiacal, anti-sodomitic, and anti-Jewish. It is possible to conflate Lopez's dandiacal and sodomitic aspects with those of a later type: namely, the effeminate male homosexual of the 1890s. Doing so, however, scants the religious and metaphysical (that is, monotheistic) basis of Trollope's revulsion. Thomas Carlyle, for example, in an important account of the dandy, reads him as a reversal of a Jewish type: that of the Johannine figure who prophesies the coming of the New Dispensation. Speaking of the Dandy's obsession with costume, Carlyle writes: "Is there not in this Life-devotedness to Cloth, in this so willing sacrifice of the Immortal to the Perishable, something (though in reverse order) of that blending and identification of Eternity with Time, which, as we have seen, constitutes the Prophetic character?"[10] It is the reversal that constitutes infidelity; it is the "*Self-worship*"[11] that constitutes idolatry.

Egoism, to use a nineteenth-century term, cuts Lopez off from the relations of desire called manly friendship that Gladstone and Trollope see as properly informing (elite) democratic governance. For example, in the chapter in which Lopez prepares to commit suicide, the narrator absents himself from Lopez's subjectivity at the same time that he refers to him as "our friend."[12] The phrase is ironic in the sense of being dispassionately observant; at the same time, the clichéd phrase, "our friend," implies the existence of an unstated but shared emotional, literary, and moral economy between author and reader. Granted, Trollope calls up the assumption in order to negate it. But this double irony has a social point. When the pundit notices Ferdinand loitering on a train platform, suspicious, he asks him why he is there. Ferdinand answers that he is awaiting the arrival of a "friend" on the Liverpool train. When the train from Liverpool arrives, the narrator remarks that "it seemed that our friend's friend had not come" (2:234). Repeating the word, Trollope emphasizes the utter isolation that has pushed Ferdinand to this moment of desperation. He also suggests that Ferdinand's drive for money, status, and influence has had as its most compelling motive a desire for personal and social acceptance. This suggestion qualifies the general tendency to represent Lopez as, in Victorian parlance, a blackguard. Ferdinand's friendlessness further suggests that the responsibility for his death may be shared by those who shut him out. Near the end of the novel, for example, after her husband has been forced to resign as prime minister, Lady Glencora says of Lopez: "I have a sort of feeling, you know, that among us we made the train run over him" (2:425).

Ferdinand may be short of friends, but he does exercise influence, for instance on an ally in the City named Sexty Parker. When Ferdinand extracts Parker's signature on a personal loan of £750 in the opening chapter, Parker is unable to explain to himself why he has agreed to put himself at risk. Lopez appears to succeed with Parker by force of personal magnetism, a Victorian term that includes the force of sexual attraction.[13] Much later in the novel, after Ferdinand has brought Parker to financial ruin, Parker's wife describes the pair's relationship as vampiric (2:64). The proper relation of friends is very different. Consider, for example, Trollope's description of Arthur Fletcher, the independently wealthy but hardworking and successful young lawyer of good background, whom Emily's father, Abel, prefers as a candidate for his daughter's hand:

He was a fair-haired, handsome fellow, with sharp, eager eyes, with an aquiline nose, and just that shape of mouth and chin which such men as Abel Wharton regarded as characteristic of good blood. He was rather thin, about five feet ten in height, and had the character of being one of the best horsemen in the county. He was one of the most popular men in Herefordshire, and at Longbarns was almost as much thought of as the squire himself. . . . He looked like one of those happy sons of the gods who are born to success. No young man of his age was more courted both by men and women. . . . So much had been done for him by nature that he was never called upon to pretend to anything. Throughout the county those were the lucky men,—and those too were the happy girls,—who were allowed to call him Arthur. (1:162)

In this and adjacent passages, Trollope heaps material qualities—race ("blood," "nature") being prominent among them—to explain Arthur's appeal. But the desire of both men and women to court Arthur, though clearly dependent on his physical embodiment, does not need to be accounted for. Indeed, a defining characteristic of manly friendship is that it does not depend upon direct verbal expression or mental analysis. The physical and erotic aspects are the cause-without-a-cause that provides a substratum for friendship among the county set. And not just in the county since Arthur is destined to win a Tory seat in Parliament.

The Prime Minister appeared in serial publication between November 1875 and June 1876 at a time when Disraeli alarmed the Opposition first by secretly arranging for Britain to purchase a controlling share of the Suez Canal Company and, second, for continuing to support the Turkish government while massacres of Christians were under way in the Balkans.[14] Trollope began writing the novel in April 1874, only six weeks after Disraeli became prime minister. Trollope links it to the rivalry between Gladstone and Disraeli in the ways in which he characterizes the two leading male protagonists of the novel: Lopez and the prime minister, the duke of Omnium.[15] Pictures of the contrasting qualities of Lopez and the duke operate like transparent overlays from which, when superposed, the lineaments of the new prime minister emerge.

In the eighteenth century, Henry Fielding, one of Trollope's favorite authors, built the mock-heroic satiric fiction of *Jonathan Wild* (1743) on the likeness between the master criminal, Wild, and England's leading politician of the period, Robert Walpole. In *The Prime Minister,* Trollope exploits this use of analogy by implicitly comparing Lopez and the duke with Disraeli. In introducing Lopez as "a very great man" (1:1) of extravagant ambition, lady-killer looks, and dandiacal dress and deportment (1:6), Trollope recalls the similar qualities for which Disraeli was known as a young man.[16]

In the 1830s, Disraeli was involved in an affair with the politically influential Henrietta Sykes.[17] At the same time, he apparently also enjoyed posing as a sodomite—to use the charge later alleged by the marquess of Queensberry against Oscar Wilde.[18] At dinner with the prime minister, Lord Melbourne, Disraeli shared with him a letter "detailing Arab sexual practices" from Disraeli's friend in Egypt, Paul Emile Botta. Benjamin Haydon, the painter, who was present, recorded in his diary that Disraeli "talked much of the East, and seemed tinged with a disposition to palliate its infamous vices. . . . I meant to ask him if he preferred Aegypt, where Sodomy was *preferment,* to England, where it very properly was Death" (Ridley, 130). A week later, Haydon learned that on that same night a man named Baring Wall had been arrested on charges of indecency with a policeman.[19] Writing again in the diary, Haydon links Disraeli's sexual dubeity with his extravagant taste in dress: "I think no man would go on in that odd manner, wear green velvet trousers and ruffles, without having odd feelings. He ought to be kicked. I hate the look of the fellow."[20]

On first glance, the duke of Omnium might seem to be the opposite of Disraeli. While Trollope disapproved of Disraeli, he admires the duke as a man too honorable to be a successful politician. In ways, though, Disraeli's marriage to Mary Anne Wyndham Lewis resembles the duke's to Lady Glencora. Both women brought independent wealth to their marriages; neither was a love match. Both women were personally protective of and determined to advance the political careers of their respective husbands. And both were a bit of "a rattle," to use Disraeli's phrase when he first met Mary (Ridley, 110). The emotional isolation that the duke experiences in the premiership resembles the widowed Disraeli's state of mind when he finally achieved the prime ministership late in life. In a letter to Lady Bradford in February 1875, he said, "I live for Power and the affections," but the voluminous epistolary flirtations that he carried on with her and Lady Chesterfield at this time are mild.[21] An implied impotence overhung the person of the aging Disraeli (Weintraub, 534). Allusion to Disraeli at this time of his life helps explain an otherwise odd aspect of Trollope's novel. Although the duke is middle-aged, he is described as though he were a generation older. Lady Glencora, who should know, refers to him, for example, as being as "dry as a stick" (2:185). And as his government wanes, she observes that "he was beginning to have the worn look of an old man. His scanty hair was turning grey, and his long thin cheeks longer and thinner" (2:259).

One of the leading signs of the elderly Disraeli's gradual withdrawal of affect occurs in the complaint that he was tired of the need to keep his secretaries amused. And yet he also complains to Lady Chesterfield: "I cannot endure my solitary dinners and evenings" (Weintraub, 539). Moreover, Disraeli was fortunate at the time to be served by the most devoted and skilled of his personal secretaries, Monty Corry, who had entered Disraeli's service after they met during a dull country party while Corry was still in his twenties.[22] Disraeli memorializes Corry in a passage from *Endymion* (1881), whose first reader had been Corry himself (Blake, 734). Disraeli remarks: "The relations between a Minister and his secretary are, or at least should be, among the finest that can subsist between two individuals. Except the married state, there is none in which so great a confidence is involved, in which more forbearance ought to be exercised, or more sympathy ought to exist."[23] Like Disraeli, at the end of his term the duke reserves his most intimate exchanges for his secretaries, an intimacy from which both Lady Glencora and the novel's readers are excluded (2:260).

Like Lopez, the Disraeli of Gladstone's pamphlet, conflated with Oriental perpetrators of mayhem, is an impostor. He is also Jewish, dandyish, and implicitly sodomitic. The "Bulgarian Horrors" of Gladstone's phrase were a series of massacres of thousands of Bulgarian civilians at the hands of Turkish irregular troops in the spring of 1876. On June 23, 1876, a Liberal paper, the *Daily News,* broke word of the atrocities in England. News of the massacres created a sensation, and questions were raised in Parliament. Disraeli was skeptical about the allegations of the press, in part because his own officials were not keeping him properly informed. As well, the news was unwelcome since he believed that it was crucial to British foreign policy to support the Ottoman Empire in the Middle East. As a result, he delayed responding before Parliament recessed in August.

On September 6, Gladstone published an incendiary pamphlet attacking the government's handling of what he referred to as "the nation's crisis."[24] Forty thousand copies were sold in the first week, two hundred thousand by the end of the month (Blake, 598). Gladstone used the occasion to project a model for the new post-Reform Bill electorate. In the pamphlet, Gladstone represents the nation as a live body, both collective and individual, and possessing a moral character. This nation includes the new working-class male voters, who are represented as coming to political consciousness and agency through sympathetic identification with their Christian cousins to the east. In "us versus them" mode, Gladstone attacks the vacationing leisure classes while praising "the working men of the country, [who] . . . have to their honor led the way, and shown that the great heart of Britain has not ceased to beat. And the large towns and cities, now following in troops, are echoing back, each from its own place, the mingled notes of horror, pain, and indignation" (9). This newly militant nation is aligned with universal principles: with "the Councils of Europe" (36), with "Western Christendom" (10), with "civilization," with "the broad and deep interests of humanity" (13), and "the laws of God or, if you like, of Allah"

(38). Each of these terms, which straddle Christian and humanist concerns, express a moral truth that the British government has defiled. This desecration makes its behavior idolatrous. It also makes Gladstone something of a Hebraist. For while the Jewish premier, deluded by hubris, has fallen down to worship the false god of "British interests" (28), Gladstone has been faithful to the monotheism of Judaeo-Christian tradition. The true God whom he worships is the nation or, rather, the nation and the God of Moses as identified in a shared covenant.[25]

In news reports and popular agitation, reference was made to acts of sodomy perpetrated in Bulgaria (Blake, 592). At a London meeting at which both Gladstone and Trollope appeared, Trollope's friend E. A. Freeman argued that, sooner than "uphold the integrity and independence of Sodom, . . . perish the interests of England, perish our dominion in India, rather than we should strike a blow or speak a word on behalf of right against wrong" (Feldman, 99). Although the very title of Gladstone's pamphlet, with its reference to "Bulgarian horrors," connotes sodomy (the word "bugger" is derived from "Bulgar"), Gladstone does not use the term in his text. Instead, he signifies it by repeated references to what is unspeakable. What he cannot bring himself to put into words is the negation of the truth of the word.[26]

He uses this tactic from the start, referring to "crimes and outrages, so vast in scale as to exceed all modern example, and so unutterably vile as well as fierce in character, that it passes the power of heart to conceive, and of tongue and pen adequately to describe them. These are the Bulgarian horrors" (10). As example and synecdoche, sodomy denotes and connotes what Gladstone later refers to as "the anarchical misrule" (31) that is the very opposite of moral authority. Similarly, he refers to "the Bulgarian horrors, . . . the wholesale massacres,

'Murder, most foul as in the best it is,
But this most foul, strange, and unnatural,'

the elaborate and refined cruelty—the only refinement of which Turkey boasts!—the utter disregard of sex and age—the abominable and bestial lust—and the utter and violent lawlessness which still stalks over the land" (22). To its shame, by "a strange perversity" (26), England has become a moral and material accessory to these outrages (10). In this context, England means not the nation or the people but Disraeli, the ministry, the queen, and English Jewry.

By 1878, it was commonplace to attribute Disraeli's pro-imperial policy to a misplaced sense of Jewish messianism. In the pamphlet, Gladstone prepares the way for accusations against Jews more generally by including a passage that, on its face, appears moderate. In it, he claims that his agitation is not religious in character, or, at least, that he is not leading an anti-Muslim crusade. He then proceeds to make the insidious assertion that what Englishmen really have to worry about is the conflation of religious with racial difference. Since he has already claimed that Disraeli's government is an accessory to the "Bulgarian horrors," what Gladstone says about the Turks is implicitly sayable about Disraeli and other English Jews.

Let me endeavor very briefly to sketch, in the rudest outline, what the Turkish race was and what it is. It is not a question of Mahometanism simply, but of Mahometanism confounded with the peculiar character of a race. They are not the mild Mahometans of India, nor the chivalrous Saladins of Syria, nor the cultured Moors of Spain. They were, upon the whole, from the black day when they first entered Europe, the one great anti-human specimen of humanity.[27] Wherever they went, a broad line of blood marked the track behind them; and, as far as their dominion reached, civilization disappeared from view. They represented everywhere government by force, as opposed to government by law. For the guide of this life they had a relentless fatalism: for its reward hereafter, a sensual paradise. (10)

Fatalism versus a progressive view of human history, spirituality versus sensuality, autocratic anarchy versus the rule of law, human beings versus "anti-human" beings, the binary oppositions with which Gladstone builds the passage are not difficult to recognize. More pertinent at this point in my argument is the hybrid construction of race, idolatrous religious belief (in this case directed toward the false promise of a false paradise), and national identity (Spanish, Syrian, Indian, or Turkish). The combination of a Jewish religious background with Semitic lineage also explains Disraeli's "alien" (Feldman, 120) character, his failure to identify with England's suffering Christian brethren in the Balkans, and his Oriental conception of political authority. As a composite racial/religious/national category, English Jews are implicated in the prime minister's infidelity.

Which particular Jews did Liberal and Radical polemicists have in mind? First and foremost, the Rothschilds, personal friends of Disraeli, who in a spectacular coup during the first year of his administration, provided the money the government needed to buy the khedive of Egypt's holdings in the Suez Canal Company and thereby retrieve what *Punch* called "the key of India."[28] Second, there is Gladstone's reference to the "leisure classes," later expanded to "the well-oiled machinery of our luxurious, indifferent life" (14). With these phrases Gladstone, though not a republican himself, mimics the anti-aristocratic, anti-plutocratic rhetoric of Radicals such as Henry Labouchère. The rhetoric refers to the queen and to other members of the royal family, to Tory aristocrats, but even more so to new peers such as Disraeli, whose elevation as earl of Beaconsfield was reported in the newspapers on the same day, August 12, 1876, that Parliament recessed. Even more pointedly, the term alludes to the Rothschilds and to Jewish businessmen in the City who supported Disraeli's foreign policy and held investments in Turkish bonds (Feldman, 104).

Gladstone mixes terms of financial wrongdoing (11, 12), with implications of idolatry, infidelity, and sexual transgression. The biblical authors of Exodus conceived an idolater as being like an adulterous wife; her betrayal is "a sort of robbery or improper usage of another's property" (Halbertal, 30). This image is also used to describe treaties with gentile groups that, contrary to God's will, the Israelites entered into after the exodus from Egypt. God had promised to care for the Israelites just as a husband is responsible for feeding and providing for his wife and family; in turn, Israel was obliged to Him alone. Gladstone underscores the fact that, following the Crimean War, England had bound itself by diplomatic and financial agreements to sustain Turkish autonomy. At this moment in the text, Turkey, which at the outset of the pamphlet is gendered neutrally, becomes a she, metaphorically the adulterous wife of Exodus:

Twenty years ago, France and England determined to try a great experiment in remodeling the administrative system of Turkey, with the hope of curing its intolerable vices, and of making good its not less intolerable deficiencies. For this purpose, having defended her integrity, they made also her independence secure; and they devized at Constantinople the reforms, which were publicly enacted in an Imperial Firman or Hatti-humayoum. The successes of the Crimean War, purchased . . . by a vast expenditure of French and English life and treasure, gave to Turkey, for the first time perhaps in her blood-stained history, twenty years of a repose not disturbed either by herself or by any foreign Power. . . . The insurrections of 1875, much more thoroughly examined, have disclosed the total failure of the Porte to fulfil the engagements, which she had contracted under circumstances peculiarly binding on interest, on honor, and on gratitude. Even these miserable insurrections, she had not the ability to put down. In the midway of the current events, a lurid glare is thrown over the whole case by the Bulgarian horrors. . . . The proofs are now sufficiently before us. And the case is this, Turkey, which stood only upon force, has in the main lost that force. . . . Power is gone, and the virtues, such as they are, of power; nothing but its passions and its pride remain. (12)[29]

In terms of the marriage metaphor, the passions are those of adultery, whoring, even nymphomania; they are also sodomitic since the sin of Sodom refers not only to sexual relations between men or between a human being and an animal but to any improper expression of the relationship that should subsist between a husband and a wife.[30]

Gladstone accuses Turkey of commercial fraud against its French and English guarantors. No longer a proper contract, England's obligations to Turkey are just as idolatrous as the ancient Israelites' "covenants with Assyria and Egypt and the alliance with the Chaldeans" (Halbertal, 16). Gladstone applies the same tropes to the prime minister's relationship with the British people: his government has drawn "free drafts" (8) upon the public's trust. The commercial language implicitly draws on traditional associations of Jews with the crime of counterfeiting (yet another idolatrous practice) and usury,[31] the latter allegation already posed against Disraeli and the Rothschilds in 1875 because of the generous interest the Rothschilds made on the Suez deal (Feldman, 104n.).[32] In private, Gladstone was convinced of what he called "Dizzy's crypto-Judaism" (Feldman, 102). Nor did he lack allies publicly to accuse the government and Jewish financiers of conspiring to undermine English values and genuine interests. In the spring of 1877, Freeman wrote:

No one wishes to place the Jew, whether Jew by birth or by religion, under any disability as compared with the European Christian. But it will not do to have the policy of England, the welfare of Europe, sacrificed to Hebrew sentiment. The danger is no imaginary one. Every one must have marked that the one subject on which Lord Beaconsfield, through his career, has been in earnest has been whatever has touched his own people. A mocker[33] about everything else he has been utterly serious about this. . . . His zeal for his own people is really the best feature in Lord Beaconsfield's career. But we cannot sacrifice our people, the people of Aryan and Christian Europe, to the most genuine belief in Asian mystery. We cannot have England or Europe governed by a Hebrew policy. (quoted by Feldman, 101)

Henry Labouchère is best known today as the M. P. who in 1884 introduced the amendment to the Criminal Law Amendment Act under which Oscar Wilde was charged and convicted a decade later. But Labouchère was just as antagonistic to Jews as he was to men with sexual and emotional ties to other men. In November 1877, he claimed in his newspaper, *The Truth,* that the government and bondholders were in collusion to bring England into war on Turkey's side against Russia: "These conspirators are powerful, influential, and wealthy, and they have their organs in the press." Their aim was "the continuance of Semitic rule in Europe, not in the interests of England, but on account of affinity of race and feeling between the Jews and the Turks" (quoted by Feldman, 104).

After British military involvement was averted, Bulgaria liberated, and Russian gains at Turkey's expense limited as a result of the Berlin Conference of 1878, Disraeli came home a popular premier. But the culture war that flared around the Eastern Question continued into the next parliamentary campaign. The Eastern Question brought Gladstone back to the fore of British politics. Even before the election was called, he took part in the Midlothian campaign in Scotland in late 1879. Lord Rosebery, Gladstone's host in the constituency of Midlothian and later prime minister during the Wilde trials, adapted American-style campaign tactics that he had witnessed while in the United States. In addition to mass meetings organized by Rosebery, the national press also played a major role, providing "four- or five-column reports of the major speeches."[34] The Midlothian campaign marks a significant moment in the modernization of British electoral politics. Gladstone returned to the attack on the government's foreign policy (Disraeli was now accused of having "lured Turkey on to her dismemberment"). Fortunately for Gladstone, after Berlin, as a result of mistakes beyond Disraeli's control that were made by English representatives abroad, the government incurred a series of catastrophes. One was the slaughter of twelve hundred British soldiers at Isandhlwana by the Zulu army in January 1879; another was the massacre of the head of the British mission and his staff in Kabul in September of the same year (Blake, 655–75). Both incidents illustrated to British voters the downside of an aggressively imperial foreign policy. During the campaign, Gladstone also played the Radical card, exploiting the anti-sodomitic rhetoric of republican political discourse in an assault on contemporary "luxury" (Jenkins, 427). For Gladstone, luxury denotes national infidelity. It also denotes excessive consumption, especially in the upper classes; the mechanisms of finance capital; and sensual indulgence.[35] Agricultural and commercial depression, exacerbated by Liberal and Tory economic policies during the decade, ensured a landslide victory for Disraeli's opponents; and party leaders were forced to bow to Gladstone's return as prime minister.

After the Reform Bill of 1867, enacted under Disraeli's leadership, enfranchised one million new voters, Gladstone attempted to overcome endemic corruption in the electoral process by consolidating the new voters into a collective national subject governed by a shared sense of public duty that would be both English and Christian. His objective was to ensure that the Liberal party would emerge as the majority party in Great Britain at the same time that its leadership remained in the hands of members of the old Whig families and their allies. The new electorate were to be subordinated within a singular, gendered, ethnic, and religious definition of "the nation." The one notable exception to this tendency in Gladstone's thinking is the commitment to Home Rule for Ireland that he made in 1886—a commitment that split the Liberal party (Jenkins, 542). Disraeli also believed that the democratic possibilities of expanded suffrage needed to be contained. Disraeli, however, had begun his political career as a Radical; and his government of the mid-1870s introduced pro-labor union and other legislation that benefited workers.[36] Unlike late Victorian Radicals and republicans such as Labouchère, Disraeli sought to unify the newly enlarged body politic within the terms of the existing constitution. He believed in retaining the House of Lords and embellishing the appeal of monarchy. New voters were to be linked to royalty and the aristocracy by affiliation with the Conservative party, understood to be the custodian of the national interest, which Disraeli saw in terms that combined *realpolitik* with imperial glamour and devotion to the queen.

Liberals and Radicals bridled at Disraeli's invention of the politics of imperialist populism. In assessing Disraeli's replacement for the Tory-liberal consensus, however, one needs to keep in mind the fact that his culturally hybrid, pro-imperial policy recognized the validity of social difference in England and, at times, elsewhere. That the most salient difference for him was Jewish and that he failed to recognize a number of other differences, including the legitimacy of national aspirations in India and the Celtic regions within the United Kingdom, qualifies but does not negate this feature of his concept of citizenship—particularly as a countervail to the drive toward a masculine Christian/moral unification of the body politic. This idea is particularly significant in contrast to the tactic of Liberals and Radicals of the 1870s and later, namely to attack Disraeli on the basis of *his* difference as a Jew. In other words, part of the Liberal/Radical strategy of developing a new national subject was based upon posing this position against the position of other subjects. In this way, inciting anti-Semitism played an important part in the fashioning of modern politics in Britain. The Liberal position conflated racial with religious elements: Disraeli's Jewish identity versus the Christian identity of true Englishmen. Moreover, by means of the flexible category of "the Oriental," duplicity, betrayal, and infidelity ascribed to Jews were readily transferable to other non-Christian groups as well: to Muslims, both inside and outside the empire, and to polytheists. Conversely, the Satanism and bestiality ascribed to the Turks in Gladstone's pamphlet were transferable to members of other groups such as Jews. In this context, the Liberal Christian construction of citizenship was potentially much more mischievous than Disraeli's.

Although Gladstone was an Anglican, Liberalism generally was associated with Protestant nonconformity. But, as the name Labouchère suggests, the Liberals' Radical allies included freethinkers and republicans. The Radicals, moreover, disliked Disraeli, if anything, even more than Gladstone did. The animus of secular humanists against Christianity and the Bible extended to Jews as well. At a time when Jews were migrating from eastern Europe to the East End of London, G. W. Foote, in his penny weekly, *The Freethinker*, published cartoons grossly caricaturing God the Father as an eastern European Jew, and so on. In another secularist publication, *Le bible amusante*, Gabriel Antoine Jogand-Pagés (pseud. Leo Taxil) and his illustrator, "Frid'rick," link Jewish specialty with Sodom. They picture Abraham bidding "farewell to Lot at a railway station, where a sign in the background reads "*Sodome et Gomorrhe—Train de plaisir*" (Fig. 7).[37]

The Prime Minister has a double plot. The first focuses on the personal and political life of the prime minister and his wife. The second focuses on the marriage between Emily Wharton, daughter of a well-to-do Tory gentleman, and young Ferdinand Lopez. Emily's father describes Lopez as a hybrid of southern European and African types, a characteristic way in which theorists of race described Jews.[38] This proliferating difference marks the shift in England at mid-century from the identification of Jews with Judaism, a religious belief and accompanying cultural practices, to identification as members of the Semitic race. Ironically, Disraeli himself helped to codify and disseminate this view in *Coningsby* and elsewhere.[39] Although I am unaware of evidence that Trollope read the work of the key racial theorist of mid-century, Joseph Arthur de Gobineau, Gobineau's work synthesizes attitudes, widespread at the time, that are reflected in the characterology of Trollope's novel. Gobineau believed that the existing races were already thoroughly hybridized. He believed that members of all races possessed a "racial instinct," which he called "the law of repulsion," that recoiled from cross-breeding. "But the very qualities of the white race, its civilizing urge towards social intercourse and its expansion through conquests, ended up by creating an opposite tendency ('the law of attraction'). It followed that the white race, and therefore civilization itself, were fragile and ephemeral, since these 'alloys' or infusions of inferior blood soon produced devastating effects. The laws of 'historical chemistry' decreed that the

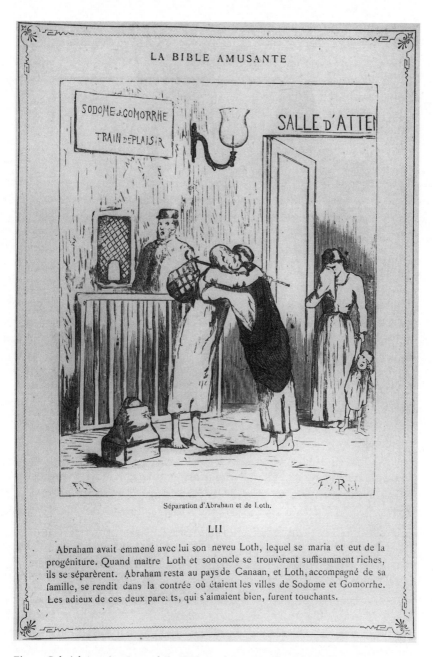

Fig. 7. Gabriel Antoine Jogand-Pagés (pseud. Leo Taxil) and his illustrator, "Frid'rick," cartoon, *Le bible amusante.*

. . . [resulting] sub-races must be degenerate." Since Semites were among the races already degraded by infusions of "black blood,"[40] Abel Wharton echoes current scientific thinking when he refers to Lopez as a "swarthy son of Judah" (1:37).[41] Within the action of the novel, the law of attraction shows itself to be far stronger than the law of repulsion. Speaking in the voice of Desdemona's father, Brabantio, Wharton wonders what "magic" can have caused his daughter to "Run from her guardage to the sooty bosom/Of such a thing. . . ."[42]

One of the ironies of *The Prime Minister* is the fact that its plot reworks the use of the Victorian marriage plot[43] in *Coningsby* even though Trollope despised Disraeli's fiction (*Autobiography*, 259–60). In his novel, Disraeli figures national reconciliation through the marriage of the young, aristocratic politician Harry Coningsby to the daughter of a newly rich, economically and politically progressive Midlands manufacturer. Trollope doubles the device. In her failed first marriage, Emily marries outside her class and background. The second time around she makes the marriage she "should have" made in the first place. In *Coningsby*, Disraeli adapts the marriage plot to provide a model for the conciliation of national differences in a single, hybrid entity. The Wharton-Lopez marriage, however, results not in social dilation but in irreconcilable differences. Emily's second marriage affirms the propriety with which old stock repel newcomers. Her second husband is her cousin and childhood sweetheart, Arthur Fletcher, whose attentions she has long refused. The lack of attraction is due to the fact that he so predictably represents her father's wishes, identification with landed values, and Anglo-Saxon solidarity.[44]

Midway through the novel, Ferdinand and Arthur become rivals for the same parliamentary seat at Silverbridge, Lopez as a Liberal, Fletcher as a Tory. Fletcher wins. Subsequently, Lopez's financial speculations collapse, and he is forced to prepare to leave the country. Instead, he commits suicide. After a prolonged period of mourning and with aid from both families, Arthur finally overcomes Emily's reluctance to remarry. Their marriage reaffirms traditional family ties. Relinquishing the ideal of national conciliation, *The Prime Minister* moves backward in time and away from the challenges of the post-1867 period. Instead of illustrating the ability of Victorian Britain to expand its range of affections, opportunities, and loyalties, the novel phantasmatically recuperates the solidarity of county families, whose political and economic power was visibly in decline in the 1870s. This deliberate turn away from political complexities and inward to a contained Anglo-Norman-Celtic hybridity represents a moral, social, and political failure. It also signals the end of the Tory-liberal consensus of the mid-Victorian period.

In *The Prime Minister*, Trollope thematizes the decadence of England's commercial, aristocratic, and political elites by frequent references to suicide. For one, there is the description of Lopez's death, which in its absoluteness recalls the destruction visited upon the inhabitants of Sodom. The representation of Lopez's death at the Tenway Junction is a fantasy of the total destruction of an alien interloper. The narrator characterizes Lopez's suicide in terms of his failure to fulfill the terms of the code of gentleman. He lacks "honour" and "honesty," Trollope's key terms of moral and social value. The condemnation of pride, vanity, duplicity, and greed meld additionally with an anthropological discourse since these failures, though contaminating Anglo-Saxons as well, are defined as the property of the Jew.[45]

After the death of his infant son, Lopez remarks: "I wish to God that where he is going I could go with him" (2:103). But he is not the only character attracted to self-annihilation. In the chapter in which he is introduced, Fletcher tells Emily's father: "The best thing to do would be to shoot myself" (1:166). After Lopez's death, Emily refuses to return to normal life. Within the moral discourse of the novel, this reluctance is portrayed in terms of injured vanity. Emily is unable to acknowledge the enormity of her error in judgment and is therefore unable to move on. Her passivity exemplifies a "perversity" (2:247) intrinsic to her gender.[46] Something more and other, though, is at stake. What Emily has risked and lost when she loses her dream of sexual fulfillment in marriage is the desire to differentiate herself, her wants, needs, and course of life from the route already mapped for her. Choosing an exogamous marriage partner means affirming the desire to be and to act differently from the ways that come to her already given. Losing Lopez means losing this aspiration. She remarks: "I sometimes feel that I must kill myself" (2:218). Being gradually compelled to recognize the very different kind of "love" (2:221) she feels for Arthur means giving up the dream of self-individuation. Hence the disturbing note of coercion when she finally yields—on order from him.

Interestingly, the word that Arthur uses to describe Emily's despondency is drawn directly from the republican rhetoric of Gladstonian and Radical discourse: namely, the word "luxury," a term that signifies the idolatrous misdirection of worship both by the inhabitants of Sodom and by latter-day politicians identified with them in satiric attacks. Emily's idolatry is her mistaken worship, first of Lopez, second of her will to live beyond the limits prescribed to her by her social position, a will that, after her disastrous marriage, can be affirmed only by negation.

Arthur urges:

"Every friend you have wants you to marry the man you love and to put an end to the desolation which you have brought on yourself.[47] There is not one among us all, Fletchers and Whartons, whose comfort does not more or less depend on your sacrificing the luxury of your own woe."

"Luxury!"

"Yes; luxury. No man ever had a right to say more positively to a woman that it was her duty to marry him, than I have to you. And I do say it. I say it on behalf of all of us, that it is your duty. I won't talk of my own love now, because you know it. You cannot doubt it. I won't even talk of yours, because I am sure of it. But I say that it is your duty to give up drowning us all in tears, burying us in desolation. You are one of us, and should do as all of us wish you. If, indeed, you could not love me it would be different. There! I have said what I've got to say. You are crying, and I will not take your answer now. I will come to you again to-morrow, and then you shall answer me. But, remember when you do so that the happiness of many people depends on what you say." Then he left her very suddenly and hurried back to the house by himself. (2:459–60)

Why does Emily cherish her grief? And why are the Fletcher and Wharton families so determined to wrench it from her? After falling out of love with Lopez and losing her son at birth, Emily enters a period of "melancholy and dejection" (2:223). This state is reinforced by the failure of her marriage and the suicide of her husband. For Emily, the end point to which the novel moves marks the extinction of the desire to differentiate herself from her family. Both Trollope and Emily make clear that the desire ridden by this ambition has been explicitly sexual. As she says to her husband the night before his death: "There are different kinds of love, Ferdinand. There is that which a woman gives to a man when she would fain mate with him. It is the sweetest love of all, if it would only last" (2:221).

Emily's melancholy registers the fierceness of her struggle to live gender and sexuality differently. The same strength disturbs the ease of her kinfolk, and it promises no sexual love to her second husband (2:221). The violence required to suture Emily within her family implies a larger sacrifice for the author and his readers, namely, sacrifice of the pleasures of widening social participation. This sacrifice leaves Trollope, his readers, and the genre of the realist novel within a double bind. Progress, modernization, imperial expansion all depended upon cultural and social hybridity. These aspects of modernity also called for a sacrifice of identity that an old-fashioned

Tory such as Abel Wharton is incapable of making. At the same time, the processes were ongoing regardless of whether members of the upper classes were prepared to accept them or not. The forced migration for economic reason of population from rural areas to town and cities; the wave of immigration of eastern European Jews to the East End of London;[48] the continuing assertion of Irish national aspirations; suffrage feminism and social purity agitation; the move during the 1880s of working-class leaders toward large-scale strike actions and the development of socialist and communist agendas; these changes and others were at hand. Liberals thought of themselves as managing necessary political and social accommodations. But if proponents of the Tory-L/liberal consensus failed in the effort, worse if they were to disidentify from this raison d'etre, then *their* decadence would become all too evident.

Julian Wolfreys interprets the melancholy that suffuses both of the novel's plots as arising from the fact that both Tories and Liberals were immobilized as a result of economic contradictions (174). James Kincaid has observed that precisely those parts of the Liberal coalition that sought change—Radicals and Irish Home Rulers—are excluded from the duke's coalition at the outset.[49] The prime minister is well intentioned. As he says, "I suppose what we all desire is to improve the condition of the people by whom we are employed, and to advance our country, or, at any rate to save it from retrogression" (2:319). But he lacks a political agenda. The main legislative goal of the new term focuses on electoral reform: "the assimilation, or something very near to the assimilation, of the country suffrages with those of the boroughs" (2:325). The objective is necessary and worthwhile, but it does not constitute a political program.

More substantive democratization could occur only at the expense of the interests that the Tory-liberal consensus served. Hence the tinkering with the electoral mechanism, political malaise among well-intentioned leaders, and a sense of the futility of political action. Political agency proved to be elusive when it implied self-diminishment if not extinction on the part of existing oligarchies. At the same time, it became increasingly evident through the 1870s that not to act meant to accept economic stagnation and decline, the gradual loss of Britain's standing abroad, and the increasing irrelevance of leading institutions. This double bind is reflected in the prime minister's anxiety and guilt about doing nothing. He responds by retreating to a conception of gentlemanliness not as a mode of agency but as a kind of being.[50] Basing his political identity on the affirmation of moral purity, he insists on quixotic acts such as naming new Lords exclusively on the grounds of merit. These efforts produce resentment and resistance among members of the Cabinet. In this context, the assertion of disinterestedness functions as a rationale for failing to act in more far-reaching ways.

The duke sows the seeds of dissolution of his government by refusing to do favors for or to befriend fellow Cabinet members. One may say that this refusal is made in defense of the concept of the gentleman and of Parliament as a government of and by gentlemen (Wolfreys, 171). In the beginning, the duke implicitly seeks to ally himself with men whose gentlemanliness will be defined and governed by a shared sense of dedication to the common good. But he finds few such men; instead, he lives, as Disraeli lived while prime minister in the 1870s, a life of ever greater personal isolation. Actual gentlemen depend on friendship in the practical, at times venal, sense that the duke refuses. Again, the duke is caught in a double bind. He does not find mutual "sympathy" (1:67) at the level at which he pitches it; and at the level at which its existence is necessary for elite male governance to function, he repudiates political friendship as a mode of corruption. The duke construes trading in personal favors as a mode of sodomitic exchange between men. This is the end to which the eighteenth-century Radical Whig ideal of a government of friends, of elite friendship as the very representation of proper governance, of government *as* friendship, arrives after working-class men begin to vote in large numbers.[51]

Emily is not the only melancholic in Trollope's novel. In place of Disraeli's continual practice of engaging even those with whom he lacked "community of feeling,"[52] the duke withdraws both from Lady Glencora and from his male political associates. He is in mourning for the ideal of governance by gentlemen/friends. His melancholy is yet more profound than Emily's since, while she is at least aware of her lost objects, the duke is unable to attach the object (elite governance) to embodied individuals. There is no scope for erotic identification between the duke of Omnium and the players in his Cabinet. What occurs instead is erotic disidentification. Or, to be more precise, the possibilities of identification are severely circumscribed, even at the level of the most private of government workings, those between a prime minister and his private secretaries.[53]

The attempt by Lady Glencora to exercise her husband's influence and her own in the election at Silverbridge makes her, in terms of classical republican discourse, a sodomite. Lopez, for his part, is a master of wrongful influence. When we first meet him at the beginning of the novel, he is swindling his business associate, Sextus Parker. The attempt to make money through financial transactions is both cause and effect of Lopez's perversity, in the traditional sense defined by Aristotle in his discussion of usury in the *Politics*. Aristotle distinguishes between money secured in exchange for an object, which he regards as natural, and money received in return for the use of money, which he regards as unnatural.[54] This source of income was traditionally associated with Jews as a sign of their perversity. The ability to generate income from capital, however, is also the defining economic activity of the Christian bourgeoisie. To condemn Lopez and other Jews as usurers, then, is likewise to condemn the Sexty Parkers of this world. This originating economic crime exacerbates while motivating Lopez's defilement of the Wharton family and his attempt to get into Parliament. The key crime is economic. To revert for a moment to Karl Marx's humanist rhetoric of the 1840s, the sin involved is one of "egoism."[55]

This moral offense is the defining characteristic of what Marx refers to as "Judaism" and of capitalist economic activity in general. Late in the novel, Sexty's wife seconds Marx's critique: "Them men, when they get on at money-making, . . . are like tigers clawing one another. They don't care how many they kills, so that they has the least bit for themselves. . . . It ain't what I call manly,—not that longing after other folks' money. . . . Why, it's altered the looks of the man [that is, her husband] altogether. It's just as though he was a-thirsting for blood" (2:74).

At the same time, in *Capital*, Marx defines bourgeois finance as a mode of idolatry. Money is a fetish, which substitutes for the living labor that, in Marx's theory of surplus value, is the real worth of money.[56] The ability of capital to multiply, as if by magic, is the central mechanism of what middle-class thinkers describe as progress or improvement. Trollope, however, turns against the means and, implicitly, the end. In his degenerating world, this activating energy of middle-class existence is portrayed as a kind of foreign infection that destroys the moral grounds of middle-class entitlement. It is important to recognize that, in light of the example of Sander Gilman's employment of the term "Jewish self-hatred," Trollope's negation of social desire may be thought of as a mode of *bourgeois* self-hatred. Trollope despises the drive to self-differentiation without which he, the genre in which he writes, and his readership could not exist.

Nowhere is the verbal excess that attaches to descriptions of Lopez in the novel more evident than in the description of his death at Tenway Junction. Lopez is described as walking backward down a platform into the path of an onrushing railway engine. He is literally taken in the rear in a phantasmatic projection of the deindividualizing effects of sodomitic assault. Displaced to the sodomitic side of the antithesis, between men of honor and economic egoists, between those who are English and those who are condemned not to be, Lopez is reduced to mingled dust and ash. As I have suggested, however, his destruction likewise implies judgment on those who are positioned on the other side of the antithesis: namely, Christian, English gentlemen, whose bodily, gendered, and (hetero)sexual integrity is nominally defined in contrast to his abjection.

After Lopez disappears under the wheels of the train, the remains elude identification. As a result, for two days Emily remains in limbo, unaware of her husband's whereabouts and unable to recognize the fact that he is dead. This liminal state of consciousness provides a sort of literal metaphor of the psychic process of melancholy. At this moment, the lost object is already lost at the same time that it is not decisively lost. Nor does it exist either outside or inside the grieving subject. This infliction on Emily and, through her, on her family and second husband is equally as important as the novel's action in effacing Lopez:

It seemed as though the man had been careful to carry with him no record of identity, the nature of which would permit it to outlive the crash of the train. No card was found, no scrap of paper with his name; and it was discovered at last that when he left the house on the fatal morning he had been careful to dress himself in shirt and socks, and with handkerchief and collar that had been newly purchased for his proposed journey and which bore no mark. The fragments of his body set identity at defiance, and even his watch had been crumpled into ashes. Of course the fact became certain with no great delay. The man himself was missing, and was accurately described both by the young lady from the refreshment room, and the suspicious pundit who had actually seen the thing done. There was first belief that it was so, which was not communicated to Emily,—and then certainty. (2:236)

It is not only a husband's "identity" that is reduced to Sodom-like ashes. Jewish culture is preeminently a culture of the book. Without the historic and eschatological prophecy of the Hebrew Bible, without the commentaries of the Talmud, Jews would not have survived as a group: "The unfinished book was our survival."[57] Trollope's insistence on erasing Lopez's textual existence tropes a metaphoric unnaming of the people for whom everything depends on the word. In this light, the extravagance of his annihilation is a rhetorical act of extraordinary violence. The forcefulness of this aggression against members of a specific group needs to be kept in balance together with the destruction of social desire. The destruction of the latter is internal to bourgeois existence and in that sense is self-inflicted, but it is also directed in fantasy toward an external threat, whistling in the wind of actual changes that Trollope if not Abel Wharton recognized to be inescapable.

On the day of his death, Lopez's gentlemanliness is reduced to what Thomas Arnold refers to as "the surface of things," manners and a wardrobe.[58] In the pamphlet, Gladstone makes the same kind of allegation against the prime minister. "What we have to guard against is imposture: that Proteus with a thousand forms" (28). Disraeli's "learned language" is a "dress" that conceals a sodomitic "beauty": "British policy . . . means the re-establishment of the same forms and the same opportunities, which again mean, on the arrival of the first occasion, the same abuses and the same crimes" (35). Shortly before Lopez's death, the narrator represents him within the same binary oppositions that structure Gladstone's attack on Disraeli. In moral and epistemological terms, Lopez knows nothing of the "honesty" and respect for truth that Trollope offers as his leading norms (2:227). Even while still alive. Lopez is not a man but instead, like Gladstone's Disraeli, an actor (2:227). He is "utterly unmanly and even unconscious of the worth of manliness" (2:227).

The results of the inquest, however, undercut the seeming fixity of values such as honesty and truth. In the same chapter that includes the description of Lopez's death, Trollope shows how euphemism is invoked in order to salvage the respectability of the Wharton family. Both the coroner and the counsel hired by Emily's father "to avoid a verdict of felo de se" make clear to the railway officer who witnessed Lopez's death that he is "not to speak his own mind" (2:237). Instead, both middle-class professionals question him in such a way as to make him look like a fool. At the inquest, Trollope shows truth to be a product of politics, both personal and public. Medical and legal procedure are used to efface meaning and to instate misrecognitions. Idolatry, private and public, ends in mortality and a motivated effort to confound moral judgment. Progress means improvement *and* mystification, hyper-organization and individual subjectification. In this context, inclusion and cohesion as social values lose emancipatory significance. Liberals too succumb to melancholy. And those Tories who keep their heads above water retreat to the safety of family marriages.

The Prime Minister vividly demonstrates the loss of consensus in post-Reform England. In Trollope's novel, the "love" for old institutions and ways of life that he associates with Toryism is portrayed as having hardened into a refusal of anything that is "not English" (1:36). That is the point of making Abel Wharton the most outspoken anti-Semite of the novel. The Tory story is one of outright phobia, on the one hand, and on the other, of

misguided and unsuccessful attempts at differentiation that end by rein-
forcing the cultural and social insularity of the Whartons and the Fletchers.
At the same time, Liberal "striving to build things new" (a phrase that owes
a debt to Revelation, the final book of the Bible) has degenerated into the
inept, self-defeating ambition shown by the newcomer, Lopez.

Where does this double negation leave Trollope? Most likely, with the
pundit, the only witness "who had actually seen the thing done." It is a
sign of an altered political situation that Trollope's line of sight coincides
with the pundit's vantage, which belongs to members of a particular upper-
working-class occupation. In this sense, the seemingly objective position of
the novelist/narrator at this moment in the novel, a generic position of
realist irony, can be seen as validating and being validated by democratic
change in the 1870s. To this extent, Trollope's position resembles that of
radicals and secular humanists such as Thomas Hardy as described by Joss
Marsh in her recent book.[59] At the same time, the triumph at the inquest
of middle-class respectability over the working-class truth-seer indicates
little confidence that democractic reform necessarily means change for the
better.

The ascendancy of euphemism at the inquest eclipses Trollope's central epistemological and ontological norms of "truth" and "honesty." The
language of realism no longer claims, as Gladstone's pamphlet does, to
retain the special authority of the word in Judaeo-Christian tradition. Nor
does the term gentleman any longer denote consistency, character, and
honor. At the same time, Trollope's position exceeds the ideological limitations of both Tories and Liberals in the novel by stylistic means. These are
what respectable Victorians would call its vulgarisms—the use of cockney
(for example, in the speech of Mrs. Parker), slang, technical language, the
language of advertising, and the argots of London, the big city in which
Ferdinand swims. Trollope's use of them moves him quietly outside the
liberal-conservative consensus; outside, too, of the work that mid-Victorian
novels such as Coningsby attempted to do in managing national difference.

Chapter 5

The Music of Sapphic Friendship in
George Eliot's Daniel Deronda

In the preceding chapter, I used terms such as decadence and degeneracy to describe the condition of England in the 1870s as presented in Anthony Trollope's novel *The Prime Minister* and in William Gladstone's attack on Disraeli. In these works, both Gladstone and Trollope associate national decadence with non-Christian outsiders. Gladstone singles out Ottoman Turks and their allies abroad. At home, he and Trollope finger English Jews, Disraeli in particular. As I argue in the preceding chapter, by analogy both men associate the prime minister, English Jews, and Ottoman Turks with the figure of the s/Sodomite, the Protestant Englishman's abjected other.[1] In addition, Gladstone attacks the decadence of the leisure classes, and Trollope's novel registers the breakdown of the Tory-liberal consensus that had shaped Parliamentary government in the middle years of the century. But it is George Eliot who, in her final novel, *Daniel Deronda,* goes further in underscoring the decadence of the old alliance of church, land, and aristocracy.

Like Trollope's novel, which was published in 1876, the same year as *Daniel Deronda,* Eliot's has a double plot. One plot is English and domestic, focusing on the entry into adulthood of Gwendolen Harleth, the female protagonist. Entering adulthood in this context means finding a suitable mate in marriage. Harleth seems to make an ideal social choice by marrying the aristocratic Grandcourt. But even before her wedding day, she realizes that she has made a catastrophic mistake. In terms of domestic romance, the interest of her story subsequently revolves around the emergence of handsome young Daniel Deronda as a rival vis-à-vis her husband. From some perspectives, the relationship between Daniel and Gwendolen looks flirtatious, from others adulterous. At the end of the novel, Gwendolen, now a widow, thinks that Daniel's interest may offer her a second chance at marital happiness. Daniel, however, abruptly quits her for another woman and a newly found vocation abroad. In retrospect, Gwendolen recognizes that her relationship with him has been that of male mentor to female protégé, the same terms as those in which Daniel had imagined it when he first intervened in her life at the beginning of the novel.

Daniel is the link between the first plot and the second plot, which focuses on the consequences of his search for his biological parents. In the course of this quest, he develops ties among the population of new Jewish immigrants to London: with Ezra Cohen and his family; with Mirah Lapidoth, who becomes another protégé; and with her brother, the proto-Zionist zealot, Mordecai. While the second plot ends with Daniel's marriage to Mirah, this linkage is typical of the sort of male homosocial triangulation in which two men, passionately committed to one another, find a socially acceptable setting for their devotion in the marriage of one to the sister of the other.[2] Far more important, in the second plot, is Mordecai's transformative effect on Daniel.

Given Gladstone and Trollope's figurations of Disraeli, one might expect the Jewish plot of *Daniel Deronda* to stigmatize Mordecai and others as corrupters of English purity. To the contrary, however, the Englishman Grandcourt is the leading degenerate of the novel; and Gwendolen from the outset is figured in the tropes of a perverse romanticism and the antisodomitic rhetoric of classical republican discourse. The novel is infused with Radical anger.[3] But Eliot is equally disabused with the excesses of Liberal attacks made on Disraeli and other English Jews after he became prime minister in 1874.[4] When Daniel leaves behind his country and his class to undertake the project of Jewish nation-building in Palestine, he is saying "no" to England as much as he is saying "yes" to his recovered cultural tradition. In her conservative aspect, Eliot values Jewish cultural memory. At the same time, in her cosmopolitan aspect, she turns away from English insularity in favor of the cultural syncretism, at once Judaic and Greek, that she carefully traces in Mordecai's mystic nationalism.

To say that Eliot values Jewish tradition is not to say that she endorses orthodox Jewish belief. Jane Irwin, the editor of the notebooks in which Eliot researched the Jewish materials of the novel, argues that Eliot was drawn to Judaic tradition precisely because of its heterodoxy. In other words, Eliot was interested in exploring a form of social and cultural solidarity that conserved the principle of individual choice. Eliot admired Jewish tradition for its reliance on "difference of opinion, controversy" in interpreting Scripture and the law.[5] Mordecai, who is the prophet of Jewish national rebirth in the novel, emphasizes this aspect of Judaism.[6] And Eliot describes Daniel as a young man, "exercised in all questioning and accused of excessive mental independence" (561). Mary Carpenter contrasts Daniel's questioning and self-questioning approach to the consensual nullity of English Anglican belief and character[7] while Irwin remarks that, within a heterogeneous, democratic polity,

a diversity of views is essential for "separateness with communication" (792), a reforming process which leads to ever more diversity. When Deronda says that Mordecai has "raised the image of such a task . . . to bind our race together in spite of heresy" (819–20), what does he mean? What could *heresy* mean to the unorthodox, nay atheist, George Eliot? For her, heresy was not meant to be hunted out and suppressed by the dominant orthodoxy; it meant "sect," retaining the original senses of the Greek root αἵρεσις: choosing, choice, course taken, course of action or thought, philosophical or religious sect. Deronda must be speaking of a racial bond which does not inhibit his freedom of choice. Indeed, Mordecai's impassioned discussion of the development of the Jewish people culminates in his declaration that "the strongest principle of growth lies in human choice" (598). (*Notebooks*, xxxvii–xxxviii)

The novel's critique of social and political elites is carried on from a moral stance that seems to exist outside the demoralization that Eliot portrays. Victorian attacks on decadence, however, are compromised by the perverse tropology they put into operation. As a result, their analyses quickly turn into fresh instances of cultural decadence. *Degeneration* (1892), Max Nordau's attack on artistic modernity, is only an extreme, albeit unwittingly comic, example of this sort of discursive effect. This general tendency also captures Eliot's critique of decadence in *Daniel Deronda*. But Eliot's novel is likewise decadent in a second sense insofar as it is characterized by antithetical thinking and an experimental approach to human relationships, in particular, to friendship. These features plus the work's Oxford bearings indicate that it is written from within the culture of contemporary aestheticism. In this way, the novel serves as an important point in the engagement of female intellectuals with the philosophic tradition of male friendship writing. Eliot's text opens a door for subsequent feminist aestheticist work such as Vernon Lee's fictional analysis of the Aesthetic Movement in *Miss Brown* (1885) and much New Woman fiction of the 1890s.

Eliot's stance is signaled in a comment that she makes in a letter in which she chastises Walter Pater's first book, *Studies in the History of the Renaissance* (1873) as "quite poisonous."[8] Just as Eliot, accusing Pater of "false principles and criticism and false conception of life," poses as an objective critic of Pater's thought, the narrator of *Daniel Deronda* positions her- or himself as the voice of moral reason in the face of contemporary decadence. Meanwhile, the narrative itself is infected with sadomasochistic sensation and other markers of what, by the 1890s, would be defined by sexologists as the sexual perversions.[9] The aestheticist character of *Daniel Deronda* has tended to be overlooked because of Eliot's reputation as the leading figure in the tradition of moral realism in the English novel. Even in revisionary critical work such as Nancy Henry's study, *George Eliot and the British Empire,* the truth that Eliot associated with a careful, analytic view of everyday life in rural and small town England is taken to be the regulative norm of representation in her work.[10] When aestheticist feeling and decadent thinking infiltrate novelistic realism, however, conventional representation starts to break down. In terms of Eliot's characteristically essayistic approach to psychological analysis and topographical description, in *Daniel Deronda* explicit referents are doubled by implicit or explicit aesthetic analogies, which in turn open onto ideas, affects, and sensations that are improper, indeed "quite poisonous." A surprising example of this sort of effect, which I describe below, is a long meditation on *amour fou* that Eliot embarks on in response to the infatuation of a minor character, Rex Gascoigne, with Gwendolen. Eliot treats Rex's first love as though it were Sappho's when spurned by Anactoria.

The "Greek" character of Mordecai's Judaism and his love of Daniel both register the revival of classical ideals of friendship that one finds at Oxford among men such as John Addington Symonds, Walter Pater, and his friend, the young Jewish writer and artist, Simeon Solomon. Eliot's novel solicits the attention of the young Oxford intellectuals who were reading Pater. And her reflections on Rex's passion bring into view another kind of friendship—that between women—and another Oxford link, this time with the young poet, A. C. Swinburne.[11] Swinburne's evocations of sexual passion, especially sadomasochistic, in love between women is far more emphatic than the portrayal of male love in Pater's early work.

Passionate female friendship is as much on Eliot's mind in this novel as is the cult of male friendship at Oxford. And Eliot is as interested in communicating with independent-minded young women as she is with young Oxford graduates. At the same time, she shows reserve in portraying friendship between women. Mirah's friendship with Mrs. Meyrick is unusual but proper. In contrast, Gwendolen's friendship with her mother, with its incestuous tremors and components of masochism and androphobia, edges into decadent territory. This relationship is not far removed from the poisonous mother-daughter connection that Radclyffe Hall portrays in her second novel, *The Unlit Lamp* (1924).

To suggest the impress in the novel of embodied passion between women, it is necessary to go beyond the limits of its literal portrayal of female friendships. Eliot pursues the intensities of passion between women indirectly through the use of analogies with the art of operatic music, often involving cross-voiced arias and cross-gendered roles or performances. For example, she indexes an alternative to literary verisimilitude, in chapter 61, where Mirah sings "*Lascia ch'io pianga,*" Rinaldo's aria from Handel's *Rinaldo* (796). The introduction of an alternative artistic medium to give utterance to what cannot directly be said in words is another feature of the novel as aestheticist. Eliot's emphasis on musicality causes the novel to strain, as Pater says all the arts do, "to pass into the condition of some other art, by what German critics term an *Anders-streben*—a partial alienation from its own limitations, through which the arts are able, not indeed to supply the place of each other, but reciprocally to lend each other new forces."[12] For Pater, as for Eliot, all art aspires to music; music is "the object of the great *Anders-streben* of all art, of all that is artistic, or partakes of artistic qualities."[13] Singing is important in the novel. Daniel has a good voice, and his long lost mother is a leading Italian diva. Mirah sings well enough to perform in private recitals and to attempt to make a living as a teacher of voice. Even Gwendolen sings. Music, moreover, is associated, traditionally and in Swinburne's poem "Anactoria," with Sappho, who was renowned both as a poet and a musician. In order to explore Eliot's use of musical analogy, however, it will be necessary to consider how she uses it in other fiction and in her letters, in which she enjoys sharing with female correspondents her pleasure in the contralto voice.

Finally, Eliot's tact in touching on female friendship in *Daniel Deronda* is one effect of the medicalization of unorthodox sexual desires. "Contrary Sexual Instinct" had been defined only a few years before Eliot wrote the novel—and the original definition dealt with female not male inversion. The scientific definition of sexual love between women as a perversion made caution imperative in dealing with it. At the same time, one senses in the novel a fascination on Eliot's part with friendships in which gender difference can be thought of as operating within rather than between individuals. In other words, while the sexual invert, that is, the individual with a man's mind in a woman's body, posed a psychiatric conundrum and, possibly, a problem for criminologists, the notion of the crossing of male and female characteristics in a single individual had the potential to further enrich and diversify the experience of friendship.[14]

Eliot regards the female singing voice as a capability with power to move women beyond the norms of Victorian middle-class womanhood. In Mirah's case, the aria permits her to cross both gender and racial boundaries since at this point in the novel she is absorbed in a secret, forbidden love for a man whom she believes to be a Gentile. Through music, women can "lend each other new forces." Earlier, Gwendolen decides that she would like to take voice lessons from Mirah. When she mentions this wish over the breakfast table, however, her husband reacts by asserting a clubman's sense of propriety: "I don't see why a lady should sing. Amateurs make fools of themselves. A lady can't risk herself in that way in company. And one doesn't want to hear squalling in private" (648). Grandcourt's response links singing with female revolt; the phrase "squalling in private" connotes domestic quarreling, which is exactly what starts when he implies that Mirah is Daniel's mistress. Gwendolen doesn't believe him, but, as soon as he leaves the house, she makes a socially unconventional morning call on Mirah to learn for herself whether there is any truth in Grandcourt's slur. When Gwendolen returns, Grandcourt meets her. Angered by the indiscretion of her visit, he demands that she never visit Mirah's home again: "You have been making a fool of yourself this morning; and if you were to go on as you have begun, you might soon get yourself talked of at the clubs in a way you would not like. What do *you* know about the world? You have married *me,* and must be guided by my opinion" (655).

Eliot marks her own emphases as she continues:

Every slow sentence of that speech had a terrific mastery in it for Gwendolen's nature. If the low tones had come from a physician telling her that her symptoms were those of a fatal disease, and prognosticating its course, she could not have been more helpless against the argument that lay in it. But she was permitted to move now,[15] and her husband never again made any reference to what had occurred this morning. He knew the force of his own words. If this white-handed man with the perpendicular profile had been sent to govern a difficult colony, he might have won a reputation among his contemporaries. He had certainly ability, would have understood that it was safer to exterminate than to cajole superseded proprietors, and would not have flinched from making things safe in that way. (655)

In this passage, Eliot links Grandcourt's curbing of his wife with contemporary abuses of British power abroad. In an obvious reference to the Governor Eyre controversy, Eliot compares Grandcourt's treatment of his wife with that of Eyre, who made unconstitutional use of martial law in putting down an uprising by the black ex-slave population of Jamaica in late 1865. Under cover of this imposition, Eyre "secured the court martial and execution of a personal and political enemy, George William Gordon, a mulatto member of the Jamaica House of Assembly."[16] Like Eyre, Grandcourt subdues Gwendolen's "nature" to a motionless state of outward compliance. At work in the passage are a number of hierarchical binary oppositions: (male) physician to (female) patient; scientific (male) gaze to (female) object of study; mind to body; man to woman; husband to wife. Other contrasting terms are also in play: aristocrat versus commoner; and colonial governor versus racialized others, whether indigenes, black ex-slaves, or mulattoes like Gordon.[17]

The passage offers a good illustration of how Eliot uses analogy and hypothetical grammatical construction in the narrator's commentary in order to widen her range of reference so that a situation involving the domestic politics of her fictional characters also serves to illuminate political struggles both in 1876, when Disraeli was under attack by Gladstone during the months when the novel was being published, and in 1865–67, the period in which the action of the novel is set (*Notebooks,* 351–54). The linkages, moreover, are not merely similitudes. Eliot clearly sees a logical connection between the unchecked authority of male heads of households at home in England and the unjust exercise of life-and-death power by male colonial administrators abroad.

Eliot is not altogether negative about marriage. Good marriages, however, usually contain a transgressive, un-English element. For example, the one successful upper-class marriage that she describes is that of young Catherine Arrowpoint. To achieve marital happiness, however, Catherine must first reject the proposal of Mr. Bult, "a political man of good family who confidently expected a peerage, and felt on public grounds that he required a larger fortune to support the title properly" (279). With Mr. Bult out of the way, Catherine chooses to marry Herr Klesmer, a gifted composer and pianist, introduced in the novel as "a felicitous combination of the German, the Sclave, and the Semite."[18] Likewise, although Mirah's place in her relationship with Daniel is secondary, her capabilities as a singer enable her to give voice to a cross-dressing, cross-voiced same-sex passion.

The place for such expression, in the world of the novel, is at the opera house or in private recitals. In the mid-nineteenth century, these bourgeois and aristocratic settings provided a privileged site for the expression of illicit female desire. One such instance occurred when Hector Berlioz restaged Christoph Willibald von Gluck's *Orpheus and Eurydice* for the contralto Pauline Viardot. After originally writing the part of Orpheus to be sung in Italian by a castrato, the eighteenth-century composer transposed it downward for male tenor voice when it was performed in French in Paris in 1773. Viardot not only persuaded Berlioz to rescore the part for her, in performance she introduced a cadenza of her own devising, an innovation that directly contradicted Gluck's Enlightenment program of purifying opera of excess vocalizing.[19] Nineteenth-century critics, however, argued that Viardot's "torrents of *roulades,* the chains of notes, unmeaning in themselves, were flung out with such exactness, limitless volubility, and majesty, so as to convert what is essentially a commonplace piece of parade, into one of those displays of passionate enthusiasm to which nothing less florid could give scope."[20] Eliot was a fan of Viardot, and after she moved to London in 1870, the pair became personal friends.

The contexts in which Eliot took pleasure in this cross-dressed role are evident in a letter from Berlin, where she saw Johanna Wagner, the niece of Richard Wagner, sing the role of Orpheus. Writing to her closest female friend, the feminist Sara Sophia Hennell,[21] Eliot, reports on the performance: "The voices—except in the choruses—are all women's voices, and there are only three characters—Orpheus, Amor and Euridice. . . . The music is delightful" (*Letters,* 2:191). Eliot frames her pleasure in both crossdressed roles within a friendly exchange with another woman: "'Die Wagner' . . . is really a fine actress and a fine singer; her voice is not ravishing, but she is mistress of it. I thought of you that evening and wished you could hear and see what I know would interest you greatly." Teasingly, at the end, she says: "I refer rather to Gluck's opera than to Johanna Wagner" (2:191). As Wendy Bashant points out, when Eliot discusses singing, she usually emphasizes the experience of listening rather than watching. In this instance, however, she bonds with another woman over the memory of hearing—and *seeing*—Johanna Wagner in the role of Orpheus. This memory stayed with Eliot. Twenty years later, when she was searching for a suitable piece for Mirah to sing in *Daniel Deronda,* "she considered the aria in the third and final act of Gluck's opera, '*Che farò senza Euridice!*': 'having heard Johanna Wagner sing [it] at Berlin when in her glory there.'"[22]

Both early and late in her career, Eliot returns to arias and the opera. In her first book of fiction, she draws upon both in the long short story, "Mr. Gilfil's Love-Story" (1857) and again in *Armgart* (1871), her verse-drama about an operatic diva. In these contexts, Eliot uses Orphic material to signal female revolt against the constrictions of male heterosexual presumption. When Caterina sings the aria in "Mr. Gilfil's Love-Story," for example, Eliot writes: "It happened this evening that the sentiment of these airs . . . [in] which the singer pours out his yearnings after his lost love, came very close to Caterina's own feeling. But her emotion, instead of being a hindrance to her singing, gave her additional power. . . . Her love, her jealousy, her pride, her rebellion against her destiny, made one stream of passion which welled forth in the deep rich tones of her voice."[23] By the mid-1870s, Eliot had become more cautious about the transfer of male emotion to a female subject. In *Daniel Deronda,* "the Alcharisi," Daniel's long-lost mother, is yet another diva who has triumphed in a trouser role, in this case that of Leonora in Beethoven's *Fidelio.* The Alcharisi is usually regarded as an unnatural mother, who also happens to be filled with Jewish self-hatred. But Eliot also presents her as heir to a tradition of female vocalizing. The woman who would eventually become Princess Leonora Halm-Eberstein discovered herself to be a "born singer and actress" (696) as a result of the vocal training she received as a youngster from her Anglo-Jewish mother's sister, who also happens to be named Leonora.

While researching the novel, Eliot refreshed her knowledge of the Greek classics, including reading and rereading Sappho in the ancient Greek.[24] In the novel, sapphic passion appears indirectly in Eliot's commentary on a young man's failed infatuation. Rex Gascoigne, the adolescent son of a rural clergyman, has the misfortune of falling for the self-absorbed, inexperienced, but beautiful and ambitious Gwendolen. Crossing lines of gender, Eliot represents Rex's disappointed love as an echo of Sappho's frustrated passion for young Anactoria in Swinburne's "Anactoria."

Rex's love had been of that sudden, penetrating, clinging sort which the ancients knew and sung, and in singing made a fashion of talk for many moderns whose experience has been by no means of a fiery, daemonic character. To have the consciousness suddenly steeped in another's personality, to have the strongest inclinations possessed by an image which retains its dominance in spite of change and apart from worthiness—nay, to feel a passion which clings the faster for the tragic pangs inflicted by a cruel, recognised, unworthiness—is a phase of love which in the feeble and common-minded has a repulsive likeness to a blind animalism insensible to the higher sway of moral affinity or heaven-lit admiration. But when this attaching force is present in a nature . . . of a human dignity that can risk itself safely, it may even result in a devotedness not unfit to be called divine in a higher sense than the ancient. (777–78)

The "ancient" who stands behind this passage is the Greek lyric poet, Sappho, lover of both men and women. At the end of Swinburne's poem, she sings:

Blossom of branches, and on each high hill
Clear air and wind, and under in clamorous vales
Fierce noises of the fiery nightingales,
Buds burning in the sudden spring like fire,
The wan washed sand and the waves' vain desire,
Sails seen like blown white flowers at sea, and words
That bring tears swiftest, and long notes of birds
Violently singing till the whole world sings—
I Sappho shall be one with all these things,
With all high things for ever; and my face
Seen once, my songs once heard in a strange place,
Cleave to men's lives, and waste the days thereof
With gladness and much sadness and long love.[25]

Swinburne's Sappho attains a kind of material transcendence, a subjective immortality through the music of her verse. As the quotation from the novel indicates, Eliot tries to go Swinburne one better in reimagining divinity, in a post-classical, post-Christian sense. For this meaning of passion, however, one has to look beyond Rex and Gwendolen to other singers in the novel, to Mirah and to Daniel,[26] whose devotion to Mordecai takes the divinely human shape, in Eliot's view, of choosing to commit oneself to the social redemption of a people.

The way in which passages of commentary look beyond particular characters and situations to other characters in the novel is one of the ways in which Eliot alters the terms of novelistic realism. In this passage, they are stretched even further to material outside the novel's immediate story since Eliot creates an occasion to discuss sexual obsession and perversion, that is, "love . . . of a fiery, daemonic character." Writing frequently within the terms of Greek pederastic tradition, she challenges Plato's attempt to sublimate such "attaching force" in the form of devotion to the Truth. Whether it be commitment to a group or "devotedness" to another human being, even when that devotion is neither merited nor returned, Eliot values commitment to others more highly than she values commitment to abstract principles.

Swinburne is one of the "many moderns whose experience has been by no means of a fiery, daemonic character." With this phrase, Eliot takes an insider's swipe at Oxford aesthetes whom she regards as what might at a later date be referred to as asexuals or as repressed or closeted homosexuals. Swinburne, who took offense, responded by attacking Eliot in an essay published a year later. Making his own use of classical imagery, Swinburne portrayed her as a writer whose sapphism did not, alas, signal poetic genius;

instead, she is "an Amazon thrown sprawling over the crupper of her spavined and spur-galled Pegasus."[27] Swinburne's Eliot is a failed Sappho.

An equally rich vein of musical analogy attaches to Mordecai's mission. In chapter 40, Mordecai on Blackfriars Bridge at sunset discovers his soulmate when he sees Daniel rowing toward the landing. Enthusiastically describing his theory of the cultural transmission of Jewish spirit from teacher to disciple through the centuries, Mordecai goes one step further to urge that, through metempsychosis, he is possessed by a visionary medieval singer:

It was the soul fully born within me, and it came in my boyhood. It brought its own world—a medieval world, where there were men who made the ancient language live again in new psalms of exile. . . . One of their souls was born again within me, and awaked amid the memories of their world. It travelled into Spain and Provence; it debated with Aben-Ezra, it took ship with Jehuda ha-Levi; it heard the roar of the Crusaders and the shrieks of tortured Israel. And when its dumb tongue was loosed, it spoke the speech they had made alive with the new blood of their ardour, their sorrow, and their martyred trust: it sang with the cadence of their strain. (555–56)

In the passage, poetry and music become the vehicle for the transmission of cultural memory, including the experience of the persecution of Jews by Christians.

Later, when Daniel discovers his Jewish parentage and pledges himself to struggle on behalf of the Jewish people, he shows that he has been meditating on the relationship between pedagogic influence, memory, and music. In the passage, he pushes Mordecai's representation of cultural transmission even further, adapting to Jewish oral tradition the Greek pederastic notion of the "receiver" in friendship between an older man and a younger one.[28] Using also an image that Sappho uses in "Anactoria," Daniel describes himself as a musical instrument played upon by Mordecai/tradition:

It is through your inspiration that I have discerned what may be my life's task. It is you who have given shape to what, I believe, was an inherited yearning—the effect of brooding, passionate thoughts in many ancestors—thoughts that seem to have been intensely present in my grandfather. Suppose the stolen offspring of some mountain tribe brought up in a city of the plain,[29] or one with an inherited genius for painting, and born blind—the ancestral life would lie within them as a dim longing for unknown objects and sensations, and the spell-bound habit of their inherited frames would be like a cunningly-wrought musical instrument, never played on, but quivering throughout in uneasy mysterious moanings of its intricate structure that, under the right touch, gives music. Something like that, I think, has been my experience. (819)

Here Daniel speaks like a Lamarckian evolutionist, who believes in the inheritance of cultural characteristics.

At Oxford in the 1860s and 1870s, the significance of erotic pedagogy in Athenian and Spartan tradition was a topic of reflection and emulation. Eliot herself "immersed herself in the culture and literature of ancient Greece during the months just prior to her study of ancient Jewish culture" (*Notebooks*, 240). Among other texts, she read fragments of Sappho, as I have already mentioned, and Plato's *Phaedrus*, the latter one of the two most important texts within the philosophic tradition of male friendship writing. Daniel's image extends this meditation to the delicate topic of influence between rabbi and student in Jewish pedagogy. Mediated through the study of shared texts—the Torah and the Talmud—the intimacy that exists between rabbi and student has been a central feature of Jewish culture. Disraeli acknowledges the power of this connection in *Alroy,* but more often homophilia within Jewish scholarly tradition has gone unremarked.

A notable exception to this tendency occurs in the writing of Eliot's friend, the scholar Emanuel Deutsch, who is sometimes described as having inspired her portrait of Mordecai.[30] In an article that Eliot read, Deutsch includes an anecdote in his essay on the Talmud that combines Hebraic with Greek tradition.[31] The story concerns "Elisha ben Abuyah, the Faust of the Talmud, who, while sitting in the academy, at the feet of his teachers, to study the law, kept the 'profane books'—of 'Homeros,' to wit, hidden in his garment, and from whose mouth 'Greek song' never ceased to flow."[32]

"How he, notwithstanding his early scepticism, rapidly rises to eminence in that same law," finally falls away and becomes a traitor and an outcast, and his very name a thing of unutterable horror—how, one day (it was the great day of atonement) he passes the ruins of the temple, and hears a voice within "murmuring like a dove"—"all men shall be forgiven this day save Elisha ben Abuyah, who, knowing me, has betrayed me"—how, after his death the flames will not cease to hover over his grave, until his one faithful disciple, the "Light of the Law," Mëir, thrust himself over it, swearing a holy oath that he will not partake of the joys of the world to come without his beloved master, and that he will not move from that spot until his master's soul shall have found grace and salvation before the Throne of Mercy—all this and a number of other incidents form one of the most stirring poetical pictures of the whole Talmud.[33]

The story combines two key aspects of the Mordecai-Daniel connection. First, syncretistic, heterodox knowledge (Mordecai reports that the medieval singer who inhabits him "had absorbed the philosophy of the Gentile into the faith of the Jew, and . . . still yearned toward a centre for our race" [555]). Second, embodied devotion between master and disciple. In short, love and heresy. In face of this double ardor, even divine authority relents: Elisha is permitted to enter paradise. This permission is even more significant since, like Socrates, Elisha had the reputation of being a corrupter of youth, through his induction of youth into religious and personal infidelity. In the Talmud, he is described as "one" who "destroyed the young plants."[34]

If the Talmud can open space for the toleration of an Elisha ben Abuyah, Eliot can do likewise for a Sapphist. Deutsch commented that the Talmud was written in "hieroglyphical" code so as to baffle non-Jewish readers.[35] The passage in which Eliot vectors Rex's passion through Swinburne's recreation of Sappho's is but one of many, apparently addressed to heterosexual readers, which communicates differently to others. Here another friend of Eliot's is in question, Edith Simcox, who understood well the privations of passionate attachment to another woman while luxuriating in a "devotedness" that rises above allegations of "blind animalism." In her unpublished autobiography, Simcox refused the tactic of a defensive translation into philosophic abstraction of her obsessive love for Eliot, even though and perhaps even more so because that love could not be sexually expressed. Simcox was a gifted journalist, a member of the London school board, cofounder of a successful workers' cooperative in the garments trade, and a respected leader of the British trade unions movement. She was also a favorite of Eliot, her love of whom Simcox records in her manuscript. Simcox understood her sexual attraction to women in vernacular terms that would soon be consecrated in the terms of third-sex theory. In other words, she attributed her love of women to the fact that she herself was "half a man."[36]

Eliot also directs her reflections on Rex's travails to another readership, namely the young male aesthetes whom Pater and Swinburne cultivated in the 1860s and 1870s. Eliot's pleasure in the company of young, sensitive men attracted her toward this promising group. So too did her ambition to change male-dominated culture. Eliot believed that a writer's influence is most effectively wielded by making an impression on members of intellectual elites (*Letters*, 5:30). This conviction drew her toward Oxford and Cambridge, precincts to which her growing reputation as a novelist and thinker gained her entry. On May 27, 1870, during her first visit there, she heard Deutsch give a guest lecture during "a meeting apropos of Palestine Exploration." She dined with Jowett and Pater. Perhaps just as pertinently for Daniel, an oarsman, Eliot adds: "After tea we went . . . to see a boat-race."[37]

At Oxford in the 1860s, liberals such as Matthew Arnold and Benjamin Jowett attempted to draw young men into a secular clerisy that would staff the civil and foreign service of the British Empire. Aesthetes such as Swinburne, Pater, and their mutual friend, young Simeon Solomon, were committed to social transformation, to "Renaissance," as they termed it. But their approach was heterodox, validating perverse forms of desire and emphasizing individual self-culture as the norm in light of which social and political change was to be understood and assessed. Solomon himself was a young writer and visual artist, well known for two different sorts of work. One were his images of Orthodox Jewish observances; the other were images of melancholy yearning between pairs of androgynous youths, at times males, at other times, females, including Sappho.[38] In the standoff between Jowett and the aesthetes, Eliot was affiliated with the latter in her contempt for British imperialism as vectored through upper-class, Anglo-Saxon male privilege. But she recoiled at the emphasis of Oxford aesthetes on personal pleasure and reacted with distaste to their celebration of the delights and sufferings of passionate male friendships.

The elaborate discussion of culture in chapter 16 of *Daniel Deronda* directly echoes the culture debate at Oxford in the 1860s. Daniel's refusal of conventional routes to advancement plus his dilemma as to what to do with his life are representative of members of the generation whom Pater, as a young man in his twenties, tutored. Heretic though she might be herself, however, Eliot uses the Jewish plot to correct aestheticist errors. Shortly after the epiphanic encounter at Blackfriars Bridge, Eliot, in a passage that overlaps Daniel's consciousness, thinks: "Deronda might receive from Mordecai's mind the complete ideal shape of that personal duty and citizenship which lay in his own thought like sculptured fragments certifying some beauty yearned after but not traceable by divination" (571). A reader of Pater would immediately recognize in the sentence a reference to a leading trope of *Studies in the History of the Renaissance,* which republished, in altered form, a number of the radical essays of the 1860s mentioned by Eliot in her journal (140). Pater uses the discovery in Renaissance Italy of buried remnants of antique sculpture as an image of the Renaissance itself. But the trope also figures the rediscovery of the androgynous beauty of the youthful male nude within the context of male friendship and pedagogy. Of Winckelmann on his first journey to Italy, Pater remarks: "Hitherto he had handled the words only of Greek poetry, stirred indeed and roused by them, yet divining beyond the words an unexpressed pulsation of sensuous life. Suddenly he is in contact with that life, still fervent in the relics of plastic art. Filled as our culture is with the classical spirit, we can hardly imagine how deeply the human mind was moved, when, at the Renaissance, in the midst of a frozen world, the buried fire of ancient art rose up from under the soil."[39]

In the mind of Eliot, such "fire" was dangerous despite the fact that she frequently refers to the fiery force of Mordecai's influence on Daniel. Hence, in adapting the passage, she frames it within the terms of an intellectual friendship. Mordecai's "mind" will lend an "ideal shape" to Daniel's own, imparting a sense of "citizenship" that emphasizes a recognition of one's "duty." Eliot defines citizenship in terms of responsibility to a social body.[40] In this context, citizenship may seem to denote not rights or freedom but the sort of subordination to a social entity that Pater warns young men against in the Conclusion: "The theory or idea or system which requires of us the sacrifice of any part of this experience, in consideration of some interest in which we cannot enter, or some abstract theory we have not identified with ourselves, or what is only conventional, has no real claim upon us."[41] And it is true that Eliot sees Daniel's commitment as arising in part from recognizing his racial heritage. But at this point the particular character of that heritage makes a difference since, for Mordecai and for Eliot too, this is a diasporan heritage, informed by other cultures, especially classical Greek culture and overcoming the corruption of that culture by the myth of Aryan supremacy.[42] When reestablished in a national center, Jewish culture promises to become "a covenant of reconciliation" (597). As Mordecai says: "Let us . . . choose our full heritage, claim the brotherhood of our nation, and carry into it a new brotherhood with the nations of the Gentiles.[43] The vision is there; it will be fulfilled" (598).

Eliot's conflation of citizenship with duty differs from subjection because it is a choice and, in that respect, achieves the objective, endorsed by Pater as the most important in modern culture, of communicating "at least an equivalent for the sense of freedom."[44] What differentiates this choice from an ideological effect is the fact that the choice is heretical. Daniel's choice violates the invidious demands both of an implicitly Protestant English national identity and of a tribal Judaism. Moreover, his choice is ambiguous about the boundaries within which he experiences intellectual friendship since the possession of his interiority by Mordecai described in the passage is so intimate that it must be both psychological and embodied.

Throughout her life, Eliot was involved in close mentor-protégé relationships with both men and women. In friendships of her youth, such as her connection with Maria Lewis, she played the part of pupil. With Simcox, Eliot became mentor—as she did with a number of other young men and women at this time in her life.[45] Representing the Mordecai-Daniel relationship provides Eliot with an opportunity to explore the complex intensities of same-sex friendship. At the same time, this focal point works as part of her bid to secure the engagement of Pater's circle of readers. Within this context, the relationship is carefully hedged so as to protect her from the sorts of allegations of impropriety that enmeshed Pater at Oxford in 1874 (Dellamora, 60–61).

As Christopher Craft observes, the theory of sexual inversion was first put forward in an article about *desire between women* by Carl Westphal in 1870: "Westphal defines inversion or homosexuality or contrary sexual feeling as a congenital perversion in which 'a woman is physically a woman and psychologically a man, and on the other hand, a man is physically a man and psychologically a woman.'"[46] Through her acquaintance with the psychological research of her partner, George Henry Lewes (he carried on extensive discussions with Westphal in Germany in 1870), Eliot was familiar with the standard features of female sexual inversion as it would be described in sexological literature of the late nineteenth century.[47] Eliot reacted with ambivalence to his work—the categorization of same-sex desire militated against her insistence on the affirmation of personal commitment as an individual choice.[48] In a letter, she referred to Westphal's field of psychiatry as a "(to me) hideous branch of practice. I speak with all reverence: the world can't do without hideous studies."[49] Interestingly, what might be moral revulsion here is expressed in aesthetic terms—a substitution characteristic within aestheticist rhetoric that was frequently singled out for criticism. By placing her reference to herself in parentheses, Eliot both minimizes and underlines it. Why should the medical definition of sexual inversion matter (personally) to George Eliot? Moreover, why does she acknowledge the importance of studies such as Westphal's? Because same-sex desire exists and for that reason alone, if no other, it is a proper, even necessary, object of study.

In *Daniel Deronda,* the leading instance of female friendship occurs between Mrs. Meyrick, her daughters, and Mirah. Although Eliot takes care to quarantine the connection within a safely domestic context, it is highly unusual. First, the situation itself, in which a widow with three young daughters agrees, at the request of a young male friend, to harbor a young woman in distress, someone unknown to them, who happens to be Jewish "but quite refined" (240), and who has just attempted suicide. Second, the Meyricks' background of mixed nationality makes them unusual, that is, "not" English. At the same time, the friendship develops in ways that show how patronizing typically English attitudes can be, for example, the Protestant interest in the conversion of the Jews.[50] Early in their friendship, Mrs. Meyrick expresses the hope that Mirah will convert to Christianity: "'If Jews and Jewesses went on changing their religion, and making no difference between themselves and Christians, there would come a time when there would be no Jews to be seen,' said Mrs Meyrick, taking that consummation very cheerfully." Mirah replies in protest, "I will never separate myself from my mother's people" (425). Daniel and the Meyricks learn from Mirah to appreciate the value of a distinctively different Jewish existence. This lesson is one of the ways in which friendship counters "the rule of contrary" (425).

The connection between Daniel and Gwendolen is understood by Sir Hugo Mallinger, Daniel's guardian, to be flirtatious; Grandcourt sees it as implicitly adulterous. It may be, however, that Eliot uses the mask of Daniel's relation to Gwendolen as an opportunity to explore the dynamics of a tutelary friendship between two women, in which one functions as a sort of "spiritual mother" to the other.[51] At the same time, transcoding same-sex friendship as an opposite-sex attraction that is at once flirtatious, socially risky, and personally transformative enables Eliot to manage the discomfort she apparently feels in representing female intimacy.

Eliot seems to be particularly sensitive to the possibility that the older friend might be regarded as physically repulsive. Accordingly, in the same letter in which she gushes about three women playing male and female leads in Gluck's *Orpheus,* she also comments to Sara: "One would prefer Mercury as a tenor to Amor in the shape of an ugly German soprano" (*Letters,* 2:191). The expression is odd, as though one were justified in preferring a male singer only because a particular female one might be "ugly." Moreover, the term tenor appears to be a euphemistic substitution for the word castrato. If this suggestion is correct, then Eliot's aesthetic distaste for female ugliness becomes even more emphatic—as well as morally dubious. Finally, as the reference to cross-dressing in the letter to Sara Hennell suggests, it may not be Daniel as a man or Daniel as a screen-figure for a woman but Daniel as a focus of cross-gendered identification that is crucial for Eliot. Eliot likes her mentors to be manly-womanly.

By means of the relationship between Mordecai and Daniel, Eliot communicates to female readers the possibly radical effects of friendship.

Hence the elaborated rhetoric in the novel of androgynous fusion between men or of soul-marriage, terms that function simultaneously as images of intellectual power and artistic genius.[52] At the same time, Eliot is of two minds about male intimacy. Much as male friendship fascinated her, its physical embodiment appears to have repelled her. Daniel characteristically recoils when touched by a man, especially if that man happens to be Jewish. The reaction registers a double phobia, both sexual and racial. Eliot makes Mordecai's body as unappetizing as his "soul" is attractive.[53] He is tubercular, wasting, and "yellow" (553), a color that connotes both bodily decay and racial miscegenation, since light-toned blacks of mixed blood were often called "yellow" and Jews were believed to be of mixed, including African, blood.

Daniel's aversion to male touch and Eliot's distasteful descriptions of Mordecai's physicality suggest a Victorian disapproval of improper mixing whether it be sexual or racial. Perverse inversions and reversals, however, also mark Eliot's portrayal of the most privileged inhabitants of the novel. In her portrayal of upper-class English life, Eliot inverts the proper relationship between English subjects and s/Sodomites in English nationalist ideology. Within Jewish culture, the contrast that exists between the children of Israel and the inhabitants of Sodom and Gomorrah is registered in the passage, already cited, in which Daniel describes himself as a dispossessed relative of Abraham, "the stolen offspring of some mountain tribe brought up in a city of the plain." In critiquing contemporary England, Eliot reverses the relation whereby Christians had long claimed God's Covenant with his people for themselves while transferring the people of Israel across the binary divide by which they formerly had distinguished themselves from the men of Sodom. If Mordecai may carry a taint of sodomy in the sexual sense, Grandcourt carries it as a representative of national infidelity.[54]

In *Daniel Deronda,* Eliot writes for the first time under the impress of what Foucault refers to as "the perversion-heredity-degenerescence system" that came quickly into place after 1870.[55] Based in evolutionary biology, ethnographic anthropology, sociology, and psychiatry, this emergent "system" was antithetical to the standard plots of the mid-Victorian novel. It came to be associated instead with aesthetic modes that follow upon realism: naturalism, symbolism, decadence, and modernism. In place of the securing of family and property in the happy ending called for by the marriage plot, the system traces the degeneration of blood lines. This reversed representation of patriarchal genealogy negates contemporary mystifications of national identity, including the religious grounding of national identity in the English appropriation of Genesis covenant narratives. Interruptions and disruptions of proper genealogy characterize the novel. Daniel's guardian, for example, fails to provide the male heir he needs in order to secure his estate to his immediate heirs. Instead, his nephew, the degenerate aristocrat whom Gwendolen marries, will inherit Monk's Topping. Grandcourt fathers four children out of wedlock but fails to leave a legitimate male heir. Before his death by drowning, he names his bastard son as his principal heir, an act of moral restitution that puts paid to fantasies of proper aristocratic descent. As for Mallinger, he is so sexually insecure that he takes satisfaction in the rumors that his ward is his natural son. Daniel's fears about being illegitimate block him from choosing a line of work as an adult. He achieves manhood only when he rejects the life that his training as an English gentleman marks him out for and instead declasses himself by committing himself to the project of the return of Jews to their ancestral home in Palestine.

Gwendolen too is contaminated by anti-sodomitic rhetoric. In the opening book of the novel, her fondness for "luxurious ease" (44) frames her within the terms of classic republican rhetoric, which labels modern life as sodomitic. Linking Gwendolen's moral irresponsibility with her critique of British colonial exploitation, Eliot associates the love of luxury with illegitimate inheritance and the abuse of racial others. "On the point of birth Gwendolen was quite easy," comments the narrator. "She had no notion how her maternal grandfather got the fortune inherited by his two daughters; but he had been a West Indian—which seemed to exclude further question" (52). Gwendolen prefers to be ignorant of the basis of her leisure in the enslavement of blacks on sugar and coffee plantations in the West Indies (886n.3.1).

Gwendolen is also associated with sexual perversion by her connection with the incident that first gave Eliot the idea of the novel. Eliot suggests that the germ of *Daniel Deronda* was a moment in 1872 when, visiting Homburg, Germany with Lewes, she "witnessed . . . Miss Leigh, Byron's grandniece" at the gaming tables. Writing to John Blackwood, her publisher, Eliot described the young woman as "only 26 years old, and . . . completely in the grasp of this mean, money-raking demon. It made me cry to see her young fresh face among the hags and brutally stupid men around her."[56] The romantic, aestheticist association with Byron connotes perversion, in this case allegations of incest with his half-sister, Augusta, mother of the woman whom Eliot observed.[57] Eliot knew these allegations both through acquaintance with members of Byron's circle and as a result of the sensation prompted by Harriet Beecher Stowe's 1869 essay, which disclosed the secret. In *Daniel Deronda*, an implication of incest returns in the linked fates of Mirah and Daniel, twinned by their parallel search for lost mothers. It returns too in Mirah's imaginary identification with her brother, Mordecai, and Daniel's with both. At the end, Daniel marries a spectral invert—the "soul" of a man (Mordecai) housed in the attractive body of his sister.

Eliot introduces Daniel in a scene of instruction with his private tutor. A casual question by the boy diverts the lesson plan into a discussion of sexual illegitimacy that alters his sense of himself and of the social world that he inhabits:

> Deronda's circumstances, indeed, had been exceptional. One moment had been burnt into his life as its chief epoch—a moment full of July sunshine and large pink roses shedding their last petals on a grassy court enclosed on three sides by a Gothic cloister. Imagine him in such a scene: a boy of thirteen, stretched prone on the grass where it was in shadow, his curly head propped on his arms over a book, while his tutor, also reading, sat on a camp-stool under shelter. Deronda's book was Sismondi's History of the Italian Republics:—the lad had a passion for history, eager to know how time had been filled up since the Flood, and how things were carried on in the dull periods. Suddenly he let down his left arm and looked at his tutor, saying in purest boyish tones—
>
> "Mr Fraser, how was it that the popes and cardinals always had so many nephews?"
>
> The tutor, an able young Scotchman who acted as Sir Hugo Mallinger's secretary, roused rather unwillingly from his political economy, answered with the clear-cut, emphatic chant which makes a truth doubly telling in Scotch utterance—
>
> "Their own children were called nephews."
>
> "Why?" said Deronda.
>
> "It was just for the propriety of the thing; because, as you know very well, priests don't marry, and the children were illegitimate." (202–3)

Daniel, the identity of whose parents has been concealed from him, is jolted by the term into a sense of unease that is relieved only late in the novel when he learns that he is the child in wedlock of two Jewish parents. In the meantime, speculating that he is Sir Hugo's illegitimate son, he fantasizes a family romance in which his unknown mother figures as the innocent victim of a worldly seducer.

The shame, ignorance, and resentment provoked by this exchange with his tutor places Daniel in an uncertain relationship to the identity of gentleman that his mother purchased for him by entrusting him to Sir Hugo, one of her English admirers. The euphemism of the reference to "nephews," of the silence surrounding the facts of his descent, conforms to

propriety in one sense while undermining the code of the English gentleman in others. As Daniel surmises, "There was something about his birth
which threw him out from the class of gentlemen to which the baronet
belonged" (209). But if Sir Hugo's presumed betrayal of a young woman is
the act of a gentleman, what honor or ethical standing does the term have?
Note, moreover, that it is an *English* gentleman of which we speak here.
The path of advancement, through Eton and Cambridge University, into
professional or public service, is one that Daniel finds increasingly uncom-
fortable and unsuitable although, as long as he does not know his family
history, he is unable to define an alternative path for himself. Shamed as
illegitimate, Daniel becomes a de facto rebel, albeit passive and somewhat
indeliberate, against the norms of the class in which he has been brought
up. As Sir Hugo asks him when he decides to leave Cambridge to pursue
further studies on the Continent, "So you don't want to be an Englishman
to the backbone after all?" (224). Daniel's later adoption of the Jewish national cause as his own needs to be understood in its full force as a rejection
of the male gender-norms of Sir Hugo's class.

The illegitimacy of the aristocratic class is also marked in the reference
to "a Gothic cloister." Up until now, Daniel has delighted in Sir Hugo's
estate at Monk's Topping, "one of the finest in England, at once historical,
romantic, and home-like. . . . The Mallingers had the grant of Monk's
Topping under Henry the Eighth, and ages before had held the neighbour-
ing lands of King's Topping, tracing indeed their origin to a certain Hugues
le Malingre, who came in with the Conqueror—and also apparently a sickly
complexion which had been happily corrected in his descendants" (203–4).
This account provides a reminder of the violent origins that attend aristocratic property and lineage.[58] The Mallingers were opportunistic beneficia-
ries of Henry the Eighth's attack on the late medieval church, an attack
that sundered the unity of religious community and faith, while unlawfully
enriching a few. The monks of the former abbey, then, are one more group
among those whom Eliot refers to as "superseded proprietors." Dynastic
history is one of repeated acts of violence, subjection, and dispossession,
sometimes of members of one ethnic or religious group by another, at
others of colliding factions within a single polity. These injustices constitute
aspects of Mr. Fraser's favored topic of "political economy" that he prefers
not to analyze.

In the argument of Jean Simonde de Sismondi, a liberal Protestant
Swiss historian, the papal church invited its own eclipse in part as a result
of the irresponsible sexuality of leading clergy. And although Eliot focuses

on sins of adultery and fornication, Sismondi, other historians, and Protestant polemicists of the mid-nineteenth century also remark the sodomitic excesses of Catholic prelates, "nephews" in this case being a euphemism for catamites. Even the name, "Monk's Topping," can be read as alluding to clerical perversity. The pedagogic context in which the scene is set, with a lovely thirteen-year-old boy lounging on fallen rose petals at the feet of his tutor, quietly underscores pederastic suggestion in the passage as does Eliot's later comment that the purity of the boy, caught in a portrait, makes one "shudder anew at all the grossness and basely-wrought griefs of the world, lest they should enter here and defile" (205).[59]

The legitimacy of the established church in England is also put in question. In the parts of the novel that focus on upper-class life, national identity appears to be based on domestic genealogy—a succession, literally and figuratively, of family portraits. But, within the terms of the novel, national identity cannot be restricted to such limited terms. Even the fact that Daniel's tutor is Scottish registers the fact that English identity is one aspect of British identity. The British identity of *English* subjects connotes English cultural, economic, and political dominance of the Celtic inhabitants of Scotland, Ireland, and Wales. The question of the place of subordinated national cultures within the United Kingdom was a troubling one in the years in which the novel is set, with Irish M. P.s pressing for Home Rule while the Fenians resorted to violence in Ireland and in English cities with large Irish populations such as Manchester and London (*Notebooks*, 353). Daniel's personal situation also has a context in constitutional debates of the day. In 1858, Jews were first permitted to sit in the House of Commons. And in 1867, Disraeli, although technically a convert to Anglicanism, became England's first prime minister of Jewish descent. These changes plus the emergence of a distinctive Anglo-Jewish cultural presence brought into focus the question as to what place Jews with full political rights would and should play in English public life.[60] Under the new conditions, too, what would be the proper role of Jewish tradition in English culture? How would this hybrid relation change English culture?

The tendency for such discussions to be cast within biologically inflected terms of "race" provides an additional, complicating factor. The narrator says of the portrait of the boy: "You could hardly have seen his face thoroughly meeting yours without believing that human creatures had done nobly in times past, and might do more nobly in time to come" (205). Much later, when Daniel visits the Hand and Banner club with Mordecai, the working- and lower-middle-class intellectuals there are engaged in a discussion about the meaning of the word progress. As the conversation continues, the general question is pursued within the context of national movements, of which the proposed return of the Jews to Palestine serves as an example.[61] One still unanswered question is whether or not the values of a liberal constitution can be reconciled with appeals to race as the ground of claims to land and national sovereignty. Eliot like John Stuart Mill attempts to conciliate the affirmation of cultural and geographical rootedness with a liberal ideal of civic nationality. Within these terms, she does not directly address the question of race as it informs Mordecai's discourse.[62] Were she to do so, she would need to call Mordecai's vision of a restored Jewish homeland into question since a racial definition of citizenship (a nation of brothers) is at odds with the notion of civic nationality (a nation of friends).

Eliot's sympathy with the politics of Jewish return is potentially in conflict with the anti-imperial stance of her references elsewhere in the novel to the Jamaica Uprising. Edward Said has shown how closely Mordecai's reasoning parallels that of Jewish nationalists such as Moses Hess in *Rome and Jerusalem* (1862) and, earlier, Ernest Laharanne.[63] According to Said, by ignoring the rights of the Arab inhabitants of Palestine, Hess and Laharanne position Arabs as yet another class of "proprietors" to be "superseded" in the Western partition of the rest of the world. This oversight on Eliot's part also puts in question Daniel's relationship to the prerogatives of an English gentleman. Jewish resettlement could be achieved only if Western great powers were to replace the Turks as the dominant force in the region. In other words, writers such as Hess and Laharanne envisage Jewish nation-building within the terms of a colonizing, Western project. The primary value of Daniel to the resettlement effort will lie in the access he enjoys as an upper-class English gentleman to sources of support based in England. In the Hand and Banner chapter, Jewish characters repeatedly compare the effects of Jewish diaspora and nation-building with the effects of the spread of English settlers throughout the globe. These characters overlook the injustices likely to result from Western-sponsored migration of Jews to the Middle East.

Leonora's rejection of motherhood as the literal conduit of Jewish identity signifies feminist revolt from the subordination of women within a traditional religious culture. In the present context, her choice also challenges notions of polity based on blood relationship. For both Mordecai and Eliot, the key element within tradition is not the creation of a nation-state but the function of transmission and the role of transmitter, "the

Masters who handed down the thought of our race—the great Transmit-
ters, who laboured with their hands for scant bread, but preserved and
enlarged for us the heritage of memory and saved the soul of Israel alive as
a seed among the tombs" (580). Given Eliot's importance as a leading novelist and her belief in the responsibility of the artist to transmit cultural
values, she necessarily supplements Mordecai's masculinist view with an
awareness of the fact that women are likely to have different perspectives
about the meaning of cultural transmission. Leonora, for example, has been
driven from Orthodox Judaism because of her father's view of women's
role within that tradition as a biological "instrument" (726) for the passage
of male seed from father to son. The subjection of Jewish women that
angers Leonora enfolds her daughter-in-law, Mirah, both as sister and as
wife, despite the fact that Mirah chooses to accept these roles and even
though Eliot appears willing to second Mirah's choice.

The marriage of Mirah and Daniel at the end of the novel is consistent
with the view that Eliot endorses different paths for exceptional and ordinary women, the latter among whom might well be best suited for traditional lives as daughters, sisters, wives, and mothers (Bodenheimer, 178).
Her comment to a close friend, the feminist Barbara Bodichon, in a letter
of October 2, 1876, suggests such a view: "My impression of the good there
is in all unselfish efforts is continually strengthened." And yet, because of
her voice, Mirah is not ordinary. In the immediately succeeding sentence,
Eliot suggests what may be her view of the upshot of the Daniel-Mirah
expedition: "Doubtless many a ship is drowned on expeditions of discovery
or rescue, and precious freights lie buried. But there was the good of man-
ning and furnishing the ship with a great purpose before it set out" *(Letters,*
6:290). As for Daniel, when Gwendolen, in the penultimate chapter, asks
him whether he will return, he says: "If I live, . . . *some time*" (874, italics
Eliot's). The "if" portends. . . .

How is one to reconcile the Eliot presented in this chapter: affirmative
of perverse desire, Jewish-identified, feminist, and radical, with the woman
whom Bernard Semmel describes as "one of the more sensitive and articu-
late exponents of the social-conservative politics of tradition—and of the
politics of national inheritance"?[64] Eliot's views were not uniform. For example, although at one time she had held Disraeli in contempt (Haight, 59,
63), at the time of Disraeli's victory over Gladstone in 1874, she wrote to
her close friend, the feminist Barbara Leigh Smith: "Do you mind about
the Conservative majority? I don't" *(Letters,* 6:13–14). Of course, feminists
had reason for dissatisfaction with Gladstone. In 1870, "the watershed year"

in mid-Victorian efforts to extend suffrage to women, "a Suffrage Bill passed second reading in the House on a vote of 124 to 91. Despite the fact that Liberals were nominally in support, Gladstone . . . brought out his determined opposition, and the majority melted away. 'It would be a very great mistake to carry this Bill into law,' he said, and though he gave no reasons the whole tone of the House changed forthwith. . . . So ended the early hopes of parliamentary success."[65] At the same time, however, Eliot was also prepared to flatter Jowett by letting him form the impression that she was no advocate of "women's rights" (Haight, 465).

The logic of Eliot's apparent self-contradiction lies in part in her personal situation. Literally engaged in an adulterous liaison with Lewes that lasted twenty-four years, the pair presented themselves to the public as husband and wife. Although both, particularly Eliot, paid a high price for their transgression, she eventually was received by Masters of Colleges at Oxford and Cambridge, by leading authors, and by aristocrats and politicians. Eliot's ambition depended upon public acceptance, but it also required sexual and gender transgression. Eliot's "marriage" out-of-law brought to her side an effective business manager, intellectual interlocutor, protector, and friend. The needs of his wife and her children also helped turn her attention to writing fiction in the first place. At the same time, Eliot was shielded from the legal, moral, and psychological subordination that attended conventional marriage.

Eliot's intelligence and critical energy put her at odds with conventional expectations of women at the time. In this light, sexual involvement carried with it unavoidable debits. In the relationship established between Lewes, Eliot, and Simcox in the 1870s, however, one finds what might be described as carefully managed obsession and risk. Lewes mediated between Eliot and her passionate young admirer—enjoying certain benefits along the way. For her part, Eliot was able to enjoy close friendships with Simcox and a number of other women. As in the pre-Lewes years, Eliot was emotionally entangled with both women and men but now in ways that no longer exploited and diminished her. For her part, Simcox knew the limits, though she persistently challenged them.

Rex Gascoigne's "devotedness not unfit to be called divine" is apposite Simcox's abjected relationship with Eliot (McKenzie, 101). Eliot's preceding reference to "a human dignity that can risk itself safely" bespeaks her approval of Simcox's submission and tells as well of the edification and pleasure that Eliot took in being able to risk herself with a younger woman. On the occasion of their last long conversation alone, Simcox kissed her passionately. Then Eliot "said I gave her a very beautiful affection—and then again she called me a silly child, and I asked if she would never say anything kind to me. I asked her to kiss me—let a trembling lover tell of the intense consciousness of the first deliberate touch of the dear one's lips. I returned the kiss to the lips that gave it and started to go—she waved me a farewell" (McKenzie, 97). The farewell, acknowledging connection but also distancing it, is Orphic. The gesture, combining recognition and warding off, is Eliot's preferred stance in relation to an intense, embodied friendship with another woman.

Daniel Deronda expresses a strong intuitive awareness of the power of this sort of tie between women. When Daniel brings Mirah to the Meyricks, he thinks of a classical context in which his action makes sense. "Then there occurred to him the beautiful story Plutarch somewhere tells of the Delphic women: how when the Maenads, outworn with their torch-lit wanderings, lay down to sleep in the market-place, the matrons came and stood silently round them to keep guard over their slumbers; then, when they waked, ministered to them tenderly and saw them safely to their own borders. He could trust the women he was going to for having hearts as good" (236). Eliot sees the relation between women like herself and women who were beginning to be called sexual inverts as one between "matrons" and "Maenads." (In Greek myth, the Maenads had torn Orpheus apart when, after he lost Eurydice a second time, he became a lover of boys. The dismembered body came to rest on the island of Lesbos.) The key word that structures this relation and makes an exchange of tenderness possible is "borders." Both terms depend upon this separation, which creates the possibility of a wildness that is not less or other than human but more intensely so. In this way, attachment between women eludes condemnation as perverse.

This carefully delineated limit structures Eliot's final novel, requiring that the actual effectiveness of an intimate mentor-protégé relationship between an older woman and a younger one be displaced into the depiction alternatively, in realist terms, of male friendship, male-female romance, and conventional male-homosocial marriage. Nonetheless, the music of a possible alterity, of other ways of structuring experience, continues to be heard. One receives remarkable other thoughts from Eliot, as Daniel does at this moment for, having intervened in a fate-altering way in the life of another, he thinks—in this book, which is obsessed with the power of thinking to transform personal and social existence: "The moment of finding a fellow-creature is often as full of mingled doubt and exultation as the moment of finding an idea" (236).

Chapter 6
Aesthetic Politics in Henry James's The Tragic Muse

Between 1876, the year of publication of *Daniel Deronda,* and 1890, the date of publication of the American first edition of *The Tragic Muse,* a number of changes occurred that forecast a much different play of relations between politics, desire, and aesthetics in James's novel than in Eliot's.[1] One of the key factors was the passage of the Labouchère Amendment to the Criminal Law Amendment Act of 1885, a law that drastically narrowed the range of speech in which it was permissible to express or affirm male same-sex desire. The amendment created the legal conditions whereby a leading artist could be publicly discredited and possibly convicted of "gross indecency with another male person" on the basis of personal correspondence or aesthetic material, for example verse or fiction, published or unpublished.[2] The Labouchère Amendment transformed the conditions of artistic expression in England.

In a negative sense, the amendment democratized aesthetic politics by subjecting artists and their work to commonsense views of the connection between morality and criminality as those views were shaped and propounded by journalists and editors, on the one hand, and by Tory and Radical politicians on the other. Two different aspects of democracy are in volatile play in relation to the moment of this novel. One is the formation of particular affinity and interest groups: namely, Irish nationalists, socialist and communist trade unionists, feminists, and emergent male homosexuals. The tendency for such groups to form is both desirable and inevitable in a democratic state. Another tendency, however, just as inevitable and not desirable, is the manipulation by political demagogues of the new situation created as these formations come into existence. The likelihood of the latter occurring was exacerbated in the late 1880s as a result of large-scale expansion of the male electorate by the Third Reform Bill in 1884.[3] In relation to James's novel, the most significant of these demagogues is Henry Labouchère himself. In his attacks upon members of the royal family, aristocrats, Jewish publishers and financiers, and subjects of male same-sex desire, Labouchère functions as an invisible but powerful antagonist of the complex aesthetic politics of James's novel.

This politics, as will emerge in the course of the chapter, is both descriptive and prophetic. The female protagonist of the novel, Miriam Rooth, in her talent, freedom of spirit, ambition, charisma, and air of foreignness, sums a number of characteristics of "the Souls," a new cultural and social elite, comprised of both outsiders and insiders, which included, among others, professional and society women, wealthy Jews, and male homosexuals. The leading art form of this group was not West End theater, where Miriam will make her career (and where Wilde would soon make his), but the society portrait, whose leading practitioner was James's friend, John Singer Sargent. Accordingly, it is not accidental that the art that beckons Nick Dormer, the male protagonist of the novel, is the art of portrait-painting.

The most significant sign of James's commitment to democracy is the affirmation in his work of the importance of individual choice. Within the defensive circumstances created by the Labouchère Amendment, however, James does so with caution. While there are many significations of queer desire in the novel, James always retains the option of deniability. His challenge to younger readers to change their lives comes not in the form of outrageous examples—such as Oscar Wilde was to provide in the same year in his novel *The Picture of Dorian Gray*. James instead emphasizes negative decisions. Nick's choice is not whether he should accompany his young friend, the Oxford aesthete Gabriel Nash, to southern Italy and Sicily, known at the time for the sexual availability of its adolescents and young men. Instead, Nick revolts by choosing not to pursue a career in politics and not to marry the wealthy young widow whom his mother and his political mentor, Mr. Carteret, have chosen for him. For good measure, in the 1908 Preface, James further points out that Nick fails to notice that she is falling in love when she sits for him for a portrait.[4]

These are important refusals. Nonetheless, Nick's revolt from upper-middle-class expectations is compromised, in the first place by James's decision to maintain the respectability of his bohemian characters. In the letter in which he agreed to produce the novel for serial publication in the *Atlantic Monthly*, James writes: "The scene will be in London, . . . [the] *monde*, considerably the 'Aesthetic.' There you are. It won't be improper; strange to say, considering the elements."[5] James evacuates any vagaries, sexual or otherwise, that may have occurred between Nick's graduation from Oxford and his election to Parliament. In the sculpture court of the Paris Salon, where the novel begins, Nick is reminded "of old associations, of other visits, of companionships that were closed—an insinuating eloquence which was at the same time, somehow, identical with the general sharp contagion of Paris."[6] James's "eloquence," however "insinuating," is mute.

Nick's secret dissipation has nothing to do with ballet dancers or rent boys. Instead, art is forced to carry the burden of secrecy and confession that, in the popular press of the day, was carried by sexual scandal. James writes: "Nick made afresh [to Nash], with more fullness, his great confession, that his private ideal of happiness was the life of a great painter of portraits" (294). Art as a dirty secret makes sense in the philistine terms of Nick's mother, Lady Agnes, who, according to her son, subscribes to "a general conviction that the 'aesthetic'—a horrible insidious foreign disease—is eating the healthy core out of English life (dear old English life!)" (421).[7] Within the broader outlook of Nick, the rhetoric of aesthetic decadence seems out of place. That is, it is out of place unless the rhetoric of the aesthetic life as poisonous, as a contagion or infection, which pervades the novel, actually accords with what James thinks. The author of this novel acknowledges that art corrupts. But the corruption can be redemptive insofar as it seduces individuals out of the norms and roles into which they have been socialized. In this respect, art has an important part to play in the work of widening the possibilities of choice, both individual and social.

Nick's eventual choice of portrait painting as a career is prophetic of the esteem that painters such as Sargent, James Jebusa Shannon, and Giovanni Boldini were to achieve during the coming decade.[8] Nonetheless, this choice is problematic, first of all, because Nick's theory of "the idea" in painting seems not to so much French and modern as conventionally Victorian. In the essay of 1887 in which James introduced the expatriate American, Sargent, to a North American audience, James writes: "Mr. Sargent simplifies, I think, but he simplifies with style, and his impression in most cases is magnificent."[9] Representation depends upon a stylization that is at once aesthetic and personal and which depends in turn upon sensation or "impression." Nash makes a cognate point in *The Tragic Muse* when he urges Nick that what makes portraiture special as an art form is that it offers a double representation of both the sitter and the painter: "Unlike most other forms, it was a revelation of two realities, the man whom it was the artist's conscious effort to reveal and the man (the interpreter) expressed in the very quality and temper of that effort. It offered a double vision, the strongest dose of life that art could give" (310). Nick's view of portrait-painting is rather different: "If I were to do exactly as I liked I should spend my years copying the more or less vacuous countenances of my fellow-mortals. I should find peace and pleasure and wisdom and worth, I should find fascination and a measure of success in it" (294).

Nick's blankness on the topic of style and on the basis of painting in sensation is especially significant in a Victorian context. As Christopher Newall points out, no Victorian painter was able to surmount the deadening effects of an endless stream of portrait commissions. As Sir John Everett Millais commented to the painter, Frank Holl, in 1888: "You have been ill, and I don't wonder at it, with the quantity of work you have done this year. Portrait-painting is *killing work* to an artist who is sensitive, and he must be so to be successful, and I well understand that you are prostrated by it."[10] Sargent himself eventually abandoned portrait painting.[11] The one artist who was able to overcome the limitations of the profession was another American expatriate, James McNeill Whistler.[12] But Nick is neither American nor a Whistler.

Earlier, Nick, using terms reminiscent of those used by James in 1873 when he described the impact upon him of seeing a copy of Walter Pater's *Studies in the History of the Renaissance* in a bookshop window in Florence (*Letters*, 1:391), describes his former classmate as a "poison" that threatens his very existence: "At Oxford you were very bad company for me, my evil genius; you opened my eyes, you communicated the poison. Since then, little by little, it has been working with me: vaguely, covertly, insensibly at first, but during the last year or two with violence, pertinacity, cruelty. I have taken every antidote in life; but it's no use—I'm stricken. It tears me to pieces, as I may say" (143). Cast in terms of an ideological opposition between politics and art, the rhetoric, Orphic and Dionysian, of this passage likewise connotes by reversing Nash's infatuation with Nick.

When they meet at the Paris Salon after a long interval apart, Nash says, "I have an idea you need me" (33). Nick, with his younger sister, Biddy, at his elbow, responds as flirtatiously as circumstances permit. Protecting the public presentation of his own masculinity, Nick positions Nash so that it is he who will signify the emotional register—and in ways that offend Biddy. Nick asks:

"You're not in London—one can't meet you there?"
"I drift, I float," was the answer; "my feelings direct me—if such a life as

mine may be said to have a direction. Where there's anything to feel I try to be there!". . .

"I should like to get hold of you," Nick remarked.

"Well, in that case there would be something to feel. Those are the currents—any sort of personal relation—that govern my career."

"I don't want to lose you this time," Nick continued, in a manner that excited Biddy's surprise. A moment before, when his friend had said that he tried to be where there was anything to feel, she had wondered how he could endure him.

"Don't lose me, don't lose me!" exclaimed the stranger, with a countenance and a tone which affected the girl as the highest expression of irresponsibility that she had ever seen. (34)

Nick's combination of flirtation with gentlemanly reserve typifies James's portrayal of him. In the opening description of Nick, James notes the "wandering blankness" (19) of his gaze, which "those who liked him" (the withholding of gender is conscious) characterize as "dreaminess" (20). Nick is an attractive (white, Anglo-Saxon) screen, onto which the reader, male or female, is invited to project desire. This screen is especially seductive to aliens: to Irish, Jewish, or American onlookers, including the author.[13] In the 1908 Preface, James sadly confesses that although Nick is supposed to be the primary focus of the reader's attention, for some intangible reason he fails to fascinate: "I strove in vain, I feel, to embroil and adorn this young man on whom a hundred ingenious touches are thus lavished: he has insisted in the event on looking as simple and flat as some mere brass check or engraved number, the symbol and guarantee of a stored treasure. The better part of him is locked too much away from us."[14]

Despite the readerly dalliance afforded by the narrator, James distances himself from this kind of allusiveness by "Biddy"-izing (that is, by heterosexualizing) the narrative.[15] Similarly, Nick is seduced into the pursuit of beauty not by Nash but by the beautiful young actress to whom Nash introduces him. Miriam is a counter *pharmakon* to Nash's (male) homoerotically inflected variety of aestheticism. Nonetheless, as a source of contagion she is myriad—connoting illicit desire between women, as I argue below, and, in her professional capacity, turning the theater into a site/sight of infection capable of either saving or destroying an aesthetically (re)constituted body politic.[16]

In another sign of James's caution, Nash famously disappears at the end of the novel—just as, to the mind of his friend, the uncompleted portrait that he paints of Nash "had a singular air of gradually fading from the canvas" (556). The Cleveland Street Scandal of 1889–1890 gave a number of upper-class men with sexual and emotional ties to other men reason to disappear from England to the Continent. Nash too is disappeared, so to speak, by the violence inherent in the new law. Not only does Nick participate in this effacement, partly literal, partly phantasmatic, so also does James in the 1908 Preface by omitting mention of Nash. Turning the canvas to the wall (562), however, does not mean that Nash will not come back. The inevitable return of an aesthetic stance that has been declared illegal beckons in James's novel at the same time that the machinery of the novel works hard to defer the possibility indefinitely (556).

What remains is influence. And influence, more than anything else, is what James's novel is "about." In the course of the novel, Nash influences Nick to throw over a promising political career as well as the woman who accompanies it, Julia Dallow, a beautiful, wealthy, intelligent, and ambitious supporter, who plans to marry him. Instead, Nick decides to become a painter of portraits—even though Nash believes that this choice will lead, in the end, to Nick's being reabsorbed into upper-class English life both as a successful artistic professional and as Julia's husband. Influence, then, is ambiguous. It works its effects, but these can also be resisted, derailed, or, at the least, rerouted. Influence operates in another way in the case of the other artist in the novel, Miriam, who has an artistic gift that Nick lacks and who is also possibly Jewish and, for sure, bohemian. In the course of the novel, Miriam moves from the status of an ambitious amateur actress to success on the West End stage. Through the "infinite variety" (419) of her personality, Nick believes—or at least feels—that Miriam, prompting "a feast of fraternity" (496), will exert a pervasive influence on her audiences.

Influence in this sense is another form of aesthetic politics. The novel contains extended passages in which various characters reflect on the influence exerted by different artistic media and genres: dance, sculpture, portrait-painting, and theater. The genre of the novel is validated not on the usual basis of its verisimilitude (unless invisibility is taken to be a mode of verisimilitude) but as the textual space in which the merits and effects of diverse media can be both suggested and represented.[17] In *The Tragic Muse*, this function displaces the sort of conventional political concerns, both overt and analogical, that preoccupy George Eliot in her final novel. Like the invisible influence of a Nash or a Wilde (or a Pater, who provides an original of which Nash's often fatuous aesthetic maxims are a second- or third-generation copy), the arts portrayed in James's novel create their effects through an erotic attraction that functions independently of and is, at times, at odds with reason. For example, by the end of the novel, Nick's cousin, a young diplomat named Peter Sherringham, has decided to forget his entanglement with Miriam, who is willing to consider marrying him only if he is prepared to defer to the demands of her professional calling. This sacrifice is one of which Peter is incapable. Nonetheless, when he attends a premiere with Nick, he experiences "a cessation of resistance which identified itself absurdly with liberation" (498–99). As a result, he makes one last appeal to her to marry him. When she refuses to leave the stage to minister to him and his career, Peter attempts to inoculate himself by marrying Biddy. He also arranges a transfer of post to a tropical country where, if lucky, he will contract a quick-acting, fatal disease.

Nick for his part understands Miriam's effect on the audience in terms of desire: "the night had turned into a feast of fraternity and he expected to see people embrace each other" (496). In this sentence, desire becomes the switch point for possible social transformation. The phrase "feast of fraternity" recalls the urban festivals of the French Revolution. And aesthetic politics assumes the form of aesthetic education, the concept within liberal political theory that, as Linda Dowling argues, finds a basis for democratic values in the formation of aesthetic taste. Although contemporary commentators tend to focus on the basis of liberalism in contract theory,[18] the eighteenth-century Whig writer Lord Shaftesbury sought a social principle on whose basis government by popular assent could be established. He found this ground in the moral-aesthetic concept of taste. A subjective universal that combines aesthetic refinement with sympathy and affection for others, taster, according to Shaftesbury is "a *sensus communis . . .* of public weal, and of the common interest; love of the community or society, natural affection, humanity, obligingness, or that sort of civility which rises from a just sense of the common rights of mankind."[19] In the nineteenth century, the American poet Walt Whitman affirmed this sense as one that includes touch and intimacy. As he says in an essay of 1888: "It has become . . . imperative to achieve a shifted attitude . . . towards the thought and fact of sexuality, as an element in character, personality, the emotions, and a theme in literature. I am not going to argue the question by itself; it does not stand by itself. The vitality of it is altogether in its relations, bearings, and significance."[20] Focusing on Miriam as a subject and object of desire, James is concerned to suggest the "relations" within which sexuality takes on meaning.

To choose Miriam as focus appears to offer one additional way of heterosexualizing the connection between sexual, aesthetic, and conventional politics. But male characters in the novel who insist on claiming Miriam for their desires tend to be characterized as unimaginative and self-absorbed. Peter's response in particular is dangerously narrowing, not least because to him it seems to be so obviously the only right one. Actresses, however, are not only objects of male desire. James was familiar with the sapphist aesthetic circle assembled by the American actress Charlotte Cushman at her home in Rome at mid-century.[21] As a sapphist, Cushman made her greatest impression in trouser-roles such as that of Romeo in Shakespeare's play.

The performing arts foreground the role of erotic attraction in art. They also diffuse it, making it recognizable at the same time that it maintains a sort of invisibility. This capability is one meaning of Miriam's "infinite variety." It resists cognitive scrutiny while permitting errant desires to be articulated. In describing the first encounter of Biddy and Miriam, James invokes the metaphor of another theatrical form, the dance, to show that, in Miriam's presence, Biddy can signify otherwise than heterosexually. During the scene in which Nash and Nick flirt with each other, Biddy stares at Miriam with her pre-Raphaelite "pale face . . . , low forehead and thick, dark hair." Indecorously, Miriam returns the intrusive look. "What she chiefly had, however, Biddy rapidly discovered, was a pair of largely-gazing eyes. Our young friend was helped to the discovery by the accident of their resting at this moment, for a little while—it struck Biddy as very long—on her own." As though she were Peter, enjoying the young actress's points, "Biddy's slightly agitated perception traveled directly to [Miriam and her mother's] shoes, . . . which showed a great deal of stocking and were ornamented with large rosettes. . . . They suggested to her vaguely that the wearers were dancers" (32).

Miriam resents being neglected by Nash, who is absorbed in Nick. Biddy notices that

her air was unconciliatory, almost dangerous. Did it express resentment at having been abandoned for another girl? Biddy, who began to be frightened—there was a moment when the forsaken one resembled a tigress about to spring—was tempted to cry out that she had no wish whatever to appropriate the gentleman. Then she made the discovery that the young lady had a manner, almost as much as her cicerone, and the rapid induction that it perhaps meant no more than his. She only looked at Biddy from beneath her eyebrows, which were wonderfully arched, but there was a manner in the way she did it. Biddy had a momentary sense of being a figure in a ballet, a dramatic ballet—a subordinate, motionless figure, to be dashed at, to music, or capered up to. It would be a very dramatic ballet indeed if this young person were the heroine. (34)

At moments, comic and ironic, such as this, representation overflows heterosexual markers. It is not Nash's interest in "another girl" that piques
Miriam. If he can ignore her to focus on a young man, Miriam, apparently
mimicking his desire, can target the young man's sister.

Miriam's magnetism fascinates Biddy. Does she know she's being
cruised? Well, no, not expressly, although in nineteenth-century ballet most
often it is male dancers who dash at or caper up to motionless female
figures. Biddy continually picks up vibrations that one would expect not to
register on the sonar of a typical young English lady. Signified in terms of
nervous magnetism, of the East, of bestiality, of the demimondaine, of folk
art, of music and the dance, even of what can be passed off as "manner"—
the exchange is not specific enough to be labeled perverse in the sense of
lesbian; but it is queer.[22] Not surprisingly, when Miriam shortly afterward
performs for Lady Agnes and her friends, Biddy is ravished. Similarly, we
recognize that Biddy is being straightened out at the end of the novel when
the narrator informs the reader that during Miriam's premiere as Juliet
Biddy's attention is fixed not on the actress but upon Peter sitting in the
stalls (573). Even here, however, attention is triangulated since Peter's
"gaze" is "fastened to the stage" (573).

Biddy's first impression of Miriam registers another aspect of aesthetic
politics in the novel, namely the way in which aesthetic perception functions as a mode of class, racial, and national distinction. Biddy feels no
inhibition in staring at Miriam, but when Miriam returns the glance, Biddy
feels that her cognitive privilege has been usurped. James does not expressly
comment on Biddy's sense of superiority to Miriam, but he does notice
how unselfconsciously Biddy wears the badge of Anglo-Saxon presumption.

Such presumption becomes more overtly problematic when it crosses
the threshold from impression to representation. Late in the novel, when
Miriam is sitting to have her portrait painted by Nick a second time, her
mother angles for Nick to give her the finished work. As Mrs. Rooth surveys
the contents of his studio, he is

reminded of the story of her underhand commercial habits told by Gabriel Nash at
the exhibition in Paris, the first time her name had fallen on his ear. A queer old
woman from whom, if you approached her in the right way, you could buy old
pots—it was in this character that she had originally been introduced to him. He
had lost sight of it afterwards, but it revived again as his observant eyes, at the same
time that they followed his active hand [as he paints Miriam], became aware of her
instinctive appraising gestures. There was a moment when he laughed out gaily—
there was so little in his poor studio to appraise. Mrs. Rooth's vague, polite, disap-

pointed bent back and head made a subject, the subject of a sketch, in an instant; they gave such a sudden pictorial glimpse of the element of race. He found himself seeing the immemorial Jewess in her, holding up a candle in a crammed backshop. There was no candle indeed, and his studio was not crammed, and it had never occurred to him before that she was of the Hebrew strain. (484)

At this moment, the artist's gaze reads the apparently inherent truth of racial difference. To Nick's credit, although he does so spontaneously ("his observant eyes . . . became aware"), he is self-aware enough to notice that visibility incorporates discursive truths of racial identity ("He found himself seeing").

His recognition of this fact does not, however, free him from its effects. When Nick refers to "the idea" (457) that portraiture conveys, he means the characteristic humanity of individual sitters. In this context, characteristic refers both to individual difference and to what young Marx refers to as species-being.[23] For James, species-being is racially differentiated. The scientific classification of racial types serves as a set of boundaries within which to understand individual examples.[24] This truth is based on the epistemological advantage that Nick enjoys as a member of the English upper classes. Mrs. Rooth is a "Hebrew . . . subject" because Nick recognizes her as such, and Nick reads her that way because that is how he sees her. James slyly cuts this self-enclosed system by noting that Nick sees Mrs. Rooth's perceptions as being likewise based in an "instinctive" racial knowledge, only in her case the knowledge supposedly is Jewish. A question implicitly rises from the juxtaposition of Nick's "observant eyes" with Mrs. Rooth's "instinctive appraising gestures." Which assessment is more true: hers of the exchange value of objects or his of racial taxonomy? And if both are true, then what gives the truth of Anglo-Saxon insight greater worth than that of bred-in-the-bone Jewishness? The answer is tautological: namely, Anglo-Saxon presumption. In other words, the answer is prejudicial, and art underwrites the prejudice within the terms of genre painting, for which Mrs. Rooth "holding up a candle in a crammed backshop" is an appropriate subject. The genre of the novel likewise undergirds insular arrogance insofar as the author himself is producing a naturalist text, that is, one that represents character in light of scientific laws of racial difference. Novelistic representation can indicate logical flaws in this method, but it cannot escape them.

Art also bears responsibility for invidious racial distinctions insofar as nineteenth-century science often draws its descriptions from literary sources.[25] James, however, invokes the artistic media of dance and the the-ater as defenses against the presumption to which he and his text are bound. To Peter, Nick, and Biddy, Miriam's mobility, which is defined as nomadic, doubtfully aristocratic, and, to a degree, "Hebrew" (58), makes her a fascinating alternative to the postulated fixity of Anglo-Saxon charac-ter. Not a subject in national or religious terms, like Nash she is a "cosmop-olite," a "citizen" (33, 139) of the world. Miriam's indeterminate Jewish lineage makes possible the "infinite variety" essential to the protean de-mands of her chosen profession.

This distinction, however, although freeing her from constraints ob-served by other characters, paradoxically recaptures her within the limits of race. As Hannah Arendt has argued, the shift in the nineteenth century from political and religious definitions of Jewish difference to character-ological ones leads to locating it in biology, that is, within the terms of racial taxonomy.[26] Miriam's exemplary function is further limited by con-tradictions within evolutionary thought, which, as Robert Young points out, despite valuing hybridity more highly than homogeneity, also argues that hybrids tend toward extinction.[27] Offspring of hybrids are sterile or revert to a prior type. In this way, the freedom promised by dramatic per-formance and Miriam's social performativity is liable to spring back upon itself. Likewise, Nick characterizes his wish to escape the demands made on young men of the professional class in terms of biological variation: "I'm a wanton variation, an unaccountable monster" (143). He attempts to break the pattern through friendship with an aesthete, Nash, and an actress, Mir-iam, and by becoming an artist himself. At the end of the novel, however, Nick threatens to revert to Anglo-Saxon type as an upper-middle-class pro-fessional, a society portraitist, married to Julia. As such, his art will repro-duce the factitious superiority of members of the very class that threatens to stifle him. The limits of variation put in doubt the ability of art—either pictorial or dramatic—to represent much less to accomplish cultural hy-bridity. For example, when Nick begins painting Miriam for the first time, he finds himself "troubled about his sitter's nose, which was somehow Jew-ish without the convex arch" (307).[28]

The "spell" (356) that Miriam works on the English public is her abil-ity to represent beyond the limits of racial and other kinds of characteriza-tion. This perverse freedom holds out a promise to Sherringham, Nick, and others that they too can live differently. In order to do so, however, they will have to run counter to type or, rather, they will have to find other resources within Anglo-Saxon tradition, for example, the plasticity with which Shakespeare, England's greatest playwright, was able to project a seemingly infinite range of characters.

The inducements to a conventional career in the foreign service or in Parliament are also cast within terms of perversion though in a different sense of the word. Explaining Julia's attempt to "seduce" Nick, James, in a notebook entry, describes her offer as "bribery." After Nick is returned from the constituency of Harsh: "Julia is delighted with him—this is the way she likes him—she is in love with him—she is ready for anything. She will marry him on the spot if he asks her. He is very conscious of this and he thinks he ought to ask her. She has done everything for him—for his election—she has been charming, effective, wonderful. She hasn't given money, of course—only Mr. C has given that. But she *will* give money—she will give him her fortune. She tries to seduce him—she is full of bribery."[29] Julia's offer of the exercise of political influence in exchange for material benefits, including marriage, falls within the terms that had long characterized anti-sodomitic classical republican discourse. Again, the key element is not an exchange involving a specific sexual practice but rather the effeminizing effects of the exchange.

If a female patron can undermine a young man's virility so too can "Mr. C," Nick's male mentor, Mr. Carteret. Carteret, who entered political life around time of the passage of the first Reform Bill in the early 1830s, is the decrepit embodiment of two generations of political reform. He is also a bachelor, whose single object of passion in life appears to have been Nick's deceased father, Sir Nicholas, a Liberal parliamentarian whose career was foreshortened by an early death (74). Carteret offers to smooth Nick's path financially—if only he will marry Julia and heed his father's deathbed injunction to continue his political "work" (76). Nash, who recognizes the perverse desires that organize these triangulations, complains that it is Carteret's "depraved tastes" (144) that make him willing to bankroll Nick's career. James registers the cruelty that inhabits Carteret and Lady Agnes's expectations. When he learns that the term of Nick's engagement with Julia has been indefinitely postponed, Carteret brutally informs him that "you should have held her—you shouldn't have let her go" (388). In a single breath, Carteret scores Nick's lack of manliness and asserts the social imperatives that demand that Julia become his wife.

Aspects of the sodomitic rhetoric of the Liberal campaign against Disraeli in the 1870s contaminate Nick's description of his own abilities as a political orator facing the enlarged, post-1884 electorate. "I speak beautifully. I can turn it on, a fine flood of it, at the shortest notice. The better it is the worse it is, the kind is so inferior. It has nothing to do with the truth or the search for it; nothing to do with intelligence, or candour, or honour. It's an appeal to everything that for one's self one despises," the young man went on—"to stupidity, to ignorance, to density, to the love of names and phrases, the love of hollow, idiotic words, of shutting the eyes tight and making a noise" (88).[30]

In Nick's comments, Gladstone's accusations of Jewish idolatry and infidelity to English values return to taunt the Liberals. Nick finds himself and his allies likewise failing in devotion to the truth, substituting for it "hollow, idiotic words." Idolatry in this case, however, is not merely metaphysical. After the passage of the Second and the Third Reform Bills, the British constitution was far more democratic than previously. Parliament, however, continued to be an elite preserve. By taking political mentorship, in the persons of Carteret, Lady Agnes, and Sir Nicholas, into the bosom of the Liberal party, James implies his ironic view that the politics of reform will serve to entrench the members of an already existing establishment.

It was generally assumed that extension of the ballot to artisans and other working-class male voters in 1867 and 1884 would result in the emergence of the Liberal party as the party of national governance. This outcome, however, depended upon the effective organization of a modern party structure within the ridings and Parliament. In fact, this did not happen. Instead, the Liberal party functioned as a coalition of disparate groups whose specific interests and goals were often at odds.[31] As a result, critics of the status quo such as James were likely to be frustrated with the Liberals on two related but different and somewhat contradictory grounds. First, Liberal governments were often ineffective, failing to deliver promised support to particular constituencies. At the same time, commitment to objectives of particular importance to some groups of Liberal party supporters could split the party and make it impossible for Liberal prime ministers to govern. This situation was exacerbated by the fact that, from 1868 onward, England was involved in an unresolved constitutional crisis. While the House of Commons became more susceptible to popular pressure, the House of Lords continued to exercise its prerogative to throw out legislation passed by the lower chamber. As Gladstone wrote in a memorandum to Queen Victoria in August 1884: "The House of Lords has for a long period been the habitual and vigilant enemy of every Liberal Government." He warned that if "the hereditary power" were unwilling to modify its behavior "an organic reform" might radicalize the Constitution, weakening "the foundations even of the throne" (Jenkins, 495, 496).

Consider, for example, the case of adult female suffrage. Liberals had long been identified with this cause, but in 1884, when there was a strong move to include it in the Third Reform Bill, Gladstone "employed overkill," warning Liberal parliamentarians that if the amendment were carried "the bill would be dropped and the government would resign" (Jenkins, 492). Gladstone justified this stance on the grounds that the Lords would use the amendment as a pretext to defeat the general bill, but it is equally plausible to believe that Gladstone in fact found the change too radical for his taste.

In one perspective, Gladstone's action was hypocritical. From another point of view, pressing the just cause of women at this particular moment in time threatened to derail another long deferred act of justice to working-class men. The dangers posed to Liberalism by the advocacy of a single issue crystallized in 1886 when Gladstone, taking the opposite tack, decided to endorse Home Rule for Ireland as a major legislative goal of his new administration. The decision split the party along permanent lines, losing the Liberals the remnant of Whig support they enjoyed in the upper chamber, and in effect assuring Unionist control of Parliament. James, whose views of Irish nationalism were complex,[32] followed the Home Rule question with "intense curiosity" during the years in which he was writing The Tragic Muse (*Letters*, 3:193). Regarding the elderly Gladstone as "a *parson* perverted" and "a dreary incubus," James in late 1885 doubted whether English politicians had sufficient imagination to achieve a political solution: "It is a huge black monster, and civil war seems to me to be really in the air."[33]

As I argued in *Masculine Desire*, strong affinities existed between aestheticism, male same-sex desire, and l/Liberalism.[34] But it is also the case that the passage of the Labouchère Amendment in 1885, under a Conservative government, was an initiative undertaken by a Radical Liberal. Passage of the amendment demonstrated that a confluence of demagogic politics, left-wing journalism, socialist and republican anger, and effective campaigning by labor union leaders and social purity feminists could help fashion a new and stigmatizing visibility for men whose sexual and emotional interest in other men had not, in the past, provided the basis of a social category. In other words, in a democratic age, not only could affinity groups mobilize to affect party policy and parliamentary legislation, it was also the case that politicians could help bring such identities and identifications into existence—in this instance by criminalizing them. To James, this was yet one more turn of the screw linking group politics and the radical press with sensational attacks on individual privacy. Already in the 1870s, he had seen the combination at work when his father became embroiled in the Tilton-Beecher scandal launched by the socialist feminist Victoria Woodhull.[35] In 1885, the Liberals were embarrassed when one of their leaders, Sir Charles Dilke, was exposed as being simultaneously involved in affairs with three different women, two of them married (*Letters*, 3:99). And the movement for Home Rule was damaged in 1889 when Charles Stewart Parnell, leader of the Irish party within the House of Commons, was named as correspondent in an undefended divorce case.[36]

Jewish upward mobility also drew criticism from the left.[37] Anti-Semitic slurs were common—for example, in *Reynolds's Newspaper,* which also attacked upper-class queers in the Cleveland Street Scandal in 1890, and in the pages of Labouchère's journal, *Truth.*[38] Angered by Disraeli's pro-Turkish foreign policy in the late 1870s, Labouchère complained that Jews were "members of a masonic band, which collectively exercises vast influence and is . . . an *imperium in imperio.*"[39] Assimilating Jews sometimes adopted Anglo-Saxon surnames, a practice that infuriated Labouchère as being at once counterfeit and contaminating. For example, after the editor and part-owner of the *Daily Telegraph,* the first London daily penny paper, deserted Gladstone in favor of the Tories over the Turkish issue, Labouchère began an unremitting series of public attacks. Since the editor had changed his name from Levy to Lawson, Labouchère dubbed the paper the *Daily Levy.* In September 1879, after Labouchère published an unflattering obituary of Lawson's uncle in *Truth,* Lawson attacked him with a walking stick as he hailed a cab outside the Beefsteak Club. Hiring leading members of the government to represent him, Lawson sued Labouchère for libel. Labouchère defended himself in court and was released after the jury failed to reach agreement.

The incident offers a paradigmatic example of how genealogical issues inflect racial animosities and debate. Hesketh Pearson, Labouchère's biographer, argues that Labouchère scorned Lawson for "attempting to obliterate his own racial tracks."[40] Labouchère's attacks on Lawson and his newspaper were, however, motivated not by this disdain but by the fact that, as editor, Lawson criticized Gladstone while defending his family's financial investment in Turkish bonds under the assumption of an impersonal "WE." According to Labouchère, the effacement of ethnicity in the name change plus the use of the first person plural in editorials enabled Lawson to identify covert "Jewish" interests with the impartial judgment of the public. For his part, Labouchère was determined to expose "the people who claim to speak for the English nation."[41] During the trial, he was able to show that Levy had changed his name to Lawson in order to ingratiate himself with his bachelor uncle, Lionel, another part-owner of the newspaper, who had already assumed the cognomen. In another blow to proper genealogy, Labouchère was also able to adduce that Edward Lawson had been named trustee of Lionel's illegitimate son. As for Edward, who had been married in a Christian church, he was, in Labouchère's view, like Disraeli, a Marrano, that is, a false convert.

Although Pearson, who published his account in 1937, believed himself to be free of prejudice, a contemporary reader may well think otherwise.[42] But Pearson's account of this incident does not show merely the resentment of some for the ways in which newcomers identified themselves with the nation. It also shows the sort of social advances possible for Jews at a time when popular anti-Semitism was common. These advances testify to social permeability at the same time that they exacerbated xenophobia. Lawson and Labouchère, for example, were both members of the Beefsteak Club at the time of the assault. For his part, Lawson went on to become high sheriff of Buckinghamshire a few years later in 1886, was created a baronet in 1892, and was raised to the peerage as Baron Burnham in 1903. Lawson purchased a country house, Hall Barn, near Beaconsfield, where King Edward VII paid him annual visits.

James and Sargent became friends in the early 1880s when the young painter was causing a sensation in Paris.[43] A few months before passage of the Labouchère Amendment, at Sargent's suggestion, James had been pleased to entertain Count Robert de Montesquiou in London (Fig. 8). Montesquiou had recently served as the prototype of des Esseintes, the homosexual dandy and protagonist of J-K Huysmans's novel, *À Rebours* (1884). James saved Sargent's letter of introduction—even though he later destroyed the rest of the correspondence that he had received from the painter. In this double action, James moved to protect his and Sargent's sexually coy exchanges from vulgar observation at that same time that James memorialized a moment when he was proud to be a player among an international set of male sexual dissidents.[44]

James and his sister Alice despised the venom of Labouchère's attacks in Parliament and in the press on members of targeted groups: aristocrats, the royals, Irish nationalists, male homosexuals.[45] Psychically and socially, moreover, James had as much reason to be appalled by the amendment as did other men such as John Addington Symonds, Edward Carpenter, and Edmund Gosse, who were aware of their sexual and emotional attraction

Fig. 8. James McNeill Whistler, *Arrangement in Black and Gold: Portrait of Robert, Comte de Montesquiou-Fezensac,* 1891. Copyright the Frick Collection, New York City. "In Montesquiou's case, the painter felt that he was expressing the very essence of the sitter's aristocratic lineage" (Kenneth McConkey, "'Well-bred Contortions,'" 365).

to other men. Earlier in his career, James had written about such ties fairly openly.[46] But not in *The Tragic Muse.*

This reserve absents from Nick's and Miriam's environment the experience of socializing in bohemian contexts open to men and women with same-sex ties that James himself enjoyed during the 1880s. For example, in the summer of 1885, James stayed with Gosse and Sargent and other expatriate American artists in the village of Broadway. James returned in each of the following four summers (F. Kaplan, 310). In Florence in early 1887, he was a regular visitor to the "at homes" of Vernon Lee (F. Kaplan, 316–17). Feminist, lover of women, and aesthete, Lee had been a childhood friend of Sargent in Rome.[47] In the essay that she wrote at the time of his death, she shows Sargent to have been an apt pupil of the generation of sexual dissidents that included men such as Swinburne, Pater, and Simeon Solomon. James also does not represent the sort of friendships—ardent and physical although not exclusive and not expressly sexual—that he himself became involved in during the 1890s (F. Kaplan, 387–429). These silences, however, do not mean that the politics of sex and gender are absent from this novel or that James effaces connections between them and parliamentary politics. Likewise, although he does not directly address the injustices involved in women's exclusion from Parliament and the national suffrage, in his treatment of Julia Dallow's frustrated ambitions and in Lady Agnes's suppressed rage, James leaves the reader in no doubt about the distorting effects on both men and women of women's civil disabilities.

In the novel, Nick is torn between the old politics of gradual expansion of the franchise and a new politics whose currency are the terms of culture, mass publicity, international finance, nationality, and race. In the 1880s, English aristocrats, whose agricultural wealth was diminishing, formed alliances with wealthy manufacturers and tradesmen, married American heiresses, and depended on the services of Jewish publishers and financiers.[48] The ascendancy of Miriam in the theater parallels the emergence of Jewish families in high society and as subjects of portraits by Sargent. Hybridity was occurring literally among wealthy and titled Englishmen. The ideology of reversion to type that at times structures James's insight belies the actual mixing under way. This mingling was tolerated because it enabled the royals and the existing aristocracy to shore up their position in face of what a Radical Liberal such as Labouchère saw as the advent of democracy and James and others saw as emergent mass politics. As the contretemps with Lawson indicates, Jewish entrants to high society were particularly vulnerable to attack in this volatile situation.

Sargent, James, and Wilde abutted each other within a select circle of upper-class aesthetes who styled themselves "the Souls."[49] Composed of aristocrats, parvenus, society hostesses, politicians, diplomats (such as the fictional Sherringham), expatriate Americans, assimilating Jews, artists, journalists, and theater people, members of the group saw themselves as constituting the cosmopolis of London. Sexually dubious tastemakers such as Montesquiou and Wilde were welcome in this society because it needed their chic to lend a sense of contemporaneity to members of old families, who feared being relegated as relics of a former age, and to enable *arrivistes* to display at once the blue china and the Japanese fans, so to speak, of cultivated taste. Sargent's approach to painting, which applied contemporary French "hot licks" over an assured armature of traditional representational skills, exactly suited the fashion members of the group required. This particular combination tends to undercut the serious—even puritan—emphasis on work that both Nick and Miriam associate with the life of the artist.[50] Work in Sargent often means the traditional modeling of the features of the face in a society portrait at the expense of stylistic disjunction with the impressionistic brushstrokes applied to clothing and decorative accessories. Portraits of young women are especially liable to suffer in this respect. Consider, for example, *Lady Agnew of Lochnaw,* which, not coincidentally, served to make Sargent's reputation in England (McConkey, 373–74) (Fig. 9). Stabilizing the identity of the sitter, this approach also guarantees value for money in the demonstrated mastery of three-dimensional representation. The ideological work of Sargent's painting undercuts pretensions to artistic freedom; it also undercut the sorts of claims that James made on behalf of the transnational Anglo-Saxon culture that he believed could surmount British narrowness and decline (F. Kaplan, 290–91).

Albert Boime argues that the values of "the Souls" can be summed in terms such as style and "the cult of self" that the French critic Louis de Fourcaud found exemplified in the sensational portraits of figures such as Mme. Gautreau and Dr. Samuel Pozzi that Sargent painted in Paris in the early 1880s. The cultural politics of "the Souls" were international, and it is in this context that James's text takes leave of what (for him) was an insular politics of group grievance and demands for reform and embraces instead a politics of beauty, form, and style—the privileged terms of the 1908 Preface. In this he was at one with Sargent, whom a critic in 1903 described as follows:

Mr. John S. Sargent is a typical example of the modern cosmopolitan man, the man whose habits of thought and life make him at home everywhere, and whose training

Fig. 9. John Singer Sargent, *Lady Agnew of Lochnaw,* 1892–93. Used by permission of the National Gallery of Scotland, Edinburgh.

has been such as to preclude the last touch of chauvinism. Such a man has become possible only during the last fifty years, and then only in the case of an occasional American. For the man born and bred in Europe of European parents must of necessity be influenced by national feelings that can not but make impossible any true detached cosmopolitanism. In the case of an American born and bred abroad, the only feelings that can possibly arise are those that come of cold selection; he is unattached to anything, and though living among and with the different European peoples, he never becomes one with them in sentiment or local bias.[51]

The passage nicely balances the advantages of being "at home everywhere" with the disadvantages of "never" becoming "at one" with the people among whom one lives. Insofar as cosmopolitanism deprives the artist of his or her national and racial affinities, James takes on the coloration of a Miriam, who is also defined, on first glance by Biddy, as being *not-European:* "She made the rapid reflection that [Miriam and her mother] were people whom in any country, from China to Peru, one would immediately have taken for natives" (31). This negative definition has as its supplement suggestions of excess: of indigenous, miscegenated, southern, Oriental, and presumably other aspects, for which Miriam's alleged "Jewishness" later serves as portmanteau.

To be defined as *not-European,* moreover, means to lose one's ability to realize in oneself and one's work the new transatlantic cultural community of which James dreamed. James needed to be able to speak of "our" shared "English race"[52] if he was to subsume English characteristics in cosmopolitan American ones while at the same time effacing his own Irish background. He could not afford to give up what today would be called the race card. Fashioning a double bind, he lived so as to free himself of national limitations upon which his ambitions depended. A double bind likewise structures the dependence of the critic in the passage quoted above on the term American. To be international, in effect, one has to be national, albeit in a different way. Cosmopolitanism is an American phenomenon that is available only to those Americans who have been expatriated to Europe. In other words, men such as Whistler, Sargent, and James must also be *not-American.*[53] The double injunction reflects back upon the emergence of the United States during James's lifetime as a leading nation-state with its own highly publicized imperial entanglements. James also lived through the period of Reconstruction in the American South, which constructed anew the definition of U.S. citizenship as "white" while likewise defining the term in such a way that previously outcast immigrant groups such as Catholic Irish, Jews, and southern and eastern Europeans could bid to be grouped under a shared racial-national identity, one of whose prime functions was to exist in contrast to the category of "colored" or "Negro" inhabitants, who by the same definition did not merit the extension of the rights of citizenship.[54]

Sexuality likewise partakes of a privileged, double-edged negativity. For Miriam, marriage is a matter of business. For James and Sargent, it is not an option at all. For them, the profession of artist requires the liminal status of the lifelong bachelor. This condition enables the queer resonances of their accomplishment while simultaneously inhibiting the play of impression and expression in their work so that, for example, in Sargent's *Young Man in Reverie* (Fig. 10), masculine values of embodiedness, receptivity, and reverie are liable to be seen not in the Nick Dormers of this world but projected onto aestheticized subjects, who are characterized in terms of gendered, racial, and class difference.[55]

The cultural values of "the Souls" may seem to be a shaky ground on which to base Nick's hope that Miriam's enlivening presence onstage could actually help English politicians deal with the deteriorating political and economic situation that James recognized that they faced at the end of the century. To the contrary, however, in the form of aesthetic utilitarianism, the rhetoric of aestheticism shared the language of economists and politicians of the day.[56] When Nash counter's Nick defense of parliamentary politics, he is not negating politics, he is criticizing a literal approach to social and economic reform: "Gabriel maintained precisely that there were more ideas, more of those that man lived by, in a single room of the National Gallery than in all the statutes of Parliament. Nick had replied to this more than once that the determination of what man did live by was required; to which Nash had retorted (and it was very rarely that he quoted Scripture) that it was at any rate not by bread-and-butter alone. The statutes of Parliament gave him bread-and-butter *tout au plus*" (457–58). Key in Nash's objection is the word "alone."

The idea that the theater could unify and moralize a people was not novel in 1890. Wagner had made the argument on behalf of opera, and Nietzsche called for the rebirth of tragedy. Wilde, who parodies aspects of James's novel in *The Picture of Dorian Gray* (1890),[57] argues in *The Soul of Man Under Socialism* (1891) that in a liberal nation-state modern drama can mobilize tolerance, "the temperament of receptivity," in contemporary audiences.[58] On this subject, James is both invested and agnostic. In the novel, he offers three very different views of the place of theater in English culture. Nash sees the theater as yet one more symptom of contemporary

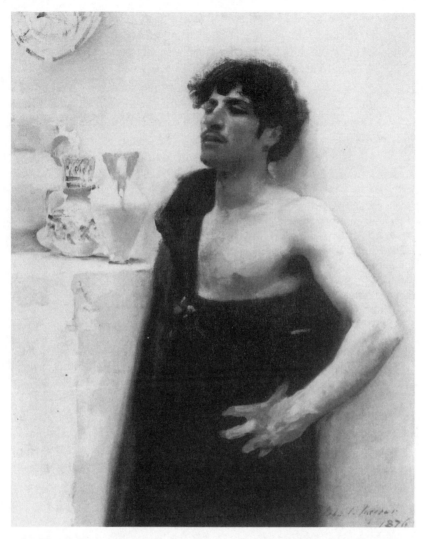

Fig. 10. John Singer Sargent, *Young Man in Reverie*, 1878 (inscribed 1876). Private collection.

vulgarity: "The *omnium gatherum* of the population of a big commercial city, at the hour of the day when their taste is at its lowest, flocking out of hideous hotels and restaurants, gorged with food, stultified with buying and selling and with all the other sordid preoccupations of the day, squeezed together in a sweltering mass, disappointed in their seats, timing the author, timing the actor, wishing to get their money back on the spot, before eleven o'clock. Fancy putting the exquisite before such a tribunal as that! There's not even a question of it" (62). In contrast, Peter Sherringham puts forward the ideal, current at the time but not realized until after World War II, of the need for a national theater. He envisages

> a great academic, artistic theatre, subsidized and unburdened with money-getting, rich in its repertory, rich in the high quality and the wide array of its servants, and above all in the authority of an impossible administrator—a manager personally disinterested, not an actor with an eye to the main chance, pouring forth a continuity of tradition, striving for perfection, laying a splendid literature under contribution. He saw the heroine of a hundred "situations," variously dramatic and vividly real; he saw comedy and drama and passion and character and English life: he saw all humanity and history and poetry, and perpetually, in the midst of them, shining out in the high relief of some great moment, an image as fresh as an unveiled statue. He was not unconscious that he was taking all sorts of impossibilities and miracles for granted; but it really seemed to him for the time that the woman he had been watching three hours, the incarnation of the serious drama, would be a new and vivifying force. (356–57)

Recontextualizing a trope, at once Shakespearean and Paterian/Winckelmanian, of sculptural visibility, James sees Peter envisaging a cultural renaissance based on Miriam's abilities as an actress.[59] As in Nick's account of the idea in portraiture, Peter's account is both individual and specifically national. But his idea of individuality, which closely resembles Wilde's concept of personality in *The Soul of Man Under Socialism,* also differs from Nick's. Peter values Miriam's ability, based in part on her sexual attractiveness, to convey to her viewers a sense that what identifies human being is precisely the capability of individuals continually to change. It is for this reason that he is preoccupied with "the idea of her having no character of her own" (356). At the same time, Peter's ideal carries the mark of his profession as a diplomat. However "disinterested" a national theater might be, it will still be a national theater, commissioned to enforce and disseminate the values of "English life." Just how limiting this condition can be is suggested in the turn that his infatuation with Miriam eventually takes. Miriam attracts Peter because of the possibility, or fantasy if you will, that an intimate relationship will enable him, for the first time, to overcome the limits of his own character, to become someone else. In the end, however, this desire is too risky to be realized. He attempts to become Miriam's sexual partner on the condition that she give up her profession and be captured within the role of a diplomat's wife. From this perspective, his vision of what theater might contribute to national life appears to have been a "momentary illusion and confusion" (357).

But is it? In ending, I return to Nick's enthusiastic response to Miriam on stage. In the warm embrace afforded her by her audience, Nick reads the signal both of her "success" (496) and of the ability of her performance to "stretch out wide arms to the future." It is important to emphasize that Nick stresses the modality of this work in terms of embodied desire: "Miriam was as satisfactory as some right sensation—she would feed the memory with the ineffaceable" (496). The phrase "right sensation" returns us to Shaftesbury's aesthetic of taste as both criterion and ground of judgment. Nick's assessment is thoroughly subjective though that is as it should be within an aesthetic whose universals likewise are subjective. Moreover, he does not duck the issues posed by the context of Miriam's performance within commercial, celebrity culture. These too are aspects of art within a democracy. Whether or not the social organization of theater—or any other art form—can serve the utopian function that Nick observes on this occasion is an open question. Under Miriam's "spell," Nick too may be experiencing "momentary illusion and confusion" (356). But, then again, perhaps something else is at work. These are questions with which James leaves his readers in *The Tragic Muse.*

Rethinking Friendship in Oscar Wilde's An Ideal Husband

Is friendship possible with a stranger? Is one's friend an enemy? Can an enemy be one's friend? On what terms can friendship be sustained between two men? Is it possible between a man and a woman? During the time that he wrote *An Ideal Husband,* Wilde had good reason to be thinking about these questions. Moreover, the play suggests that he has some answers to propose. For one thing, the action departs from the tradition of male friendship writing by affirming the possibility that marriage can provide a basis for friendship. More pointedly, Wilde suggests that, in the glare of modern publicity, marriage needs to be a friendship if it is to survive at all. Otherwise, as Lord Goring, the dandy of the play, says, "The growth of the moral sense in women makes marriage . . . a hopeless, one-sided institution."[1]

Early in the play, an adventuress named Mrs. Cheveley attempts to blackmail Sir Robert Chiltern, under-secretary for foreign affairs in the current Liberal government. As a result of this attempt, Lady Chiltern learns that her husband's career is based on a serious crime that he committed at its outset. Lord Goring, Sir Robert's best friend, discovers this fact as well. Can the marriage and the friendship survive under these circumstances? Virtuous friendship requires that Goring show himself capable of independent moral assessment of Sir Robert's action. But, as writers from Cicero to Nietzsche have observed, silent reserve about the shortcomings of one's friends is essential to the existence of friendship.[2]

Mrs. Cheveley is a former mistress of the late Baron Arnheim, a financier, implicitly Jewish. She has in her possession the letter in which Sir Robert as a young man had provided Arnheim with advance notice of the intention of the government to purchase a controlling interest in shares in the Suez Canal Company. Sir Robert had access to this information as a result of his position as private secretary to a member of Cabinet, Lord

Radley. When she meets Sir Robert early in the play, the two begin by sparring over which of them was more intimate with the baron.

Sir Robert Chiltern [with an almost imperceptible start]: Did you know Baron Arnheim well?
Mrs Cheveley [smiling]: Intimately. Did you?
Sir Robert: At one time.
Mrs Cheveley: Wonderful man, wasn't he?
Sir Robert [after a pause]: He was very remarkable, in many ways.
Mrs Cheveley: I often think it such a pity he never wrote his memoirs. They would have been most interesting.
Sir Robert: Yes. He knew men and cities well, like the old Greek.
Mrs Cheveley: Without the dreadful disadvantage of having a Penelope waiting at home for him. (160)[3]

Not yet recognizing the danger that awaits him, Sir Robert teases Mrs. Cheveley with the implications of "Greek" friendship between older and younger men. Responding with unanticipated directness, she reminds him that Arnheim was unmarried.

At the Crabbet Club in 1891, Wilde had been attacked as a sodomite by George Curzon, a fellow student of his Oxford days.[4] Wilde responded with a defense of Greek pederasty similar to the one that he would make at the first of his criminal trials in 1895.[5] Intimacy of this sort

is such a great affection of an elder for a younger man as there was between David and Jonathan, such as Plato made the very basis of his philosophy, and such as you find in the sonnets of Michelangelo and Shakespeare. It is that deep, spiritual affection that is as pure as it is perfect. . . . It is in this century misunderstood, so much misunderstood that it may be described as the "Love that dare not speak its name," and on account of it I am placed where I am now. It is beautiful, it is fine, it is the noblest form of affection. There is nothing unnatural about it. It is intellectual, and it repeatedly exists between an elder and a younger man, when the elder has intellect, and the younger man has all the joy, hope, and glamour of life before him. That it should be so, the world does not understand. The world mocks at it and sometimes puts one in the pillory for it.[6]

As the courtroom context of this speech emphasizes, after the passage of the Labouchère amendment in 1885, the social and cultural conditions that fostered such friendships were undercut. The Coda focuses on implications of this changed situation.

In *De Profundis*, the apologia in the form of a letter to Lord Alfred

Douglas that Wilde would write while in prison, he conceded that the two men's friendship had not been of the "David and Jonathan" sort. Looking backward, Wilde condemned his share in what he now characterized as an "unintellectual friendship. From the very first there was too wide a gap between us."[7] Years later, at a libel trial involving the dancer Maud Allan, Douglas passed his own verdict on friendship with Wilde from the witness box. "I think," said Douglas, that "he had a diabolical influence on everyone he met. I think he is the greatest force for evil that has appeared in Europe during the last 350 years. . . . He was the agent of the devil in every possible way. He was a man whose whole object in life was to attack and to sneer at virtue, and to undermine it in every way by every possible means, sexually and otherwise."[8] In the eyes of his former lover, Wilde had passed from friend to fiend.

Wilde is not the only mentor pertinent to *An Ideal Husband*. And he is not the only one who might be seen as friend, fiend, or both. Lord Rosebery, the Liberal prime minister who succeeded Gladstone in March 1894, was rumored to be involved in an affair with his assistant private secretary, Viscount Drumlanrig.[9] Drumlanrig, an attractive and well-liked young man, also happened to be Douglas's favorite brother. Wilde composed the bulk of *An Ideal Husband* between the summer of 1893, in a house that he shared with Douglas at Goring-on-Thames, and early 1894. He continued to revise the play until it opened in January 1895. In August 1893, Drumlanrig's father, the marquess of Queensberry, having heard the rumors, followed Rosebery, foreign minister at the time, to Bad Homburg and threatened him with a dogwhip. The Prince of Wales, who was also vacationing there, was forced to intervene to prevent the attack.[10] Early in October 1894, Drumlanrig became engaged to Alix Ellis, the daughter of Major General Arthur Ellis, an equerry to the Prince of Wales.[11] A week later, Drumlanrig was invited to a lodge in Somerset, where Alix and her parents would also be guests. While there, he met his end as a result of a self-inflicted gunshot wound. The involvement of the Prince of Wales in the upset of the preceding summer and the fact that Alix was the daughter of a member of his retinue suggests that he had a hand in arranging the match in order to avoid embarrassment to the government and the royal family. Queensberry had written "a stream of abusive letters" to Gladstone, Rosebery, and even the queen.[12] George Murray, who served as private secretary to Gladstone and subsequently to Rosebery, gossiped with Lewis Harcourt about the prime minister's private correspondence.[13] Shortly before Drumlanrig proposed, Harcourt sardonically noted in his diary: "Drumlanrig is going to marry General Ellis's daughter. It makes the institution of marriage ridiculous."[14]

The Marquess of Queensberry blamed Rosebery and other Liberal leaders and members of the royal family for his son's death. In a furious letter Queensberry wrote to his former father-in-law: "Now that the first flush of this catastrophe and grief has passed, I write to tell you that it is a *judgement* on the whole *lot of you*. Montgomery's, The Snob Queers like Rosebery and certainly Christian hypocrite Gladstone the whole lot *of you* / Set my son up against me indeed and make bad blood between us, may it devil on your own heads that he has gone to his rest and the quarrel not made up between him and myself. It's a gruesome message: If you and his Mother did not set up this business with that cur and Jew fiend *Liar* Rosebery as I always thought."[15] I cite the text of this letter as it appears in Douglas Murray's recent biography of Douglas. Murray quotes the letter from Ellmann but emends the text. Where Ellmann has "friend [?]," Murray writes "fiend" without explaining the change. Was Rosebery a "Jew friend" or a "Jew fiend"? Queensberry had good reason to refer to Rosebery as a friend of Jews, among whom were the Rothschilds and Disraeli. The latter played an important part in Rosebery's attempt "to marry an heiress."[16]

The action of *An Ideal Husband* devolves from Sir Robert's friendship with a friend/fiend of his own, Baron Arnheim. In a long speech, Sir Robert tells Goring how Arnheim drew him into crime:

One night after dinner at Lord Radley's the Baron began talking about success in modern life as something that one could reduce to an absolutely definite science. With that wonderfully fascinating quiet voice of his, he expounded to us the most terrible of all philosophies, the philosophy of power, preached to us that most marvellous of all gospels, the gospel of gold. I think he saw the effect he had produced on me, for some days afterwards he wrote and asked me to come and see him. He was living then in Park Lane, in the house Lord Woolcomb has now. I remember so well how, with a strange smile on his pale, curved lips, he led me through his wonderful picture gallery, showed me his tapestries, his enamels, his jewels, his carved ivories, made me wonder at the strange loveliness of the luxury in which he lived; and then told me that luxury was nothing but a background, a painted scene in a play, and that power, power over other men, power over the world, was the one thing worth having, the one supreme pleasure worth knowing, the one joy one never tired of, and that in our century only the rich possessed it. (182–83)

In this passage, what could be the start of a heavy flirtation between an experienced man of the world and a promising young man,[17] is registered instead as the beginning of a sodomitic relationship, in which exploitation is mutual. While the scene is obviously one of seduction, it is understood within the terms in which editors analyze the story of Lot in Victorian Bible commentaries. In these terms, the sexual aspect is important primarily as a repudiation of the natural or reproductive function of sex. Much more important, though, are other offenses. The sin of Sodom is understood as a form of idolatry, supplemented by the corollary offenses of infidelity and blasphemy. When Arnheim refers to "the gospel of gold," Wilde is aware of how literally the phrase may be understood. The worship of mammon substitutes wealth for the worship that should be directed to God alone.[18] As I argue in Chapter 4, after 1868, this way of understanding sodomy had also become part of the weaponry of Liberal/Radical political rhetoric.

It is not only desire for gold that Arnheim refers to but also love of "power, power over other men." This second formula draws additionally upon the rhetoric of classical republican discourse, to which the word "luxury" in the passage likewise refers. In this discourse, the abuse of influence within traditional patron-client relationships and within parliamentary government are both understood to be sodomitic.[19] In context, the term may be denotatively or connotatively sexual. Most important is the notion that to give or receive political patronage is as much an assault on one's virility as male-male anal sex would be. Linda Dowling argues that this transfer of meaning between sex and politics is metaphoric in a way that plays down the sexual aspect.[20] This contention is, however, logically contradictory. Why call one's political antagonist a sodomite if one does not want to emphasize that one sees him as a sexually subjected, abjected character? Once one supplements a biblical understanding of sodomy with a classical one, it becomes evident that what Sir Robert comes to idolize under the baron's influence is sodomy in its political meaning—that is, as the corrupting exercise of power by one man over another, and not just over one man but over "men" in the aggregate, an expansion that lodges the perversion directly in the world of "modern" politics, namely, parliamentary democracy.

Wilde's stance in relation to this conceptual cluster is double. On the one hand, as already in 1891, he critiques it at its center by affirming of "affection" between mentor and protègè that "there is nothing unnatural about it." The affirmation strikes at the antithesis between "natural" and "unnatural" on which the monotheistic metaphysics of Victorian biblical commentary on Sodom depends. On the other hand, Wilde's emphasis on autonomy as the key to both individual and group freedom in a modern democracy rejects the definition of governance as the exercise of power by some over others.[21] As for Robert's specific crime, Wilde criticizes but does not condemn Sir Robert; and, through Goring, Wilde explicitly advises him against confessing his offense: it is not worth the destruction of himself and his career that would ensue. Striking what the Irish playwright George Bernard Shaw, in his review, detects as "the modern note" of the play, Wilde, moreover, affirms Sir Robert's willingness to act upon a transgressive desire.[22] In reply to a rebuke by Lord Goring, Sir Robert replies: "Weak? Oh, I am sick of hearing that phrase. Sick of using it about others. Weak? Do you really think, Arthur, that it is weakness that yields to temptation? I tell you that there are terrible temptations that it requires strength, strength and courage, to yield to. To stake all one's life on a single moment, to risk everything on one throw, whether the stake be power or pleasure, I care not—there is no weakness in that" (184). Here, by introducing the term "pleasure" to the argument, Wilde implicitly adverts to his (and Rosebery's) unorthodox pleasure in young men. Still, there is necessity of a friend's reproof. Goring comments: "You were worth more, Robert" (184).

The opening night performance of *An Ideal Husband* was attended by leading members of the political class: the Prince of Wales, members of the Cabinet, and other elite males (Ellmann, 404). All of these men were aware that the criminal nub of the play referred to an incident that had occurred while Disraeli was prime minister. As Frank Harris, the "friend" to whom Wilde dedicated the first edition of the play in 1899 (148), wrote in his personal copy of the play: "This book came from a story I heard in Egypt about Lord Rothschild and Disraeli. Rothschild wanted to get back monies he had loaned to Ismael Pascha, Khedive of Egypt, persuaded Disraeli to buy Suez Canal shares from the Egyptian government through his house. Rothschild of course added his previous debt to the commission and so netted two birds in one throw. I thought of a drama on the subject and told it to Oscar Wilde who used the story in this play."[23] In 1875, Disraeli used his private secretary, Monty Corry, as a go-between in the secret purchase by the British government of a controlling interest in the Suez Canal Company.[24] Did Disraeli and the Rothschilds act as friends of British interests in this transaction? Historians such as Robert Blake say yes; but Henry Labouchère's Radical journal, *Truth,* linked Disraeli with Jewish bondholders in the City as a proponent of crypto-Jewish and Ottoman interests at the expense of British ones.[25]

Disclaimers notwithstanding, Liberal and Radical attacks of the 1870s represented Jews in England as enemies of both religion and the state. The question as to whether members of alien groups could function as citizens was pertinent to other groups as well. Of no group was the question asked more forcibly than of the Irish at a time when Gladstone split the Liberal party by insisting on legislating Home Rule for Ireland.[26] Unwilling to recognize the Irish as equals, the English political class was incapable, philosophically and politically, of dealing with them as friends. This injustice had the effect of constituting the Irish as aliens, a perennial enemy living within the United Kingdom.[27] For example, despite Gladstone's pro-Irish stance, on a number of occasions during the 1880s the Liberals brought in coercive legislation to control political unrest in Ireland. On another front, in *On the Study of Celtic Literature,* Matthew Arnold proposes the cultural assimilation of the Irish into English-language culture as a way of overcoming the existence of the Irish as "aliens in speech, in religion, in blood."[28] Arnold was candid enough to recognize that this effort depends on "brute force" (12). "Mournfully," he accepts the price of integration because he rejects the alternative, namely, the creation of "a political and social counter-power, . . . the soul of a hostile nationality" (12). This was unacceptable not only for reasons of real politik but because "a rival self-establishment" (12) would be just that, a bringing-into-being of a self that would be other. Arnold can't tolerate that prospect because alterity is acceptable in his eyes only when internalized as an aspect of oneself. The self externalized in the empirical form of regional autonomy would negate the cosmopolitanism of the Anglo-Norman-Celtic hybrid that he espouses instead. The existence of the one implies the psychic/social extinction of the other.

Given his Irish background, Wilde had reason to be aware of the violence implicit in the assimilationist position.[29] His assessment of English entanglement in Ireland is outspoken: "If in the last century England tried to govern Ireland with an insolence that was intensified by race-hatred and religious prejudice, she has sought to rule her in this century with a stupidity that is aggravated by good intentions."[30] In 1889, in a negative review of a novel by J. A. Froude in which Froude attacks Irish republicanism, Wilde remarks: "There are some who will welcome with delight the idea of solving the Irish question by doing away with the Irish people" (*AC,* 140). As for his own position, in an 1887 review of J. P. Mahaffy's *Greek Life and Thought,* Wilde makes clear that he supports neither the Fenians nor the Liberal Unionists. A proponent of "freedom and autonomy" for Ireland, on this particular point Wilde is at one with Gladstone (*AC,* 80).

Greek pederasty and the colonial relation between Ireland and England were linked in Wilde's experience of Mahaffy. J. P. Mahaffy was

Wilde's tutor at Trinity College, Dublin. As an undergraduate, Wilde benefited from his teaching and friendship. Wilde traveled with him to Greece
and corrected the proofs of his book, *Social Life in Greece* (1874). In that
work, Mahaffy includes an extensive, sympathetic account of Greek pederasty. He argues the naturalness of, so to speak, unnatural passion: "As to
the epithet *unnatural,* the Greeks would answer probably, that all civilisation was unnatural, that its very existence pre-supposed the creation of new
instincts, the suppression of old, and that many of the best features in all
gentle life were best because they were unnatural."[31] Mahaffy, however,
retreated, deleting these remarks from the next edition. A decade later,
Wilde turned against his former friend. Mahaffy had employed *his* cultural
capital as a leading classicist and a tutor at Ireland's foremost university to
become an apologist for English hegemony. In *Greek Life and Thought from
the Age of Alexander to the Roman Conquest* (1887), Mahaffy criticizes "the
ineffaceable passion for autonomy" of the Greeks, which he compares with
the vain efforts of Irish republicans to gain independence (*AC* 81). Angered,
Wilde condemns forms of "cosmopolitan culture" that are prepared to
sacrifice "a healthy national life" in the interest of imperial hegemony (*AC,*
82). He also notes that Mahaffy's lack of respect for Irish autonomy is
symptomatic of a contempt for other forms of autonomy as well. Mahaffy,
for example, disapproves of male suffrage without a property qualification
(*AC,* 81). And on the topic of male-male desire, Wilde notes a retreat on
Mahaffy's part to hypocritical prudery, to "the censure of the Puritan,
whether real or affected" (*AC,* 83).

The violence implicit in Arnold's and Mahaffy's cultural politics and
explicit in coercive aspects of Gladstone's policy in Ireland provides an
important, unstated background of Wilde's play. Although literary critics
usually ignore political reflexivity in the play, it offers a number of perspectives on late Victorian politics. Lady Chiltern translates politics into a
moral, implicitly Christian, discourse. Her view of politics at the outset of
the play coincides with the position of Gladstonian Liberalism: "Power is
nothing in itself," she contends. "It is power to do good that is fine—that,
and that only" (177). In contrast, Sir Robert's position seems to be immoral
or amoral. When Lord Goring rebukes him for having sold a Cabinet secret,
he replies: "No; that money gave me exactly what I wanted, power over
others" (184). As I've described above, this position might be called the
sodomitic view of politics even though, in practice, Sir Robert has been a
progressive politician. Moreover, Wilde is prepared to affirm Sir Robert's
transgression insofar as it has made possible the public life necessary if he

is to become himself. Political life is the apt form that Sir Robert's individualism, to cite a central Wildean norm, takes. And it has the additional advantage over Lady Chiltern's position that it does not mystify the ambition that drives politicians.

What I call Sir Robert's individualism may also be referred to as autonomy. It may also be termed "ego-mania"—as it is by Max Nordau, who, in *Degeneration* (1892; trans. 1895), attacks Wilde as an examplar of this modern disease.[32] Like Nordau, Mahaffy sees autonomy as the great enemy of political order; to him it is synonymous with anarchy.[33] In contrast, autonomy is Wilde's leading political concept and anarchy a good, not an evil. In this view, Wilde combines two different aspects of democratic politics. One is the affirmation of the political and social rights of members of groups, whether they be women and manual workers or the inhabitants of Ireland. The other is his contention that political action is always to be judged in relation to the individual. "These two laws are irreducible one to the other" (*PF*, 22). Rather than being self-contradictory, however, the affirmation of autonomy in both senses is a central tension within democratic thought and practice.

Lord Goring poses the antithetical view: namely, that politics is boring, ineffectual, and irrelevant. To date, he has defined himself against both marriage and the political career that his senile father, a member of the House of Lords, demands of him. Goring's negativity expresses Wilde's own disabused view. Home Rule had passed the House of Commons in 1893. But on September 8th the bill was rejected by members of the House of Lords in a vote of 419 to 41.[34] The unwillingness of the Lords to acknowledge the democratic basis of the power of the Commons plus the related problem of the failure to resolve the status of Ireland within the United Kingdom left Parliament and the country in a constitutional stalemate.

The negative atmosphere affecting upper-class men with an interest in male-male sex, the status of the House of Lords in the English constitution, and the associated issue of the status of Ireland combine in a series of events in 1894 and 1895 in which Rosebery managed to bring himself and his government both to the brink of breakdown. A term that links these topics is the word "partner," a name is that of Labouchère, author of the 1885 anti-homosexual amendment. This journalistic and parliamentary antagonist of Disraeli and Wilde was also an enemy of Lord Rosebery.[35] Rosebery made a serious mistake at the beginning of his premiership when, in a speech in the House of Lords, he said that Home Rule for Ireland could be achieved only after England, "the predominant member of the partnership of the three kingdoms" will be convinced "of its justice and equity" (Brooks, 8). Taking advantage of Rosebery's vulnerability as a member of the upper chamber, Labouchère promptly submitted Rosebery to a devastating embarrassment. On March 13, 1894, the day following Rosebery's unfortunate remarks about Irish Home Rule, Labouchère successfully moved an amendment to Rosebery's inaugural address as prime minister. The amendment "practically abolished the powers of the House of Lords. . . . As a start to a Premiership this could hardly have been more catastrophic" (R. R. James, 338).

A number of events during a ten-day period in late October 1894 caught Wilde and Rosebery together in a net. It was during this period that Rosebery made the popular choice of Frank Lockwood as solicitor-general. Later, Lockwood would successfully prosecute Wilde in his third and final trial in May 1895. On October 18th, Rosebery's private secretary, Viscount Drumlanrig, was found "dead from a gunshot wound at a shooting party in Somerset."[36] His death occurred at a time when there was already concern about the weakness of Rosebery's position in the Cabinet and the House of Commons. Rosebery decided to attempt to regain the initiative in a speech at Bradford on October 27. In his diary, Sir Edward Hamilton, a close friend and political confidant of Rosebery, predicted that, in the speech at Bradford, Rosebery "may, & probably will, make or mar himself" (Brooks, 178). Without prior consultation with his Cabinet colleagues, Rosebery declared that he would fight the next election on the issue of reform of the House of Lords. Both the issue and the timing were not right—as Hamilton and others could have told Rosebery had he only asked (Brooks, 176). Moreover, Rosebery's moderate and vague suggestions about the shape of reform aggravated both conservatives such as the queen and Radicals such as Labouchère.

In deciding to stake his success on the issue of reform of the House of Lords, Rosebery attempted to assert his claim to be "Leader of the Left Party" (Brooks, 181) at the expense of Labouchère. In doing so, however, Rosebery let Labouchère choose the issue on which Rosebery would rise or fall. In an unfortunate echo of his statement on Irish Home Rule in March, he asserted that the House of Commons must be the "predominant partner" (Brooks, 180) in its relationship with the Lords. Particularly in view of Drumlanrig's death only a few days earlier, Rosebery's slip of the tongue suggests that his focus on aristocratic irresponsibility was a switch point for personal anxieties exacerbated by Labouchère's long campaign against those whom, as I mention above, Queensberry, at the time of his son's death, referred to as "Snob Queers like Roseberry" [sic].[37]

While I have focused to this point on the bearing of the play on members of two groups: namely, subjects of male-male desire and the Irish, recent criticism of the play has tended to focus on its implications for women.[38] The most important personal development that occurs in the play is that of Sir Robert's wife, Lady Chiltern. Indeed, although I have referred to Sir Robert as the character central to the action, as an example of the capacity for self-transformation, Lady Chiltern is most significant. Lady Chiltern is young, a beauty, well educated, and moneyed. At the age of twenty-seven (153), she is already well on her way to becoming an ideal politician's wife, actively involved in the Women's Liberal Association. As she tells Lord Goring, she is absorbed in "dull, useful, delightful things, Factory Acts, Female Inspectors, the Eight Hours' Bill, the Parliamentary Franchise. . . . Everything, in fact, that you would find thoroughly uninteresting" (188).

Wilde's play operates on the assumption that a politician's wife will be politically active. There is no sense that such involvement is unnatural, unimportant, or inappropriate for a woman—even though women at the time were still barred from some professions, from policy-making administrative roles in the national government, from seats in Parliament, and from the vote in national elections. Wilde's axiomatic acceptance of women's presence in political life accords with his public support for removing civil disabilities against women.[39] Nor does Wilde react against Lady Chiltern's ambition—although he is more knowing about it than she is. Indeed, one of the things that she will come to recognize during the course of the play is the significance of ambition in her private and public life. With this recognition will come another, namely, that in the world of late-Victorian England, her ambitions can be fulfilled only in marital alliance with a successful politician. At the outset, Lady Chiltern screens herself from this awareness through a romantic flaw: namely, idolization of her husband (202–3). While represented as a character trait, in fact this stance is ideologically mandated. In the final quarter of the nineteenth century, women in England exercised increasing influence in parliamentary politics—as representatives in the public sphere of the values associated with their roles as wives, mothers, and daughters. Women's emergence paralleled the emergence of what Wilde referred to as "the family ideal of the State."[40] Their claim to influence depended upon their purity—hence the need for an irreproachable domestic life and hence Lady Chiltern's need to regard her husband as a "tower of ivory" (177).

The change in the status of women fueled the politics of scandal.[41] If influence in the public sphere was to be associated with moral purity and if moral purity in turn was coded as being based on women's roles within the private sphere, then it followed that corruption, should it occur, was to be looked for in the public sphere, primarily in male activity. Given the demand for purity, corruption needed to be concealed. Hence immoral behavior became the substance of political secrecy, and the disclosure of personal secrets became a determining feature of public life. The demand for moral purity in politics guaranteed that political struggles would be fought out within the terms of moral scandal. The public declaration of female virtue called into existence a world of male secrets, whose exposure could have major implications for policy decisions.[42]

Once disabused of faith that her husband is "pure" (203), Lady Chiltern threatens to leave him unless he resigns from office and retires from public life. In this way, she threatens both to deprive him of his life's work and to sentence him to public disgrace. An unfortunate side effect, as Goring points out, is that the marriage will be irretrievably damaged. As no one says but as is also evident, Lady Chiltern's career will be blocked. Lady Chiltern, however, simply wouldn't be Lady Chiltern if stripped of her life of meetings and social gatherings. Public service is an essential aspect of her existence. Accordingly, she needs to relent in order to permit her husband to carry on. Since thenceforth she will be the sharer of the secret of his criminal past, she will have to relinquish both innocence and a mistaken sense of moral superiority.

The denouement of the play permits Wilde to turn his attention to the future of friendship, both between men and between spouses. Earlier, I argued that Lady Chiltern has practical reasons to choose to stand by her husband. Within friendship writing, friendship between husbands and wives is seen within the terms of use-value.

Women are deemed not suitable for "perfect friendship" (*PF*, 190n.) Montaigne writes:

Women are in truth not normally capable of responding to such familiarity and mutual confidence as sustain that holy bond of friendship, nor do their souls seem firm enough to withstand the clasp of a knot so lasting and so tightly drawn. And indeed if it were not for that, if it were possible to fashion such a relationship, willing and free, in which not only the soul had this full enjoyment but in which the bodies too shared in the union—where the whole human being was involved—it is certain that the loving-friendship would be more full and more abundant. But there is no example yet of woman attaining to it, and by the common agreement of the Ancient schools of philosophy, she is excluded from it.[43]

Given the terms within which women emerged within the public sphere, use-friendship for a wife like Lady Chiltern takes on a new meaning. Likewise, the more nearly symmetrical relation which her public persona permits creates the conditions for better friendship within marriage.

In the final lines of the play, Sir Robert asks his wife whether she has chosen to remain with him out of love or pity. Lady Chiltern responds, "kissing him": "It is love, Robert. Love, and only love. For both of us a new life is beginning" (244). Some viewers regret this decision on Lady Chiltern's part. But Wilde's wager is that the meaning of the word, the relationship, and the institution can change.

In some ways, Lady Chiltern brings to mind Rosebery's wife, Hannah. Hannah did not play a public role in national politics. But she idolized her husband (R. R. James, 87). And she was a consummate political insider, as Hamilton remarks: "She was one of those born to direct; and with this birthright she had in a notable degree the faculty of getting other people to work and of quickening their energies" (Brooks, 124). Rosebery depended implicitly upon her loyalty and approval, which were absolute. When she died in 1890, he was shattered. In a letter, he wrote: "I have lost the best wife ever man had. I do not see the elements of consolation, except in the memory of her beautiful, unselfish life, and in the feeling of her still encompassing love" (R. R. James, 227). The final line of Wilde's play virtually repeats Rosebery's words. Hannah nourished Rosebery's extraordinary ambition (Jenkins, 588), but, after her death in 1890, it was "effectively destroyed" (R. R. James, 229). Rosebery fell prey to recurrent insomnia and depression. In words that likewise echo his response to his wife's death, in Act 3 Sir Robert tells Goring that he loves his wife "more than anything in the world. I used to think ambition the great thing. It is not. Love is the great thing in the world. There is nothing but love, and I love her" (214).

Rosebery's extreme reaction to his wife's death suggests both a sense of personal guilt on his part as well as the recognition that she played a vital role in his sexual/political economy. Hannah may have been a wife who was able to tolerate her husband's sexual friendships with younger men without withdrawing from him either her love or her practical support. Without this aid, Rosebery found himself emotionally unsecured and overexposed, hence the threat of nervous breakdown and the repeated, panicky urge to retire from public life.

Although Sir Robert tries to suppress the memory of his crime, the violence with which he speaks of it suggests that the lapse involved an assault upon his superego that resulted in permanent pyschic division. Speaking of the incriminating letter that Mrs. Chevely offers to sell him, he says: "The sin of my youth, that I had thought was buried, rose up in front of me, hideous, horrible, with its hands at my throat. I could have killed it for ever, sent it back into its tomb, destroyed its record, burned the one witness against me" (203). Interestingly, in view of the playwright's involvement at the time with Douglas and Rosebery's with Drumlanrig, the threat from one's past is associated with a young man. Despite Goring's success in derailing Mrs. Cheveley's scheme, the action of the play forces Sir Robert to recognize the traumatic effects of his earlier behavior. By the end of the play, the letter has been burned, but the sin of Sir Robert's youth has become a permanent, known factor in his relationship both with his wife and with his best friend. As a result, he too will have to change, but at least now he has the chance to do so.

Within friendship writing, idealized friendship provides the basis for active citizenship. As I indicated earlier, Lord Goring's rejection of politics departs from tradition. The shift suggests that Wilde believed that a "government of the best"[44] neither exists nor is possible even as an ideal projection in present-day democracy. As I mentioned, at the outset of the play, Goring's father, the earl of Caversham, wants his son to settle down and enter Parliament. For his part, Goring is already thinking of marrying Lady Chiltern's sister, Mabel. Perhaps, after the action of the play is over, he will choose the conventional aristocratic path into national politics. But the distance from Parliament that he maintains in the play and the fact that Sir Robert's involvement in politics is compromised reflects Wilde's earned cynicism about the possibilities of practical politics. Goring's withdrawal indicates that the advent of popular suffrage and a mass press has outmoded the view of democracy as a form, in Plato's words, of "aristocracy—a form of government which receives various names, according to the fancies of men, and is sometimes called democracy, but is really an aristocracy or government of the best which has the approval of the many" (*PF*, 95). The final lesson of friendship is that perfect friendship joins imperfect men and women and that there is no necessary analogy between private virtue and the public weal. The future of politics remains as open as the meaning of a word on which its worth continues to depend—namely, love.

Notes

Introduction

1. Dowling, *Hellenism and Homosexuality,* 9n., hereafter cited in text as Dowling.

2. Drawing on the work of J. G. A. Pocock, Dowling shows how this tradition was translated into the field of nineteenth-century literary polemic.

3. On the distinction between external and internal Others, see J. Boyarin, *Storm,* 98. Boyarin makes the point that nation-states in western Europe in the nineteenth and twentieth centuries struggled with questions about the status of internal Others such as Jews and the Romani. I extend his argument to consider the status of the Irish within the United Kingdom. For Ireland as England's imaginary Other, see Kiberd, *Inventing Ireland,* 1–32.

4. *Storm,* 86.

5. For Macaulay on Jewish emancipation, see Viswanathan, *Outside,* 5–9; Arnold, *On the Study of Celtic Literature,* hereafter cited in text and notes as Arnold.

6. Bray, *Homosexuality in Renaissance England,* 67–70.

7. Goldberg, *Sodometries,* ch. 1.

8. Dellamora, *Masculine Desire,* 211–12, hereafter cited in notes as Dellamora.

9. Schmidgall, *The Stranger Wilde,* 43–63; Buckton, "An Unnatural State," 359–83; Dellamora, ch. 10.

10. Alter, "Sodom as Nexus," 31, hereafter cited in notes as Alter.

11. But not always. See the anonymous Elizabethan sermon included by Hallam in *The Book of Sodom,* 158–67.

12. M. Carpenter, *Imperial Bibles, Domestic Bodies,* ch. 1, typescript, 30, hereafter cited in the text and notes as M. Carpenter. I would like to thank Professor Carpenter for permission to cite this material prior to its forthcoming publication in book form.

13. Trumpener, *Bardic Nationalism,* hereafter cited in notes as Trumpener.

14. Parry, *Democracy and Religion,* 2, hereafter cited in text and notes as Parry; Robert Blake, *Disraeli,* 438.

15. Clark, "Gender, Class, and the Nation," 232, hereafter cited in text as Clark.

16. In 1880, Margaret Oliphant protested the exclusion from suffrage of female heads of household: "The ten-pound franchise represented something—a solidity, a respectability—perhaps above the level of female attainment. But now that the floodgates have been opened, and all who contribute their mites to the taxation

have a right to a voice, the question is different. When every house is represented, why not my house as well as the others? and indeed, I may ask, on what ground is my house, paying higher rates than a great many others, to be left out?" ("The Grievances of Women," in Hamilton, ed., *"Criminals, Idiots, Women,* and Minors," 24.)

17. Trollope, *An Autobiography*, 302.

18. M. Carpenter points out that editors bracketed, printed in reduced type, or paraphrased material dealing with "unnatural" (30) sexual practices such as the story of Lot, Rom. 1:26–27, and 1 Cor. 6:9; rituals, laws, genealogy, "and some other matters peculiar to the Jews" (41); and "Oriental" (48) customs. The presentation of portions of the text in brackets, reduced type, et cetera, indicates editors' concerns that the English translation of the Bible, far from being pure English, was a text contaminated by Oriental practices and understandings (48).

19. Bourdieu, *Field*, 32.

20. *The Portable Folio Family Bible*, 16n. Unless otherwise specified, references to the Bible in the Introduction are to this edition, hereafter cited in text and notes as *Portable*.

21. *The Imperial Family Bible*, 20n., cited in notes as *Imperial*.

22. Marx, "On the Jewish Question," 239.

23. Cited in M. Carpenter, 30. For the wording of English anti-sodomy statutes and their history, see Goldberg, *Sodometries*, 3, 253n. In addition to citing specific wording, Goldberg includes a list of recent articles on the topic.

24. Goldberg, *Sodometries*, 3. The death penalty for sodomy was removed in 1861.

25. Jordan, *Invention*, 35.

26. Ibid., 97.

27. M. Carpenter, 28–34. It is a commonplace among commentators on legal, religious, and political texts dealing with sodomy that there are many referents for the term. Hence, Michel Foucault refers to it, in a well-known phrase, as "that utterly confused category" (*History*, 1:101).

28. *Portable*, 15n.; *Imperial*, 18, 19.

29. Jordan, *Invention*, 34.

30. In Chapter 4, I analyze sodomitic rhetoric in the pamphlet. For the significance of the pamphlet and attendant agitation, see Joyce, "The Constitution and the Narrative Structure of Victorian Politics," 179–203, hereafter cited in text and notes as Joyce.

31. It is a measure of the complexity of English attitudes to the Jewish heritage that radical working-class politicians often invited their listeners to identify with the Israelites in exile (Joyce, 186–87). Not only were Jews internal Others in England, but the Israelite existed within, so to speak, Chartists demanding their rights.

32. Viswanathan, *Outside*, 3–43.

33. Both Derrida in *Politics of Friendship* (75–111, hereafter cited in text as *PF*) and Shell discuss how the association of democracy with the term brotherhood conflates contradictory notions of universal affiliation and filiation through a shared line of blood descent. See Shell, *Children of the Earth*, vii–x, 24–40, hereafter cited in notes as Shell.

34. Viswanathan argues that Macaulay's advocacy of the rights of Jews was based on his experience of colonial administration in India. In this way, the experience of empire shapes English domestic politics (*Outside*, 5–8).

35. The term incorporation is both psychoanalytic and political. Cf. Daniel Defoe's words: "But if the Union be an Incorporation . . . to the extent of the Letter, it must then be a Union of the very Soul of the Nation, all its Constitution, Customs, Trade, and Manners, must be blended together, for the mutual united, undistinguish't, good, growth and health of one whole united Body; and this I understand by Union ("An Essay at Removing National Prejudices Against a Union with Scotland"). Cited in Trumpener, 128.

36. Young, *Colonial Desire*, 55–89.

37. See the discussion of Disraeli's racial theory in Chapter 3.

38. Arnold, vii.

39. Arnold quotes this self-characterization from the *Times*.

40. Interestingly, this description could be attached both to the young Disraeli of the 1830s and to Oscar Wilde in the 1880s.

41. Hilton, "Gladstone's Theological Politics," 32, hereafter cited in text and notes as Hilton. See also Vernon, *Politics and the People*, 334, hereafter cited in notes as Vernon.

42. Information in the paragraph is from Hilton.

43. Joyce; see also Vernon, 295–339. The editor of *The Portable Family Bible* links blood genealogy, the Covenant, and the doctrine of justification by faith in Gen. 15:6, in which, he says, Abraham is "justified by faith" (12) when he accepts God's promise that Sarah will bear a son to him. This doctrine was transferred into a demand for political fidelity once the English translation of the Bible became recognized as the foundation of the state.

44. Joyce, 179–203; see also Parry, 432.

45. Joyce, 202.

46. "The credit—or rather, the blame—for inventing the word *sodomia*, "Sodomy," must go, I think, to the eleventh-century theologian Peter Damian. He coined it quite deliberately on analogy to *blasphemia*, "blasphemy," which is to say, on analogy to the most explicit sin of denying God" (Jordan, *Invention*, 29).

47. Alter, 39.

48. See, for example, *Oscar Wilde's Last Stand*, Philip Hoare's study of the Maud Allan libel trial of 1918.

49. E.g., Wilde, *An Ideal Husband*, 170.

50. Steiner, *Passion*. Page numbers in the remainder of the paragraph refer to this title.

51. Derrida considers this connection at length in *Politics of Friendship*.

52. For the military model of pederasty in ancient Sparta and Victorian responses, see Dellamora, *Apocalyptic Overtures*, 43–64.

53. Foucault, *History*, 2:52, 35.

54. On Ascham, see Stewart, *Close Readers*, 122–60.

55. Foucault, *History*, 1:106.

56. Bergeron, *King James*.

57. Jacques Derrida, "The Politics of Friendship," 640n. For reflections on

this dynamic in the representation of male friendship in Victorian fiction, see C. Lane, *Burdens.*

58. The submersion of individual moral responsibility in collective affect within fascist politics can also be understood in terms of fusion. When commentators collapse the distinction between sexual attraction and ties between pairs of friends, on the one hand, and the loss of self in identification with, say, the nation as a band of brothers, on the other, then fascism and other forms of collective mobilization can be stigmatized as modes of "homosexual" desire. See Sedgwick, *Epistemology of the Closet,* 154–55.

59. Jenkins, *Gladstone,* 360, 387, 389, 461, 470–71. The standard account of this aspect of Disraeli occurs in Bradford, *Disraeli,* 213–19. I consider the meaning of friendship in Tennyson's Cambridge circle in *Masculine Desire,* 16–42.

60. Foucault, *History,* 2:72–77.

61. Schultz, "Truth," 40–41.

Chapter 1

1. Although Kathleen Tillotson says that Dickens may have had the novel in mind as early as 1833, by her own account, he had not thought of Oliver before January 1837 (Charles Dickens, *Oliver Twist,* ed. Kathleen Tillotson, xv, xix). For the development of the serial into a novel, see Chittick, *Dickens and the 1830s,* 61–91.

2. Feltes, *Modes of Production,* 7–8.

3. Ibid., 103n.50.

4. Foucault, "On the Genealogy of Ethics," 366.

5. "At a certain moment, the problem of an aesthetics of existence is covered over by the problem of purity, which is something else and which requires another kind of technique. In Christian asceticism the question of purity becomes more and more important; the reason why you have to take control of yourself is to keep yourself pure. The problem of virginity, this model of feminine integrity, becomes much more important in Christianity. The theme of virginity has nearly nothing to do with sexual ethics in Greco-Roman asceticism. There is a problem is a problem of self-domination. It was a virile model of self-domination and a woman who was temperate was as virile to herself as a man. The paradigm of sexual self-restraint becomes a feminine paradigm through the theme of purity and virginity, based on the model of physical integrity. Physical integrity rather than self-regulation became important. So the problem of ethics as an aesthetics of existence is covered over by the problem of purification" (ibid., 365–66). In *Oliver Twist,* "the problem of purity" is refocused on a young male protagonist.

6. J. Rose, *The Case of Peter Pan,* 3–4; see also Kincaid, *Child-Loving,* esp. pp. 389–91.

7. D. A. Miller is the best known proponent of the concept of the novel as a disciplinary structure within nineteenth-century liberal culture (*The Novel and the Police,* vii–xiii).

8. I comment briefly on man/boy relationships in *Nicholas Nickelby* in "Male

Relations in Thomas Hardy's *Jude the Obscure*," 455; for Magwitch's interest in Pip, see Cohen, "Manual Conduct in *Great Expectations*," 242–44.

9. J. H. Miller quotes Steig in *Illustration*, 96; Chittick, *Dickens and the 1830s*, 76.

10. J. H. Miller, *Illustration*, 104.

11. Dickens, *Oliver Twist*, illus. George Cruikshank, ed. Peter Fairclough, 71. Unless otherwise cited, references to the novel, including parenthetical page numbers in the text, are to this edition.

12. J. Rose, *The Case of Peter Pan*, 5.

13. Foucault, *History*, 2:194.

14. Local boards were empowered under the Poor Law Amendment Act of 1834 to indenture orphans to factory owners *(Oliver Twist*, 482).

15. Gallagher, *Industrial Reformation*, 3, 27, 32.

16. Kettle, *An Introduction to the English Novel*, 131.

17. Forster, *The Life of Charles Dickens*, 1:90.

18. Stallybrass, "Marx and Heterogeneity," 70.

19. Malthus, *An Essay on the Principle of Population*, introd. Donald Winch, 24. Winch reprints the edition of 1803. Subsequent references in text and notes, unless otherwise indicated, are to this edition.

20. Tracy, "Fictional Modes in *Oliver Twist*," 2.

21. Malthus, *An Essay on the Principle of Population . . .* , ed. Antony Flew, 32n. These laws operate on the population conceptualized as a social body (Poovey, *Making a Social Body*, 132).

22. Dickens, *Oliver Twist*, 18.

23. Foucault, *The Birth of the Clinic*, xiv–xv.

24. Cohen, "Manual Conduct," 256 n.26.

25. In particular, in William Godwin's *Enquiry Concerning Political Justice* and the Marquis de Condorcet's *Sketch for a Historical Picture of the Progress of the Human Mind* (Jones, *Languages of Class*, 105n.); Malthus, *Essays*, vii.

26. Pullen, "Malthus' Theological Ideas," 2:213–14.

27. Dickens, *Oliver Twist*, ed. Kathleen Tillotson, 382.

28. Medick, "Plebeian Culture in the Transition to Capitalism," 98.

29. Ibid., 99. Plebeian culture is a technical term used to refer to "the socio-cultural reproduction of the urban and rural lower strata during the transition to capitalism [in the eighteenth century]. Characteristic of 'plebeian culture' was the twofold meeting of traditional ways of perception, social rules, morals and customs with the new reality of early capitalist markets and production relations on the one hand, and the politics of discipline in religion, morality and commerce, enforced by the police powers of the early modern state" (86). The question of how this culture is related to the production of proletarian culture in the nineteenth century is an open one although Medick implies that it may be as important as the changes in work and wage-relations described by Marx and Engels.

30. Ibid., 101.

31. Colley, *Britons: Forging the Nation*, 318, 316–17. Subsequent page references to Colley in the text are to this work.

32. J. H. Miller, "The Fiction of Realism," 136.

33. Pelham, *The Chronicles of Crime,* 2: facing page 241; Tracy, "Fictional Modes in *Oliver Twist,*" 17.

34. *Encyclopaedia Judaica,* 6:755.

35. Foucault, "The Eye of Power," 152.

36. L. Lane Jr., "The Devil in *Oliver Twist,*" 132–36.

37. Marcus, *Dickens,* 371.

38. Marcus, *Dickens,* 359, 367, 369, 374.

39. Laplanche and Pontalis, *Language of Psycho-Analysis,* 335–36; cf. Edelman, "Seeing Things," 95–96. See also Craft, *Another Kind of Love,* viii–ix.

40. Laplanche and Pontalis, *Language of Psycho-Analysis,* 230.

41. Cohen, "Manual Conduct," 218.

42. Tracy, "Fictional Modes in *Oliver Twist,*" 12.

43. Cited in Tracy, "Fictional Modes in *Oliver Twist,*" 13.

44. See, for example, Sutherland, *Stanford Companion to Victorian Fiction,* 478.

45. Quoted by J. H. Miller, "The Fiction of Realism," 128. James's description suggests that he read a text with the illustration as retouched for the 1846 edition. The crudely touched-up plates exaggerate Cruikshank's grotesquery. It is these images that I reproduce from the novel.

46. *The Oxford English Dictionary.* In a phobic exclusion of their own, the editors claim that the meaning of "homosexual" originated in the United States in the twentieth century. The interweave of proper and cant meanings of the term indicates, however, that the word denotes/connotes (homo)sexual perversity at least from the early nineteenth century. Dickens plays on the equivocation again in *Nicholas Nickleby,* which began publication while Oliver Twist was still appearing in serial. Mr. Wackford Squeers's Academy, Dotheboys Hall includes in its syllabus "single stick (if required)" (Charles Dickens, *Nicholas Nickleby,* 26).

47. J. Rose, *The Case of Peter Pan,* x.

48. Cf. Flynn, "Foucault as Parrhesiast," 103.

49. Chittick, *Dickens and the 1830s,* 58, 81, 82, 84.

50. Dickens, *Pickwick Papers,* xv.

Chapter 2

1. Ridley, *Young Disraeli: 1804–1846,* 125, hereafter cited in text and notes as Ridley.

2. B. Disraeli, "The Mutilated Diary," in *Letters: 1815–1834,* 447, hereafter cited in text as *DL* 1.

3. B. Disraeli, *Whigs and Whiggism,* 85, 96; *DL* 2:37.

4. Ridley; Weintraub, *Disraeli.*

5. Contemporary men of letters frequently reminded Disraeli of both his Jewishness and his effeminacy. For men such as the editor, John Gibson Lockhart, a Lowland Scot with aristocratic and church connections, Disraeli was never able to overcome being Jewish. Even later, in the 1840s, when he published *Coningsby,*

Lockhart remarked to his son: "Ben Disraeli, the Jew scamp, has published a very blackguard novel. . . . Awful vanity of the Hebrew!" (Ridley, 124). Commentators enjoyed rewriting his name so as to accentuate its foreignness. In the earliest journalistic literary study of Disraeli, for example, W. Maginn writes: "O Reader dear! do pray look here, and you will spy the curly hair, and forehead fair, and nose so high, and gleaming eye of Benjamin D'Is-ra-el-i, the wondrous boy who wrote *Alroy* in rhyme and prose, only to show how long ago victorious Judah's lion-banner rose" (R. W. Stewart, *Disraeli's Novels Reviewed,* 17). Under the surveillance of a Tory journal, D'Israeli is seen to be an exponent of Jewish triumphalism. But he is also effeminate: a girlish "boy," with "curly hair, and forehead fair." He affects aristocratic hauteur, but the very signs of social distinction (the "nose" carried "so high") signify the mortified pride and social abjection of the Jew.

6. Elfenbein, *Byron and the Victorians,* ch. 6.

7. In recent years, Beckford and the *Episodes* have attracted a good deal of attention. See Haggerty, *Men in Love,* 136–51; Jack, *William Beckford;* and Mowl, *William Beckford.*

8. Beckford, *Vathek and Other Stories,* 70–71, hereafter cited in text and notes as *Vathek.*

9. Beckford, *The Episodes of Vathek,* 21.

10. Later, this disturbing attraction is rationalized by the notional fiction that Firouz is, in fact, Firouzkah, a woman in disguise. In an earlier mss version of the episode, published for the first time in 2001, Firouz is introduced as a male in early adolescence (Beckford, *Vathek and the Episodes of Vathek,* 151–96, 385). The first version functions as a critique of two key axioms within friendship tradition. The first is that the highest form of male friendship is asexual. In Alasi's passionate love for Firouz, Beckford shows both how powerful and how thoroughly disintegrative the force of attraction/repulsion within male friendship can be. At the same time, in the behavior of Roudabah, Alasi's promised bride, Beckford shows loving friendship at its rational and virtuous best. In other words, he negates the view that friendship between a man and a woman in marriage must necessarily be inferior to disinterested male friendship. Beckford's exploratory interest in male-male desire and his progressive view of the possibility of friendship and equality within a reformulated institution of marriage are aligned aspects of Enlightenment thinking in this work.

11. Foucault, *History,* 1:58–61.

12. Fothergill, *Beckford of Fonthill,* 165–66.

13. Potkay, "Beckford's Heaven of Boys," 73–86.

14. Foucault, *History,* 2:187–246.

15. Fothergill, *Beckford of Fonthill,* 206, 209, 293–96.

16. For this and other possible meanings of the word, see Ragussis, *Figures of Conversion,* 157–59. Like other Jewish commentators, Elaine Marks speaks of Jewish converts to Christianity as "crypto-Jews" (Marks, *Marrano as Metaphor,* 129). In an important study, however, Benzion Netanyahu argues convincingly that Jewish converts did, in fact, adopt Christian belief; see Kamen, "The Secret of the Inquisition," 4–6. Quoting Yirmiyahu Yovel, Elaine Marks describes a set of attitudes aris-

ing from existence as a Marrano: "A this-worldly disposition; a split religious identity; a metaphysical skepticism; a quest for alternative salvation through methods that oppose the official doctrine; an opposition between the inner and outer life, and a tendency toward dual language and equivocation" (133).

17. I have in mind the terms of Mordecai, in George Eliot's novel *Daniel Deronda,* including the commentary on the novel by David Kaufmann, *George Eliot and Judaism: An Attempt to Appreciate* Daniel Deronda.

18. On sexual inversion, see Craft, *Another Kind of Love,* 33–36.

19. Colley, *Britons,* 349; Thompson, *The Making of the English Working Class,* 909–10.

20. Crompton, *"Don Leon,"* 53–71.

21. B. Disraeli, *Alroy,* 248, hereafter cited in text and notes as *Alroy.*

22. Boyarin, *A Radical Jew,* 3, 8.

23. Viswanathan, "Raymond Williams and British Colonialism," 47–66.

24. Already in debate with the Irish nationalist Daniel O'Connell, Disraeli uses the need to protect heterogeneity as a rationale for continued English domination of Ireland. Despite his defense elsewhere of Jewish difference, Disraeli in a series of political columns in the *Morning Post* is happy to speak—as a *Protestant Englishman*—in mockery of Catholic Irish and the Scots. He dubs O'Connell's supporters "Popish rebels." And Sir John Campbell, the attorney general, is a "base-born Scotchman, . . . this booing, fawning, jobbing progeny of haggis and cockaleekie." As so often in English writing in the nineteenth century, ethnic differences close to home become metaphors of the most extreme sort of racial, implicitly sexual degeneracy. Disraeli compares Campbell with "an ourang-outang of unusual magnitude dancing under a banana-tree, and licking its hairy chaps, and winking with exultation its cunning eyes as it beholds the delicious and impending fruit" (B. Disraeli, *Whigs and Whiggism,* 85, 89, 88–89). Attacks such as this indicate that Disraeli was as capable of xenophobic assaults as were other contemporaries such as Thomas Carlyle and Charles Kingsley. Compare, for example, the latter's infamous comparison of the Irish to "white chimpanzees" (quoted by McClintock, *Imperial Leather,* 216).

25. See Beckford's note, *Vathek,* 118.

26. I. Disraeli, *The Genius of Judaism,* 256–58.

27. Turner, Disraeli's baptismal sponsor, was a leading exponent of a mythically unified definition of English nationality. In his *History of the Anglo-Saxons* (1799–1805), he uses the concept of "conversion" to efface the persecution of Jews in England while praising the process of "improving progress," whereby the Anglo-Saxon developed from the condition of a pirate into that of the modern Englishman (Ragussis, *Figures of Conversion,* 94). In refusing to heed Jabaster, Alroy/Disraeli revolts against his own godfather's demand for a unitary concept of the body politic. At the same time, in ultimately rejecting Honain, Disraeli repudiates Turner's role in turning the boy Disraeli into a renegade against his heritage (Weintraub, *Disraeli,* 31–32).

28. B. Disraeli, *Whigs and Whiggism,* 2.

29. Gellner, *Nations and Nationalism,* 125. In a classic analysis of Jane Austen's *Mansfield Park,* Edward Said sees imperial expansion as an aspect of the moderniza-

tion of the nation-state (Said, *Culture and Imperialism*, 80–97; *Orientalism*). For the convergence of Disraeli's foreign policy with cockney jingoism, see Feldman, *Englishmen and Jews*, 94–97, 115–20.

30. During, "Literature—Nationalism's Other?," 140, 141. Cf. Gellner, who suggests that "conservative traditionalists" can find common ground with nationalists on grounds of race and other commonalities (*Nations and Nationalism*, 133). One finds both elements in Disraeli's *Morning Post* articles.

31. B. Disraeli, *Whigs and Whiggism*, 44.

32. Childers, *Novel Possibilities*, 53.

33. B. Disraeli, *Contarini Fleming: A Psychological Romance* (1832).

34. During, "Literature—Nationalism's Other?," 147; but Childers disagrees (*Novel Possibilities*, 52–68). Gary Wihl has argued that generalizations about the relationship between the novel and ideology should be treated with caution ("Novels as Theories in a Liberal Society," 101–13).

35. Freud, "Creative Writers and Day-Dreaming" and "Family Romances," in *The Standard Edition*, 9:143–53, 237–41.

36. Douglas, *Purity and Danger*, 54–73; Kristeva, *Powers of Horror*.

37. Gallop, *The Daughter's Seduction*, 115, 117.

38. Kaufmann, *George Eliot and Judaism*, 7–8.

39. Ibid., 3, 2, 4.

40. The capital letter refers to Lacan's usage (Lacan, *Écrits*, 311) and, more significantly, to the following passage in the book of Jewish ritual in use in London since 1780: "All *Jewish* Parents are reckoned to be accountable for the Sins of their Sons, till they are thirteen Years old, but no longer; and therefore when Boys arrive to their thirteenth Year, they are for the first Time called up to the Law that is read on the Altar in their Synagogue on the Sabbath-Day, and read a Chapter or more in the Law themselves, . . . entering into Man's State, in Regard of becoming accountable for himself, from that Day" (Weintraub, *Disraeli*, 31).

41. Elfenbein discusses the gender anxieties and intimations of sexual perversity that accompany the idealization of the brother-sister dyad (*Byron and the Victorians*, 22, 33–35).

42. Winckelmann, *History of Ancient Art*, 1:215; Potts, *Flesh and the Ideal*, 118–32; see also Dellamora, "The Androgynous Body in Pater's 'Winckelmann,'" 51–68. For a different articulation of Potts's views, see Potts, "Beautiful Bodies," 1–21.

43. Potts, "Beautiful Bodies," 20 n.27.

44. Potts, "Beautiful Bodies," 2; see also 12.

45. Beckford describes Disraeli as a "genius" (Oliver, *The Life of William Beckford*, 299, hereafter cited in text as Oliver).

46. R. W. Stewart, *Disraeli's Novels Reviewed*, 144, 145.

47. I take Alroy's reference to "the conqueror of the world" (149) as an allusion to Alexander. The quotation is from the *Athenaeum* review (R. W. Stewart, *Disraeli's Novels Reviewed*, 144).

48. Alexander, *England's Wealthiest Son*, chs. 8, 9.

49. Crompton, *Byron and Greek Love*, 180–81.

50. Crompton, "*Don Leon*."

51. *DL* 1:411–12, 419 n.8.

52. The phrase current today is *comme ça* (D. A. Miller, *Bringing Out Roland Barthes*, 6).

53. Cited in Fothergill, *Beckford of Fonthill*, 231—addition mine.

54. For a context in contemporary Jewish cultural politics, see J. Boyarin, *Storm*, xvii.

55. Said defines *affiliation* as "a joining together of people in a non-genealogical, non-procreative but *social* unity" (Said, "On Repetition," 146).

56. Beckford, *Episodes of Vathek*, 25.

57. Pelham, *The Chronicles of Crime*, 2:236.

58. Barham, "The Wondrous Tale of Ikey Solomons," sheet six.

59. Barham ms, sheet one.

60. Feldman, *Englishmen and Jews*, 103.

61. Ibid., 106, 118.

Chapter 3

I would like to thank Robert O'Kell for having first drawn my attention to *Tancred* in 1988, when he shared with me his unpublished paper, "The Politics of 'The Great Asian Mystery.'"

1. For Disraeli's role in the invention of the political novel in England, see Harvie, *The Centre of Things*, 3, 8–13; see also 29–54.

2. The opening books are written within the genre of the roman à clef about London high society, known as silver-fork novels (Elfenbein, *Byron and the Victorians*, 219–20, hereafter cited in notes as Elfenbein; see also C. Lane, *Burdens of Intimacy*, 45–72). Wilde admired the satiric wit of the genre, at least when in Disraeli's hands. The gathering of English gentlemen at Lord Darlington's in Act 3 of *Lady Windermere's Fan* recalls both the young men's conversation in the third chapter of *Tancred* as well as Disraeli's pleasure in Oriental divans in Book 3 and following.

3. For recent critical work on Disraeli's fiction of the 1840s, see Ragussis, *Figures of Conversion*, 174–233, hereafter cited in notes as Ragussis; and Brantlinger, "Nations and Novels," 255–75. See also Childers, *Novel Possibilities*, 52–68, and Poovey, *Making a Social Body*, 132–54.

4. Information in the following two paragraphs is from the biography by Robert Blake, *Disraeli*, 167–90, 221–43, hereafter cited in text and notes as Blake. For more recent accounts, see Bradford, *Disraeli*, who introduces the topic of Disraeli's romantic entanglements with young upper-class men (213–19), hereafter cited in notes as Bradford. Ridley, *Young Disraeli*, gives attention to homoerotic attachments of Disraeli and members of a number of intersecting circles, including those of Alfred D'Orsay and Frederick Faber. In *Disraeli*, Stanley Weintraub focuses especially on the salience of Jewish issues in Disraeli's career. Page references to Weintraub are included in the text.

5. The description of Waldershare, a character recalling Smythe, in a later

novel by Disraeli might equally well be attached to Fakredeen: "Waldershare was profligate, but sentimental; unprincipled, but romantic; the child of whims and the slave of imagination, so freakish and deceptive that it was always impossible to foretell his course. He was alike capable of sacrificing all his feelings to worldly considerations or of forfeiting the world for a visionary caprice" (cited in Bradford, 219).

6. I say "Syria" because this geographic region is the object of Tancred's political program. While in the East, Tancred comes to believe that a general insurrection is necessary, under his leadership and that of Fakredeen, in order to carve a new Greater Syria out of the decaying carcass of the Ottoman Empire. The revived national-religious faith that will be both cause and effect of this transformation will regenerate western Europe as well and thereby save it from its nihilistic faith in modern progress. Tancred operates within the terms of a rhetoric of national, cultural, and racial regeneration that characterized the Young England movement and later discourses of national reform in England, the United States, and Canada. (For this discourse in the United States, see Wendy Graham, *Henry James's Thwarted Love*.)

7. B. Disraeli, *Tancred or the New Crusade*, 343. Subsequent page references appear in the text.

8. For example, Fakredeen to Tancred: "You will magnetise the Queen [of England] as you have magnetised me" (262).

9. See F. Kaplan, *Dickens and Mesmerism*.

10. This tendency makes Fakredeen's desire "Greek," at least in the sense that Michel Foucault uses the word in *History*, 2:188.

11. Sennett, *Fall*, 5, hereafter cited in text as Sennett.

12. In Kant's writing on friendship, the institution is haunted by the threat of perversion, by an excess of love between two men (Derrida, *Politics of Friendship*, 256–57, hereafter cited in text and notes as *PF*). The friendship of Tancred and Fakredeen is similarly haunted. One way in which this specter is signified is through the influence of Byron's writing and its cultural reception in England. By naming one of Fakredeen's erotic targets "Astarte," the name of the sister to whom Manfred is attracted in Byron's play of the same name, Disraeli suggests perverse aspects of Fakredeen's desires—both for Eva and for Tancred.

13. The tradition is traced in Derrida, *PF*.

14. Derrida, *PF*, ch. 9 passim, including 230–31, 252–53, 260–62. See also the final pages of ch. 10.

15. Bernheimer, "Unknowing Decadence," 51.

16. Nordau, *Degeneration*, 32; cf. Potolsky, "Pale Imitations," 235.

17. Derrida, *PF*, 230.

18. Reference to the friendship of Damon and Pythias might be referred to as either a cliché or a touchstone of the writing of male intimacy in Victorian England. The phrase is invoked by homosexual apologists such as Edward Carpenter later in the century as well as by assertively heterosexual writers such as Charles Kingsley, who, in the September 1850 issue of *Fraser's Magazine,* describes Alfred Tennyson's *In Memoriam* as a successor to "the old tales of David and Jonathan, Damon and

Pythias, Shakespeare and his nameless friend, of 'love passing the love of women'"
(B. Adams, "The 'Dark Saying' of the Enigma," 221; E. Carpenter, *Ioläus,* 33–34).

19. Derrida, *PF,* 1, 2.

20. Fakredeen is frequently compared to the "fragrant puff" of the nargilly.

21. Poliakov, *The History of Anti-Semitism,* 3:323–37, hereafter cited in notes as Poliakov; Ragussis, 185–89.

22. B. Disraeli, *Bentinck,* 346, hereafter cited as Bentinck in text and notes.

23. B. Disraeli, *Coningsby,* 267. Subsequent page references appear in the text and notes.

24. Ibid.

25. B. Disraeli, *Bentinck,* 355.

26. Ibid., 356.

27. Ibid.

28. Hence the purity both of personal friendship and racial brotherhood. This allusion to Sodom and Gomorrah, "the cities of the plain" (Gen. 19:29), refers not only to Middle Eastern cities but implicitly to London, which Tancred has left in search of Lot's angel (51). Disraeli slyly reverses the English notion of the Protestant Christian supercession of the Jews by associating Sodom (and the sin of Sodom) not with Jews but with the British metropolis.

29. Tancred's blood lust is shown in Book 6, when he leads a skirmish against a Turkish force. Not only is the fight avoidable, but the Turks have intervened at the behest of Tancred's friend, Adam Besso, in order to free his abducted daughter, Eva.

30. For a corroborative reading based in political and social history, see Saab, "Disraeli, Judaism, and the Eastern Question."

31. Here and elsewhere Disraeli draws no clear distinction between the narrator's point of view and Tancred's. At such moments, the text may also register Disraeli's point of view. These passages, where views seem to hover between different consciousnesses, need to be distinguished from Tancred's direct statements of his political ideology, which Disraeli does not endorse.

32. This moment throws light on Disraeli's seemingly evasive usage in referring to the friendship of Damon and Pythias as "ethereal." As Astarte gazes at the statue of Apollo, upon which she projects her image of Tancred, "the ethereal form" of the statue is suffused with "radiancy" (459).

33. I discuss ways in which nationalist ideology in the nineteenth century is couched within terms drawn from the story of Lot in Genesis in the Introduction and Chapter 4.

34. Robert Alter argues convincingly that the function of "the story of Sodom" within Genesis is to emphasize that in exchange for the Covenant Abraham must "do *righteousness and justice*" (Gen. 18:19, emphasis Alter's; "Sodom as Nexus," 31, 32).

35. In the ensuing paragraph, I draw upon M. C. N. Salbstein's analysis of Judaism in relation to Western and Islamic thought in the nineteenth century. See his *Emancipation of the Jews,* 17–43.

36. The Bentincks were former Whigs. Their recognition that the Tory party was the proper place for aristocrats—and their willingness to give Disraeli the fi-

nancial and other support he needed to become Tory leader—arises in response to the politics of reform following passage of the Reform Bill of 1832 (Blake, 253–54).

37. O'Connell "founded the Catholic Association, the first mass political party in history" and "developed the methods of grass roots organizing and the mass meeting which made him the first modern agitator" (Ignatieff, *How the Irish Became White*, 6).

38. Salbstein, *Emancipation of the Jews*, 22.

39. In *Islam: A Short History*, Karen Armstrong writes that the Ottoman "government merely provided a framework which enabled different groups . . . to live together peacefully, each . . . following its own beliefs and customs," a comment that William H. McNeill refers to as an "anodyne half-truth" (McNeill, "History 101," *New York Times Book Review*, September 3, 2000, 8).

40. Salbstein, *Emancipation of the Jews*, 27.

41. Quoted in Blake, 179.

42. Poliakov, 3:330.

43. Following is an example of what Poliakov, a leading historian of anti-Semitism, refers to as Disraeli's "virulent racism" (3:331): "What would be the consequence on the great Anglo-Saxon republic, for example, were its citizens to secede from their sound principle of reserve, and mingle with their negro and coloured populations?" (B. Disraeli, *Bentinck*, 356).

44. B. Disraeli, *Alroy*, 271. I discuss this phenomenon in Chapter 2.

45. Elfenbein, 22.

46. Blake, 70.

47. Salbstein, *Emancipation of the Jews*, 11.

48. Derrida, *PF*, 253–57.

49. On Disraeli's competitiveness vis-à-vis his gentile colleagues, see Poliakov, 3:333–34.

Excursus

1. Henry James, *The Tragic Muse*, 484.

2. Philip Hoare, *Oscar Wilde's Last Stand*.

3. George Eliot, *Daniel Deronda*, 597–98.

4. Notwithstanding this fact, Eliot invested in colonial railways and worked with her partner, George Henry Lewes, to send his two younger sons to South Africa to make their living (Nancy Henry, *George Eliot and the British Empire*).

5. George Steiner, *Passion*, 416, 417.

6. Cited in Jacques Derrida, *Archive Fever*, 13.

7. Fritz J. Raddatz, *Karl Marx*, 97.

8. Isaiah Berlin, "Benjamin Disraeli, Karl Marx, and the Search for Identity," 252–86.

9. I consider this problem in Kant's philosophy in my essay, "The Ends of Man," 117–36.

10. Marx reviews two publications on the Jewish question by the radical anti-

Christian theologian Bruno Bauer, a collaborator of his at the time (Paul Lawrence Rose, *Revolutionary Antisemitism,* 296).

11. For example, Marx's view licensed anti-Semitism in Russia under Joesph Stalin but also more recently. See Robert Conquest, "Stalin and the Jews," *New York Review of Books,* July 11, 1996, 46–50; Joel Greenberg, "New Israelis with Ideas as Big as Russia's Sky," *New York Times,* July 26, 1996, A5.

12. Poliakov, *History of Anti-Semitism,* 3:427, hereafter cited in notes and text as Poliakov.

13. Ibid., 3:555 n.110.

14. In contrast to Engels, who maintained an Irish mistress, Mary Burns, in a house in suburban Manchester, Marx never recognized his peasant-born housemaid, Helene Demuth, as mother of their illegitimate son. For the balance of probabilities regarding Marx's paternity out of wedlock, see Raddatz, *Karl Marx,* 134–38.

15. Ibid., 39.

16. Michel Foucault and Gilles Deleuze, "Intellectuals and Power," 15.

17. This potential requires the same sort of policing that is necessary to govern the limits of nationhood defined as a fraternity: "Typically represented as a passionate brotherhood, the nation finds itself compelled to distinguish its 'proper' homosociality from more explicitly sexualized male-male relations, a compulsion that requires the identification, isolation, and containment of male homosexuality" (Andrew Parker, et al., *Nationalisms and Sexualities,* 6).

18. Poliakov, 3:425.

19. Andrew Parker, "Unthinking Sex," 32, hereafter cited in notes as Parker.

20. Ibid., 32.

21. Parker comments on the anxieties that attended the close friendship between Marx and Engels, in which Marx was a financial dependent (29).

22. Karl Marx, "On the Jewish Question," 239, hereafter cited in text and notes as Marx. What does Marx refer to by "etc."?

23. Marx associates Jews with pimping. Attacks on usury often identified Jews with prostitution (James Shapiro, *Shakespeare and the Jews,* 99–100).

24. Although his father was an assimilating Jew, his mother, whose family came from Pressburg in Hungary, spoke Yiddish as her first language (Sander Gilman, *Jewish Self-Hatred,* 188–208, 199–200; P. Rose, *Revolutionary Antisemitism,* 297).

25. Marx, 230, 238 n.37.

26. Although Marx and Wagner did not meet in the 1840s, they moved in the same left Hegelian circles (P. Rose, *Revolutionary Antisemitism,* 364 n.20). See Marc A. Weiner, *Richard Wagner and the Anti-Semitic Imagination,* 64.

27. Gilman, *Jewish Self-Hatred,* 189.

28. I use the word "terror" advisedly—in view of Maurice Blanchot's account of Marx's "three voices": first, the voice of the humanist philosopher; second, the voice of the scientist; and, third, the apocalyptic voice of "'revolutionary terror.'" Although Blanchot regards these voices as "non-contemporaneous," it is important to recognize that, in a text such as "On the Jewish Question," the humanist and revolutionary voices mutually implicate one another (Maurice Blanchot, "Marx's Three Voices," 19).

29. As a term within medical pathology, "Jewish self-hatred" develops in the

late nineteenth century (Gilman, *Jewish Self-Hatred,* 286–308, esp. 308). Because the phrase is prejudicial, I prefer to use the term anti-Semitism. In the case of Marx, however, the phrase is unavoidable because the disavowal of Jewish identity becomes a structural feature first of his general philosophy and, subsequently, of his political theory.

30. Alter, "Sodom as Nexus," 32.

Chapter 4

1. Since the word Christian is used negatively in this chapter, I want to emphasize the importance of not reifying the term. In Gladstone's usage, Christianity is appealed to as part of the ideological work of constituting a modern, that is, a secular national subject. Within Christian tradition, there are materials that can be used to resist this abuse of religion. Daniel Boyarin, who has argued strenuously against the reification of Judaism in both philo-Semitic and anti-Semitic contexts, makes a point similar to mine here when he attempts to conciliate Orthodox Judaism with radical politics, including a radical politics of sex and gender: "Tradition, as Bertha Pappenheim understood and enacted, is precisely the critical recovery of the past that we make for the redemption of the future" (D. Boyarin, *Unheroic Conduct,* 359).

2. Trollope, "Public Schools," 476.

3. On this point, I disagree with other critics, who assume that the prime minister's formulation of the consensus in Ch. 68, "The Prime Minister's Political Creed," expresses Trollope's view of it as well. See, for example, Harvie, *The Centre of Things,* 1–2.

4. Trollope, *An Autobiography,* 305, hereafter cited in text as *Autobiography.*

5. Schwartz, "Adultery in the House of David." In analyzing how Judaic concepts of idolatry and infidelity are adapted to serve the purposes of both novelistic and political argument in this chapter, I am indebted to Moshe Halbertal and Avishai Margalit's book, *Idolatry,* hereafter cited in text as Halbertal.

6. Jewish racial hybridity was believed to include black, African blood (Poliakov, *The Aryan Myth,* 234–35, herafter cited in notes as *Aryan*).

7. J. Boyarin, *Storm,* 81.

8. Kucich, *The Power of Lies.* In their own terms, Karl Marx and Alexis de Tocqueville locate the same motive as driving both the market economy and liberal democracy. See the excursus on Marx; also, Gordon S. Wood, "Tocqueville's Lesson," 49.

9. The overdetermination of the concept of the gentleman in England (it was a term that referred to "blood" or family background *and* financial independence *and* "honour" both in the aristocratic sense of repute and in the bourgeois sense of moral integrity) produced a social ambiguity that accommodated both traditional privileges and upward mobility (Castronovo, *The English Gentleman*). The same ambiguity, however, opened the possibility of the reduction of the concept and the

substitution of signs of wealth and social access for a more complex understanding of the term.

10. Carlyle, *Sartor Resartus,* 249.

11. Ibid., 251.

12. Trollope, *Prime Minister,* 2:234. Subsequent citations occur parenthetically in the text.

13. F. Kaplan, *Dickens and Mesmerism.*

14. For Disraeli's role in the Great Eastern Crisis of 1876–1878, see Saab, "Disraeli, Judaism, and the Eastern Question."

15. For studies of the political novels of Trollope, see Harvie, *The Centre of Things;* Halperin, *Trollope and Politics;* McMaster, *Trollope's Palliser Novels;* Walton, *Patriarchal Desire;* and Wolfreys, *Being English,* hereafter cited in text as Wolfreys. Michael Ragussis discusses the Jewish cultural politics of Trollope's fiction in *Figures of Conversion.* For further information on Trollope and politics, see N. John Hall, *Trollope;* Mullen, *Anthony Trollope;* and Glendinning, *Trollope.* Mullen and Munson's *Penguin Companion to Trollope* is also useful.

16. Ridley, *Young Disraeli,* 130, hereafter cited in text and notes as Ridley.

17. Ibid., 153–54, 178–79, 185.

18. Ellmann, *Oscar Wilde,* 412.

19. Sodomy legislation was a topic of political lobbying at the time. Following passage of the Reform Bill of 1832, men with sexual and emotional ties to other men pressured Melbourne's administration to reduce or remove legal penalties against sodomy (Dellamora, *Masculine Desire,* 2, 13–14).

20. Ridley, 130; on Disraeli's posing as a sodomite, see Elfenbein, *Byron and the Victorians,* 206–46.

21. Weintraub, *Disraeli,* 529, hereafter cited in text and notes as Weintraub.

22. For their remarkable friendship, see the entry on Corry in the *Dictionary of National Biography.* Corry returned from a vacation in Algiers to be at Disraeli's deathbed. See also Blake, *Disraeli,* 449, 714, 734, hereafter cited in text and notes as Blake. Taking a different tack, Sarah Bradford sees the relationship as one of surrogate sonship (*Disraeli,* 218).

23. Cited in Blake, 449.

24. Gladstone, *Bulgarian Horrors,* 9. References to Gladstone in the text, unless otherwise cited, are to this title.

25. Gladstone was well known for his studies of Homeric tradition. Accordingly, David Feldman, following Frank Miller Turner, poses him as a Hellenist (Feldman, *Englishmen and Jews,* 102, hereafter cited in text as Feldman). But Gladstone's evangelical Anglicanism includes its own Judaicizing understanding of Christianity. In this chapter, I am interested in the extension of these concepts to secular politics in a democratizing age.

26. Insofar as truth is "information," Gladstone is able, in the next breath, to assure the reader that "the details of these abominations may be read in published Reports, now known to be accurate in the main. They are hardly fit for reproduction" (10). Regarding the abominations, one might keep in mind Patrick Joyce's comment that, in the interest of a "fictive real," after 1867 the popular press became

the repository of pornographic material whose representation in fiction would not have been tolerated ("The Constitution," 201–2).

27. Similarly, Marx identifies Judaism as anti-human. See the Excursus.

28. Weintraub, 545.

29. A shape-shifter, Turkey later becomes a "he."

30. See the discussion in the Introduction.

31. Usury was associated with the forced departure of the Jews from England under Edward I. On usury and counterfeiting in the early modern period, see Shapiro, *Shakespeare and the Jews*, 48, 98–100.

32. The incident provides the point of departure of Oscar Wilde's play, *An Ideal Husband*. See the Coda.

33. Like the unrepentant thief on Calvary, whom Daniel O'Connell, the Irish political leader, had earlier linked with Disraeli (quoted by Blake, 125).

34. Jenkins, *Gladstone*, 425, hereafter cited in text as Jenkins.

35. For historical usage of the term, see Dowling, *Hellenism and Homosexuality*, 5–7, passim. See also Jordan, *The Invention of Sodomy*, 3, 17, 63, passim Jordan, who traces the way in which the theological concept of *sodomia* contributes to defining a particular type of human subject, argues that in Peter Damian's writing the term *luxuria* is conflated with St. Augustine's concept of *libido* or "disordered" personal "desire" (63). But, in Gladstone's rhetoric, in the examples in Dowling, and in texts such as the anonymous Elizabethan sermon on the text, "Remember Lot's Wife" (Luke 17:32), luxury is also associated with institutional corruption.

36. See the discussion of Disraeli's domestic program in Weintraub, 529–32.

37. Marsh, *Word Crimes*, 140.

38. As Ann Pellegrini points out in a witty essay, Jews were criticized both on grounds of incestuous inbreeding and of indiscriminate miscegenation. "Jews could be held to represent the dangers at once of too much and too little race-mixing. At both poles—hybridization (exogamy) and conservation (endogamy)—Jews were conceptualized as exceeding the norm" (Pellegrini, *Performance Anxieties*, 21).

39. See Poliakov, *Aryan*, 224–35. Pellegrini comments: "In the increasingly secular, urban landscape of nineteenth-century Europe, categories of religious difference, Christian/Jew, were transformed into categories of 'racial' science, Aryan/Jew. Nonetheless, the transformation was not total. The opposition Jew/Aryan vacillates among boundaries based on religion and culture (Jew as standing in for Judaism; Aryan as the standard-bearer for an unnamed, but always implicit Christianity), 'race' (Jew and Aryan as opposed racial categories in the emerging 'science' of race), and language (Aryan as the name for a family of languages whose influence and highly 'evolved' character contrasts with the 'static,' 'immutable' Semitic languages)" (Pellegrini, *Performance Anxieties*, 19–20).

40. Poliakov, *Aryan*, 234.

41. As in Disraeli's own association of the Irish with Blacks, invidious racial comments frequently represented those under attack as contaminated with sub-Saharan African blood. Gladstone himself referred to Disraeli as an "Ethiopian" (i.e., a black African Jew). I want, however, to avoid reducing concepts of race in

the nineteenth century to the terms of a black/white binary. To do so obscures the salience of a wide range of differences.

42. 1:142. "The thing" of course, is Othello, Moorish and African. In Shakespeare's play, he is revered as a military leader by the Venetians because he has successfully led their troops against the Turks. His identification as "the noble Moor," however, permits Trollope subliminally to associate him and Lopez with the "bestial" (Gladstone, 22) Turks.

43. On the pervasiveness of the marriage plot, see Boone, *Tradition Counter Tradition.*

44. Arthur's name also connotes Celtic and Norman admixture.

45. The conflation of moral terms with anthropological ones is classically expressed in the essay by Marx, "On the Jewish Question." See the Excursus.

46. The word is Emily's. It signals her subjection to the judgment of the Wharton and Fletcher families.

47. Note the restriction of the term friend here to relatives and acquaintances whom Emily has known since childhood.

48. Judith Walkowitz discusses how demographic pressures in the East End helped provoke attacks on Jews during the Jack the Ripper sensation of 1888 (*City of Dreadful Delight,* 203–4).

49. Kincaid, "Anthony Trollope," 221.

50. For Kincaid's view of Trollope's subversion of the concept of the gentleman, see "Anthony Trollope."

51. In Chapter 2, I discuss the ideal as expressed in the writing of William Beckford.

52. The duke of Omnium's phrase (1:67; cf. Blake, 448).

53. Disraeli (Gladstone too, for that matter) was well known for his close friendships, at times charged, at times romantic, with aristocratic young parliamentarians and private secretaries. (On Gladstone's friendships, see Jenkins, 16–18, 48–49, 77, 360–61, 387, 471; on Disraeli's see Bradford, *Disraeli,* 213–19.) Bradford believes that Disraeli turned to friendship with young men "to combat his natural melancholia, his tendency to be 'bored to extinction'" (218). A theorist such as Judith Butler might well see this melancholy as not "natural" but rather as socially constituted. In light of her theory of heterosexual melancholy, Disraeli's melancholy may be seen as an effect of the suppression, on his part, of desire for the young men to whom he was attracted. See Butler, *Psychic Life,* 132–59. Disraeli was bisexual (Ridley, 131).

I am not implying an erotic entanglement between the duke and his secretaries comparable with Disraeli's friendships with young men. In the duke's case, what may be in question is not the suppression but the repression of any such possibility. Nor is melancholy confined to same-sex desire. For the duke, it likewise signifies the physical, emotional, and psychological distance that exists between himself and his wife (McMaster, *Trollope's Palliser Novels,* 122–25).

54. Shell, *Money, Language, and Thought,* 15, 22, 50 n.12. There are further complications, which I will not enter into here, insofar as such exchanges often depend not on money but on promissory notes, that is, on one's signature (and honor) as a gentleman.

55. Marx, "On the Jewish Question," 238.

56. "It is, however, just this ultimate money form of the world of commodities that actually conceals, instead of disclosing, the social character of private labour, and the social relations between the individual producers" (Marx, *Capital*, 87)

57. Edmond Jabès, cited by Harold Bloom, "Introduction," 21.

58. Cited by J. Adams, *Dandies and Desert Saints*, 60.

59. Marsh, *Word Crimes*, 269–327.

Chapter 5

1. For the connection between Western nationalism and the story of Sodom in Genesis, see the Introduction.

2. Eve Kosofsky Sedgwick introduced this paradigm to Victorian studies in her 1985 book, *Between Men*.

3. In the "Address to Working Men, by Felix Holt" (1868), Eliot, through the persona of her fictional creation, Felix Holt, reaffirms her political radicalism: "I am a Radical . . . .I expect great changes, and I desire them. But I don't expect them to come in a hurry, by mere inconsiderate sweeping" (524). In the key chapter in *Daniel Deronda* in which Mordecai offers his vision of Jewish regeneration, he says that "there is store of wisdom among us to found a new Jewish polity, grand, simple, just, like the old—a republic where there is equality of protection, an equality which shone like a star on the forehead of our ancient community, and gave it more than the brightness of Western freedom amid the despotisms of the East" (594–95).

4. On Gladstone, see Chapter 4. Eliot disapproved of Gladstone's attack on Disraeli: "I wonder whether you read our papers and notice the bad figure our liber[al] party has made of late on the Eastern Question. You remember me as much less of a conservative than I have now become. I care as much or more for the interests of the people, but I believe less in the help they will get from democrats" (*Letters*, 7:47, hereafter cited in text and notes as *Letters*). See also her comment in *The Impressions of Theophrastus Such* (1879), 148.

5. Eliot, *George Eliot's* Daniel Deronda *Notebooks*, xxxiii, hereafter cited in text and notes as *Notebooks*.

6. Eliot, *Daniel Deronda*, 591. Page references to this edition are hereafter cited in the text.

7. M. Carpenter, *George Eliot and the Landscape of Time*, 131–32.

8. Eliot, *Letters*, 5:455.

9. Ann Cvetkovich is an excellent commentator on affect in Eliot's novel. See her *Mixed Feelings*, 128–64.

10. Henry, *George Eliot*, 6–9.

11. For Swinburne and Sappho, see Prins, *Victorian Sappho*, 112–73.

12. Pater, *The Renaissance*, ed. Donald L. Hill, 105. Although the essay did not appear in the *Fortnightly Review* until October 1877, a draft probably was submitted

to Macmillan as part of the manuscript of the first edition of *Studies in the History of the Renaissance*, 1873 (ibid., 384).

13. Ibid., 106.

14. Eliot takes care to demasculinize Daniel in a number of ways: by denying him the lineage of an English gentleman; by making him instead a member of a circumcised people (cf. Sander L. Gilman, *Freud, Race, and Gender*, 49–92); and by associating him with the Judaic tradition of gentle, unworldly male biblical scholarship (D. Boyarin, *Unheroic Conduct*, 313–59). For the place of adolescent males in a lesbian cultural imaginary, see Vicinus, "The Adolescent Boy."

Gwendolen is not so much masculinized as associated with monstrosity: through the Maenad-like, suppressed but murderous rage that she feels against her husband and through Eliot's association of her, in the opening chapter, with the trope of fatal beauty, in this case Geraldine, the Sapphic lamia (half-serpent/half-woman) who seduces the virginal Christabel in Coleridge's poem, "Christabel" (35, 40–41; Elfenbein, *Romantic Genius*, 177–202).

15. Her husband has been blocking her way (654).

16. Semmel, *Jamaican Blood*, 13. Reports of this and other outrages led to the creation of the Jamaica Committee in England under the leadership of John Stuart Mill among others. When successive governments failed to prosecute the governor and leading subordinates, members of the Jamaica Committee attempted to bring charges themselves. In April 1867, the lord chief justice of England, Sir Alexander Cockburn, responded by charging a grand jury investigating allegations made against two of the officers involved in the trial of Gordon as follows: "I come irresistibly to the conclusion that if a man had been tried upon that evidence—I must correct myself. He could not have been tried upon that evidence. No competent judge acquainted with the duties of his office could have received the evidence. Three-fourths, I had almost said nine-tenths, of the evidence upon which that man was convicted and sentenced to death, was evidence which, according to no known rules—not only of ordinary law, but of military law—according to no rules of right or justice, could possibly have been admitted; and it never would have been admitted if a competent judge had presided, or if there had been the advantage of a military officer of any experience in the practice of courts martial" (quoted by Semmel, *Jamaican Blood*, 154). For more on the Jamaican Uprising and Eliot's relation to it, see C. Hall, "Competing Masculinities"; Heuman, "*The Killing Time*"; Linehan, "Mixed Politics"; Meyer, *Imperialism at Home*.

17. As a mulatto, of course, Gordon was himself the effect of a transgression of the boundary that separates the races.

18. Haight, *George Eliot's Originals*, 68. Haight argues convincingly that Anton Rubinstein, the Russian Jewish pianist, was the model for Klesmer. Franz Liszt introduced Eliot and George Henry Lewes to Rubinstein at Weimar in 1854 (75). She met him again in London in 1876 when she had nearly completed writing the novel (76).

19. Bashant, "Singing in Greek Drag," 227, hereafter cited in notes as Bashant.

20. Pope, "The Diva Doesn't Die," 482 n.23.

21. Zimmerman, "'The Dark Eye Beaming,'" 127.

22. *Letters*, 6:184; Bashant, "Singing in Greek Drag," 226.

23. Quoted by Bashant, 228.

24. *Notebooks,* 250 n.5.

25. Swinburne, *Poems and Ballads,* 74–75.

26. Daniel has a good voice. As a youth, he is repelled when his guardian at one point suggests that he become a professional singer (208).

27. Haight, *George Eliot,* 525, hereafter cited in text and notes as Haight.

28. For Victorian contextualizations, see Dellamora, *Masculine Desire,* 38–39, 42–43, 56–57, hereafter cited in text and notes as Dellamora.

29. As does Tancred in the novel of the same name, Daniel implicitly compares London with the biblical cities of the plain. He sees himself as a blood relation of the Abraham of Genesis, who chose to live in the mountains. Moreover, as a relative of Abraham who finds himself out of place in a latter-day Sodom, Daniel implicitly compares his situation with that of Lot and his family.

30. Haight, 469–71.

31. Eliot took notes on this essay, which Deutsch sent her in proof (Haight, 470; *Notebooks,* 24).

32. Deutsch, *Literary Remains,* 15.

33. Ibid., 15.

34. Ibid., 15.

35. Ibid., 5.

36. McKenzie, *Edith Simcox,* 91, hereafter cited in text as McKenzie.

37. Eliot, *Journals,* 140. Subsequent page references in the text to Eliot's journals refer to this volume.

38. Dellamora, illus. 94.

39 Pater, *Studies,* 153.

40. Cf. Eliot, "Address," 519, 528. As I have argued elsewhere, Pater's politics are democratic, verging on social democratic (*Apocalyptic Overtures,* 75–79). Linda Dowling makes a similar argument (*Vulgarization,* 76–78) but underplays the significance of male same-sex desire in Pater's social and cultural thinking.

41. Pater, *Studies,* 251.

42. Bernal, *Black Athena.*

43. In context, the term Gentiles also includes Islamic culture. Mordecai sees Jewry's singularity in its potential to reconcile Western with Oriental culture and interests.

44. Pater, *Studies,* 205–6.

45. Bodenheimer, *The Real Life of Mary Ann Evans,* 232–67, hereafter cited in text and notes as Bodenheimer.

46. Craft, *Another Kind of Love,* 35.

47. Haight, 423–24.

48. Eliot's first close friendship with another woman, her teacher, Maria Lewis, foundered on this point. Explaining the end of the friendship to Simcox, Sara Hennell suggested: "It was some verbal *tu quoque* leading to a misunderstanding, as if Miss Lewis had reproached her with seeming to take too much interest in somebody—of the opposite sex; whereto she angrily: 'It might as well be said that *you* have an 'interest' or are interested in your friendship for me'" (Haight, 62).

49. Karl, *George Eliot,* 466.

50. Ragussis, *Figures of Conversion*, 15–56.

51. Zimmerman, "'The Mother's History' in George Eliot's Life," 85. Gillian Beer, finding a model of heterosexual androgyny in Eliot's reference in the novel to the mystic androgyne of the Kabbalah, believes that Daniel for a time "takes on the role of mother soul" to Gwendolen (*George Eliot*, 216–17). The role is one that Eliot enjoyed playing during the period of her artistic celebrity. See the essay by Zimmerman cited above plus Bodenheimer, 232–67.

52. See the preceding note.

53. Nunokawa, *The Afterlife of Property*, 108.

54. For the full range of moral and theological meanings associated with the story of Sodom in Genesis, see the Introduction. For Gladstone's exploitation of the idea of divine covenant with a chosen people, see Chapter 4.

55. Foucault, *History*, 1:119.

56. Eliot is once again moved by thought of the spectacle of aged female ugliness juxtaposed with youthful beauty (*Letters*, 5:314; cited by Haight, 457).

57. Crompton, *Byron and Greek Love*, 203. Byron's name was, of course, also associated with allegations of pederasty and sodomy. See Crompton's book as well as Elfenbein, *Byron and the Victorians*.

58. Eliot further underscores the point in a final political statement in *The Impressions of Theophrastus Such*, 136–38. This important passage ends with a sarcastic indictment of British violence against colonial insurgents.

59. Dever, *Death and the Mother*, 143. Later, we learn that Daniel visited the Rhineland with one of his Eton schoolmasters (215). Eliot was well aware that such connections could be sexually dangerous. Oscar Browning, a friend and eventual biographer of Eliot who entertained her at Cambridge in 1868 (Haight, 408), was forced to resign his post at Eton in 1875 "under suspicion of making homosexual advances to pupils" (Ashton, *George Eliot*, 304). In the events leading up to his resignation, Eliot lent him strong moral support. Browning repaid her assistance at this time with malice when after her death he spread rumors, circulated further by Henry James and Eliza Lynn Linton, the conservative female journalist and onetime friend of Eliot, that Eliot discovered Lewes to have been unfaithful to her (Ashton, *George Eliot*, 372).

60. Galchinsky, *Origin*, 17.

61. Baker discusses the Jewish historians whose views Eliot draws on in this chapter in "George Eliot's Readings."

62. Anderson, "George Eliot and the Jewish Question," 41, 42, 48–49, 51–52; for more on the relationship between the novel and liberal political theory, see Tucker, *A Probable State*, 33–121.

63. Said, "Zionism," 539–40.

64. Bell, "George Eliot, Radical," 55; Semmel, *George Eliot and the Politics of National Inheritance*, 143.

65. Ray Strachey, quoted by D. E. Hall, *Fixing Patriarchy*, 7.

Chapter 6

1. Henry James wrote an article on Eliot's novel, "Daniel Deronda: A Conversation."

2. Smith, "Labouchere's Amendment," 165.

3. Douglas, *History of the Liberal Party*, 10. An even greater challenge resulted from the "villa Conservatism" that came into existence as a result of legislation accompanying the 1884 Reform Bill, which divided the counties and the big cities into single-member districts. As a result, the Tories gained many safe seats in the Home Counties and in the middle-class suburbs of the provincial cities (Jenkins, *Gladstone*, 498, hereafter cited in text as Jenkins).

4. H. James, Preface, 10.

5. H. James, *Letters*, 3:223, hereafter cited as *Letters* in text and notes.

6. H. James, *The Tragic Muse*, 30. Subsequent references in the notes to the novel are to this edition.

7. Cf. McWhirter, "Restaging the Hurt," 465.

8. McConkey, "'Well-bred Contortions,'" 352–86.

9. Fairbrother, *John Singer Sargent*, 63.

10. Newall, "The Victorians," 350.

11. Sargent preferred painting landscapes and genre scenes. He frequently let slip comments "mocking individuals and the very idea of portraiture alike" (Simpson, *Uncanny Spectacle*, 66).

12. Newall, "The Victorians," 339–41; McConkey, "'Well-bred Contortions,'" 365.

13. Cf. Blair, *Henry James*, 127–28, hereafter cited in notes as Blair. James was of Protestant Irish descent.

14. James, Preface, 13.

15. Characteristically, however, the foregrounding of ties of marriage and family tends to reverse itself in queer indirection(s). For example, in this passage, James uses Biddy to underscore the implicit immorality ("irresponsibility") of the exchange. James characterizes Biddy as a female ingenue. Her (heterosexual, marital) interest in Peter Sherringham is the most convincing representation of female-male desire in the novel. Nonetheless, James repeatedly deploys her sensibility as a receptor of overtones and undertones of same-sex desire.

I use the word queer rather than homosexual or lesbian in this context because I see James as resistant to these emergent definitions of sexual difference. In this sense, queer refers to his disidentification from heterosexual norms as well as to the ways in which his texts continually register ways in which attraction and repulsion evade the prescribed forms. (There is an extensive bibliography dealing with queer allusiveness in James. See, for example, Moon, *A Small Boy*, esp. 31–65; Sedgwick, *Tendencies*, 73–103; and Eric Savoy, "'In the Cage' and the Queer Effects of Gay History.")

In recent years, there have appeared a number of excellent studies of dissident sexuality in *The Tragic Muse* as well as in James's writing more generally. See, for example, Haralson, "The Elusive Queerness of Henry James's 'queer comrade,'" 191–210; Kaye, *The Flirt's Tragedy*, 177–83; and C. Lane, "Impossibility," 739–64. See also Bradley, *Henry James and Homo-Erotic Desire*; Graham, *Henry James's Thwarted Love*; Rowe, *The Other Henry James*; and Stevens, *Henry James and Sexuality*.

For a discussion of "theatricality" in *The Tragic Muse,* see Joseph Litvak, *Caught in the Act,* 235–69.

16. Blair, 140.

17. In this way, the realist novel becomes a new thing, the art novel. Michael Anesko describes how the changing material conditions of the publishing industry in England contributed to this generic transformation (*"Friction with the Market,"* 119–39). See also F. Kaplan, *Henry James,* 329–31, hereafter cited in notes and text as F. Kaplan. For further biographical information about James, see Edel, *Henry James, 1882–1895.*

In recent years, an extensive literature has developed, focusing on the so-called New Journalism of the 1880s, whose leading features were the spread of inexpensive, large circulation print media and the concurrent rise of a fragmented literary marketplace with many specialized publications. The emergence of the art novel is one aspect of the latter tendency. For convincing treatments, see Brake, *Subjugated Knowledges,* and Feltes, *Literary Capital and the Late Victorian Novel.*

18. Tucker, *A Probable State,* 1–32.

19. Dowling, *The Vulgarization of Art,* 9.

20. Fairbrother, *John Singer Sargent,* 96.

21. See Markus, *Across an Untried Sea.*

22. For the introduction of the term lesbian (or *lesbienne*) in English and French to refer to female same-sex desire, see DeJean, *Fictions of Sappho,* 245–46, 350 n.51.

23. See the Excursus.

24. This fact is dramatically evident in the assessment that he offers of his deceased sister, Alice, after reading her mss diary. Even in dealing with a sibling, racial difference, that is, Alice's Irish descent, is regarded as crucial (*Letters,* 3:481–82).

25. In *Romantic Genius,* Andrew Elfenbein, for example, argues persuasively that fin de siècle sexology draws the traits of sexual inverts from Enlightenment and romantic characterizations of artistic genius (16–38).

26. Cited in M. Kaplan, *Sexual Justice,* 161.

27. Young, *Colonial Desire,* 1–19.

28. For arguments cognate with those of the preceding three paragraphs, see Freedman, "Poetics of Cultural Decline," and David Glover, "Bram Stoker and the Crisis of the Liberal Subject."

29. H. James, *Notebooks,* 46. This passage continues from another notebook, which has been lost.

30. In contrast, in an unpublished review of Disraeli's letters to his sister, Wilde quotes the following aphorism: "Next to undoubted success the best thing is to make a great noise" (3).

31. See Hamer, *Liberal Politics,* 1–33.

32. Graham, *Henry James's Thwarted Love,* 202–6; F. Kaplan, 293–96.

33. F. Kaplan, 294; *Letters,* 3:105.

34. Dellamora, *Masculine Desire,* 196–97.

35. Habegger, *Henry James,* 54–58. On Woodhull, see Gabriel, *Notorious Victoria,* and Goldsmith, *Other Powers.*

36. Ellmann, *Oscar Wilde,* 289–90.

37. Roth, "Court Jews," 293–94; Rubinstein, *History,* 121–24.

38. The term is literally apt: the Marquis of Queensberry, for example, attacked Lord Rosebery as a "Snob Queer" (Ellmann, *Oscar Wilde,* 402); Hirshfield, "Labouchere," 137. But note that *Reynolds's* was one of the few papers that deplored Wilde's conviction and punishment (Ellmann, *Oscar Wilde,* 450).

39. Quoted in Hirshfield, "Labouchere," 136. At the other end of the social scale, large-scale immigration to the East End of Jewish immigrants from eastern Europe also fed working-class antagonism (Walkowitz, *City of Dreadful Delight,* 191–228; Blair, 123–31. And see Hirshfield, "The Tenacity of Tradition."

40. Pearson, *Labby,* 134.

41. Ibid., 135.

42. For a detailed, carefully considered view of anti-Jewish feeling in the interwar years, see Rubinstein. Rubinstein believes that prejudice in England against Jews was most pronounced in the period 1917–1922 (*History,* 192–223).

43. According to Sargent's biographer, James ardently pursued Sargent at this time though in a "strangely, though not clearly, chaste" fashion (see the discussion in Shand-Tucci, *Art of Scandal,* 80).

44. For Sargent's homoerotic interests, see Fairbrother, *John Singer Sargent,* 95–113, 153–65.

45. A. James, *Diary,* 98.

46. C. Lane, "Impossibility," 745–47.

47. Lee, "John Singer Sargent," 237. On Lee, see, for example Psomiades, "Still Burning," and Vicinus, "Adolescent Boy."

48. Boime, "Sargent in Paris and London," 97.

49. Ibid., 97.

50. Interestingly, Lee characterizes Sargent as a puritan in an idiosyncratic sense of the term ("John Singer Sargent," 235–36).

51. Cited in Patrica Hills, *John Singer Sargent,* 32.

52. H. James, "Anthony Trollope," 113.

53. For an ironic look at the imaginary character of Sargent's American identity, see Olson, "On the Question of Sargent's Nationality."

54. Ignatiev, *How the Irish Became White;* cf. Blair on James and the Dred Scott Decision, 69–70.

55. In "'In the Cage,'" Savoy describes how queer signification hovers between denotation and connotation (301). *Young Man in Reverie* (1878, inscribed 1876; private collection) was exhibited at the Grosvenor Gallery in May 1882. In the same month, *Dr. Pozzi at Home* (The Armand Hammer Collection, UCLA at the Armand Hammer Museum of Art and Cultural Center, Los Angeles) showed at the Royal Academy. The homoerotic languor of the first painting suited it for the former venue while the setting of the Royal Academy and the anonymous title, *A Portrait,* would bring forward the Old Master-ly qualities of the latter. Nonetheless, for in-the-know viewers of both exhibitions, the showing of the two paintings in important exhibitions in London in the same season would in effect have underlined the aesthetic and decadent associations of *A Portrait.*

56. See, for example, Small, *Conditions for Criticism,* and Gagnier, *The Insatiability of Human Wants.* See also Weiss, "Walter Pater, Aesthetic Utilitarian."

57. Cf. Freedman, *Professions of Taste,* 192–97. See also Ellmann, "Henry James among the Aesthetes."

58. Cited in Dellamora, "Oscar Wilde," 135.

59. For Eliot's use of this trope at a key moment in Daniel Deronda's conversion to Judaism, see Chapter 5. See also Dellamora, "Androgynous Body."

Coda

1. Wilde, *An Ideal Husband,* 207. Subsequent page references in the text refer to this edition.

2. Derrida, *Politics of Friendship,* 26–48, 53, subsequently referred to in text and notes as *PF.*

3. O'Connor discusses the passage in *Straight Acting,* 55–56, hereafter cited in notes as O'Connor.

4. Curzon was reputed to have been one of the school boys whom Oscar Browning had spooned at Eton (Ellmann, *Wilde,* 60, hereafter cited in the text and notes as Ellmann).

5. Ibid., 302.

6. Quoted in Hyde, *Trials,* 201. As Linda Dowling and Joseph Bristow have emphasized, "intellectual friendship" is Wilde's chosen term for understanding sexual and emotional ties between men (Dowling, *Hellenism and Homosexuality,* 1–2; Bristow, "Wilde's Sexual Identities," 203–4).

7. Wilde, *De Profundis,* 99.

8. Hoare, *Oscar Wilde's Last Stand,* 152.

9. For a number of perspectives, see Gagnier, *Idylls of the Marketplace,* 205–7, hereafter cited in notes as Gagnier; Murray, *Bosie,* 66–71, hereafter cited in notes and text as Murray; Ellmann, 402–3, 434–35, 437.

10. Ellmann, 381; Murray, 66.

11. Unless otherwise cited, this and following information on Drumlanrig is from Murray, 67–70.

12. Murray, 66.

13. Trevor-Roper, *A Hidden Life,* 361–62n.

14. Ibid., 262. Harcourt's entry is dated October 1, but Murray thinks the proposal occurred around October 11th. No friend of Rosebery's, Harcourt was the son and aide to Sir William Harcourt, Rosebery's major competitor for the premiership at the time of Gladstone's resignation in 1894.

15. Murray, 69.

16. According to a well-known but unverifiable anecdote, he is reputed once to have said "that he had three ambitions in life: to win the Derby, marry an heiress, and become Prime Minister" (R. R. James, *Rosebery,* 86, hereafter cited in text and notes as R. R. James).

It was Disraeli's wife who in 1868 introduced Rosebery to his future wife,

Hannah Rothschild (R. R. James, 79). Disraeli gave away the bride at Rosebery's wedding (R. R. James, 85). Rosebery told his sons that a conversation he had with Disraeli during a long walk at Raby Castle first made him consider politics as a career (R. R. James, 42–44).

17. On male flirtation in Wilde, see Kaye, *The Flirt's Tragedy,* 177–83.

18. I discuss conceptions of the sin of Sodom in Victorian biblical commentaries in the Introduction. O'Connor points out that the Chiltern-Arnheim relation is discussed less in legal terms than as a "sin" (55).

19. Dowling, *Hellenism and Homosexuality,* 4–5, 9n.

20. Ibid., 9n.

21. I discuss Wilde's view of autonomy below.

22. Eltis, *Revising Wilde,* 138, hereafter cited in notes as Eltis.

23. Private collection; information courtesy of Merlin Holland.

24. Feldman, *Englishmen and Jews,* 104n.

25. Ibid.; Blake, *Disraeli,* 582–87, hereafter cited in notes as Blake.

26. After being returned to Parliament as prime minister in the election of 1885, Gladstone made Irish Home Rule his main policy objective. At the time, he wrote in his diary: "I propose to examine whether it is or is not practicable to comply with the desire widely prevalent in Ireland, and testified by the return of 85 out of 103 representatives, for the establishment, by Statute, of a legislative body, to sit in Dublin, and to deal with Irish as distinguished from Imperial affairs; in such a manner, as would be just to each of the three Kingdoms, equitable with reference to every class of the people of Ireland, conducive to the social order and harmony of that country, and calculated to support and consolidate the unity of the Empire on the combined basis of Imperial authority and mutual attachment" (Jenkins, *Gladstone,* 543, hereafter cited in notes and text as Jenkins).

27. For an excellent analysis of the imaginary character of England's relation to Ireland, see Kiberd, *Inventing Ireland.*

28. Arnold, *On the Study of Celtic Literature,* 15, hereafter cited in the text as Arnold. I discuss this text at greater length in the Introduction.

29. In recent years, there has been a wealth of writing that explores Wilde in relation to Ireland. See Coakley, *Oscar Wilde;* McCormack, *Wilde the Irishman;* Mahaffey, *States of Desire;* Pine, *The Thief of Reason;* and Kiberd, *Inventing Ireland.*

30. Wilde, "Mr. Froude's Blue Book," in *The Artist as Critic,* 136, hereafter cited in text as *AC.*

31. Mahaffy, *Social Life in Greece from Homer to Menander,* 1st ed., 308. Pages 305–6 and 309–14 have been torn out of the copy of this book at Young University Library (UCLA). In the second edition, pp. 325–26 are missing. In a note, Mahaffy writes: "I have discussed the matter [i. e., Greek pederasty] as fully as possible in my first edition, which the student of Greek life may compare with my present remarks" (330). There follows a list of places in Greek texts that discuss the topic.

32. Nordau, *Degeneration,* 317–22.

33. Ibid., 301.

34. Jenkins, 606.

35. According to Hamilton, Labouchère's weekly publication, *Truth,* "never"

lost "an opportunity of running down R" (Brooks, *Destruction,* 178, hereafter cited in text as Brooks).

36. Gagnier, 207.

37. Ellmann, 402.

38. In the following paragraphs, I draw upon a previously published article to deal with this aspect of the play ("Oscar Wilde, Social Purity, and *An Ideal Husband*)."

39. See Eltis, 7–13.

40. Dellamora, "Oscar Wilde," 120.

41. I discuss this situation in *Masculine Desire,* 193–217 and in "Oscar Wilde."

42. The development of a working-class radical and socialist press following the widening of male suffrage in 1867 and later operated in similar fashion, posing working-class moral purity against upper-middle-class and aristocratic corruption.

43. Montaigne, quoted by Derrida, *PF,* 190n., 191n.

44. Plato, cited by Derrida, *PF,* 95.

A Note on Further Reading

Readers of this book may wish to read further in the list of books that follows.

For the human body as a social symbol, key texts are Mary Douglas, *Purity and Danger: An Analysis of Concepts of Pollution and Taboo*, Julia Kristeva, *Powers of Horror: An Essay on Abjection*, and Peter Stallybrass, "Marx and Heterogeneity: Thinking the Lumpenproletariat." On the representation of the social body in the mid-Victorian novel, see Joseph Childers, *Novel Possibilities: Fiction and the Formation of Early Victorian Culture*, and Mary Poovey, *Making a Social Body: British Cultural Formation, 1830–1864*. Robert Young's *Colonial Desire: Hybridity in Theory, Culture, and Race* emphasizes the importance of the concept of hybridity in Victorian attempts to understand issues of race and nationality.

T. H. Marshall's *Citizenship and Social Class*, which takes its point of departure from the economics of the late Victorian economist, Alfred Marshall, continues to be crucial. In a recent Verso edition, the text is accompanied by a new essay that recontextualizes Marshall's argument in light of neo-liberal politics in England in the late twentieth century. On sexual rights, see Morris B. Kaplan's *Sexual Justice: Democratic Citizenship and the Politics of Desire*.

In *Bardic Nationalism: The Romantic Novel and the British Empire*, Katie Trumpener discusses the relationship between the genre of the novel and the development of a hybrid Celtic-Anglo-Saxon nationality in Great Britain and its colonies in the nineteenth century. In *Inventing Ireland: The Literature of the Modern Nation*, Declan Kiberd shows how Ireland has long been figured as England's imaginary Other by both English and Irish writers. On the significance of the othering of internal minorities in western European nation-states, see Jonathan Boyarin, "The Other Within and the Other Without," in *Storm from Paradise: The Politics of Jewish Memory*.

In *Outside the Fold: Conversion, Modernity, and Belief*, Gauri Viswanathan discusses minority religious conversion as a mode of resistance to the development of the modern imperial nation-state. For arguments emphasizing the religious character of politics in England before and after passage of the Reform Bill of 1867, see Boyd Hilton, "Gladstone's Theological Politics," and J. P. Parry, *Democracy and Religion: Gladstone and the Liberal Party, 1867–1875*. For the construction of debates over expansion of suffrage as arguments about proper masculinity, see Anna Clark, "Gender, Class, and the Nation: Franchise Reform in England, 1832–1928," and Patrick Joyce, "The Constitution and the Narrative Structure of Victorian Politics."

On the importance of the Jewish Question to English nation-building in the nineteenth century, the standard work is *Figures of Conversion: "The Jewish Question" and English National Identity* by Michael Ragussis. See also David Feldman, *Englishmen and Jews: Social Relations and Political Culture, 1840–1914,* and Bryan Cheyette, *Constructions of "the Jew" in English Literature and Society: Racial Representation, 1875–1945.*

In recent years, an efflorescence has occurred of works in Jewish postmodern cultural studies. Among several by Sander Gilman, I have made particular use of *Jewish Self-Hatred: Anti-Semitism and the Hidden Language of the Jews* and *Freud, Race, and Gender.* Of special significance are the contributions of Daniel Boyarin: *Carnal Israel: Reading Sex in Talmudic Culture; A Radical Jew: Paul and the Politics of Identity;* and *Unheroic Conduct: The Rise of Heterosexuality and the Invention of the Jewish Man.*

Arguments about the metaphysics of monotheism in Jewish and Christian thinking, which Moshe Halbertal and Avishai Margalit trace in their book, *Idolatry,* have shaped my own discussion about the ways in which allegations of blasphemy, idolatry, and sexual perversity inform Gladstone's attacks on Disraeli between 1876 and 1880.

For a set of complex reflections on loving friendship between men in the United States and England in the nineteenth century, see Jonathan Ned Katz's *Love Stories: Sex Between Men Before Homosexuality.* Studies of sexual tensions within elite male friendship in England have tended to focus on the period of the Renaissance. A leading example is Alan Bray's "Homosexuality and the Signs of Male Friendship in Elizabethan England." Bray's earlier study, *Homosexuality in Renaissance England,* has provided the point of departure for studies by gay historians and literary critics of connections between sodomy, blasphemy, and treason. Jonathan Goldberg has made important contributions in *Reclaiming Sodom* and in *Sodometries: Renaissance Texts, Modern Sexualities.* Mark D. Jordan studies the genealogy of the concept of sodomy in medieval Christian theology in *The Invention of Sodomy in Christian Theology.* For the place of sodomy within classical republican rhetoric in England and its transfer to Tory polemic in the nineteenth century, see Linda Dowling, *Hellenism and Homosexuality in Victorian Oxford.*

Michel Foucualt discusses connections between pleasure, ethics, male Friendship, and citizenship in ancient Athens in *The Use of Pleasure*, volume 2 of *The History of Sexuality.* In *Politics of Friendship*, Jacques Derrida pursues a valuable series of reflections on the place of the concept of friendship within modern European thinking about the relationship between nationhood and citizenship. Also useful in this regard is Marc Shell's *Children of the Earth: Literature, Politics, and Nationhood.*

Derrida canvases the way in which male friendship is taken to provide the model of just government in the classical tradition of male friendship writing, beginning with Plato and Aristotle and continuing to the twentieth century. In the eighteenth century, the tradition is supplemented by the development of the idea of sympathy within liberal political theory. Also important at this time is attention to the role of aesthetics in democratic education. Linda Dowling provides a concise introduction to both topics in *The Vulgarization of Art: The Victorians and Aesthetic Democracy.* She argues convincingly that these concepts were of particular importance for late Victorian writers.

Bibliography

Adams, Byron. "The 'Dark Saying' of the Enigma: Homoeroticism and the Elgarian Paradox." *Nineteenth-Century Music* 23 (2000): 218–35.

Adams, James Eli. *Dandies and Desert Saints: Styles of Victorian Masculinity.* Ithaca, N.Y.: Cornell University Press, 1995.

Alexander, Boyd. *England's Wealthiest Son: A Study of William Beckford.* London: Centaur Press, 1962.

Alter, Robert. "Sodum as Nexus: The Web of Design in Biblical Narrative." In *Reclaiming Sodom,* ed. Jonathan Goldberg. New York: Routledge, 1994.

Anderson, Amanda. "George Eliot and the Jewish Question." *Yale Journal of Criticism* 10 (spring 1997): 39–61.

Anesko, Michael. *"Friction with the Market": Henry James and the Profession of Authorship.* New York: Oxford University Press, 1986.

Anonymous. "A Sermon Preached before Queene Elizabeth." In *The Book of Sodom,* ed. Paul Hallam. London: Verso, 1993.

Arnold, Matthew. *On the Study of Celtic Literature and On Translating Homer.* London: Macmillan, 1903.

Ashton, Rosemary. *George Eliot: A Life.* London: Penguin, 1996.

Baker, William. "George Eliot's Readings in Nineteenth-Century Jewish Historians: A Note on the Background of *Daniel Deronda.*" *Victorian Studies* 15 (June 1972): 463–73.

Barham, Richard Harris. "The Wondrous Tale of Ikey Solomons." Unpublished manuscript. Berg Collection, New York Public Library.

Bashant, Wendy. "Singing in Greek Drag: Gluck, Berlioz, George Eliot. In *En Travesti: Women, Gender Subversion, Opera,* ed. Corinne E. Blackmer and Patricia Juliana Smith. New York: Columbia University Press, 1995.

Beckford, William. *The Episodes of Vathek.* Sawtry, Cambs.: Dedalus, 1994.

———. *Vathek and Other Stories: A William Beckford Reader.* Ed. Malcolm Jack. Harmondsworth: Penguin, 1995.

———. *Vathek with The Episodes of Vathek.* Ed. Kenneth W. Graham. Trans. Sir Frank T. Marzials and Kenneth W. Graham. Peterborough, Ontario: Broadview Press, 2001.

Beer, Gillian. *George Eliot.* Bloomington: Indiana University Press, 1986.

Bell, Millicent. "George Eliot, Radical." *New York Review of Books,* April 18, 1996, 54–58.

Bergeron, David M. *King James and Letters of Homoerotic Desire.* Iowa City: University of Iowa Press, 1999.

Berlin, Isaiah. "Benjamin Disraeli, Karl Marx, and the Search for Identity." In

Against the Current: Essays in the History of Ideas, ed. Henry Hardy. New York: Viking Press, 1980.

Bernal, Martin. *Black Athena: The Afroasiatic Roots of Classical Civilization.* Vol. 1, *The Fabrication of Ancient Greece, 1785–1985.* New Brunswick, N.J.: Rutgers University Press, 1990.

Bernheimer, Charles. "Unknowing Decadence." In *Perennial Decay: On the Aesthetics and Politics of Decadence,* ed. Liz Constable, Dennis Denisoff, and Matthew Potolsky. Philadelphia: University of Pennsylvania Press, 1999.

Blair, Sara. *Henry James and the Writing of Race and Nation.* Cambridge: Cambridge University Press, 1996.

Blake, Robert. *Disraeli.* London: Methuen, 1966.

Blanchot, Maurice. "Marx's Three Voices." *New Political Science* 15 (summer 1986): 18–20.

Bloom, Harold. Introduction to *Musical Variations on Jewish Thought,* by Olivier Revault D'Allonnes, trans. Judith L. Greenberg. New York: George Braziller, 1984.

Bodenheimer, Rosemarie. *The Real Life of Mary Ann Evans: George Eliot, Her Letters and Fiction.* Ithaca: Cornell University Press, 1994.

Boime, Albert. "Sargent in Paris and London: A Portrait of the Artist as Dorian Gray." In *John Singer Sargent,* ed. Patricia Hills. New York: Whitney Museum of American Art, 1987.

Boone, Joseph Alan. *Tradition Counter Tradition: Love and the Form of Fiction.* Chicago: University of Chicago Press, 1987.

Bourdieu, Pierre. *The Field of Cultural Production,* ed. and introd. Randal Johnson. New York: Columbia University Press, 1993.

Boyarin, Daniel. *Carnal Israel: Reading Sex in Talmudic Culture.* Berkeley: University of California Press, 1993.

———. *A Radical Jew: Paul and the Politics of Identity.* Berkeley: University of California Press, 1994.

———. *Unheroic Conduct: The Rise of Heterosexuality and the Invention of the Jewish Man.* Berkeley: University of California Press, 1997.

Boyarin, Jonathan. *Storm from Paradise: The Politics of Jewish Memory.* Minneapolis: University of Minnesota Press, 1992.

Bradford, Sarah. *Disraeli.* London: Weidenfeld and Nicolson, 1982.

Bradley, John R., ed. *Henry James and Homo-Erotic Desire.* Houndsmills, England: Macmillan, 1998.

Brake, Laurel. *Subjugated Knowledges: Journalism, Gender, and Literature in the Nineteenth Century.* New York: New York University Press, 1994.

———. *Homosexuality in Renaissance England.* London: Gay Men's Press, 1982.

Brantlinger, Patrick. "Nations and Novels: Disraeli, George Eliot, and Orientalism." *Victorian Studies* 35 (spring 1992): 255–75.

Bray, Alan. "Homosexuality and the Signs of Male Friendship in Elizabethan England." *History Workshop Journal* 29 (1990): 1–19.

———. *Homosexuality in Renaissance England.* London: Gay Men's Press, 1982.

Bristow, Joseph. "'A Complex Multiform Creature': Wilde's Sexual Identities." In

The Cambridge Companion to Oscar Wilde, ed. Peter Raby. Cambridge: Cambridge University Press, 1997.

Brooks, David. *The Destruction of Lord Rosebery. From the Diary of Sir Edward Hamilton, 1894–1895.* London: Historians' Press, 1986.

Buckton, Oliver S. "'An Unnatural State': Gender,'Perversion,' and Newman's *Apologia Pro Vita Sua.*" *Victorian Studies* 35 (summer 1992): 359–83.

Butler, Judith. *The Psychic Life of Power: Theories in Subjection.* Stanford: Stanford University Press, 1997.

Carlyle, Thomas. *Sartor Resartus and Selected Prose.* New York: Holt, Rinehart, 1970.

Carpenter, Edward. *Ioläus: An Anthology of Friendship.* 1917. Reprint, New York: Pagan Press, 1982.

Carpenter, Mary Wilson. *George Eliot and the Landscape of Time: Narrative Form and Protestant Apocalyptic History.* Chapel Hill: University of North Carolina Press, 1986.

———. *Imperial Bibles, Domestic Bodies: Women, Sexualities, and Religion in the Victorian Market.* Athens: University of Ohio Press, 2003.

Castronovo, David. *The English Gentleman: Images and Ideals in Literature and Society.* New York: Ungar, 1987.

Cheyette, Bryan. *Constructions of "the Jew" in English Literature and Society: Racial Representation, 1875–1945.* Cambridge: Cambridge University Press, 1993.

Childers, Joseph. *Novel Possibilities: Fiction and the Formation of Early Victorian Culture.* Philadelphia: University of Pennsylvania Press, 1995.

Chittick, Kathryn. *Dickens and the 1830s.* Cambridge: Cambridge University Press, 1990.

Clark, Anna. "Gender, Class, and the Nation: Franchise Reform in England, 1832–1928." In *Re-reading the Constitution: New Narratives in the Political History of England's Long Nineteenth Century,* ed. James Vernon. Cambridge: Cambridge University Press, 1996.

Cline, Sally. *Radclyffe Hall: A Woman Called John.* New York: Overlook Press, 1997.

Coakley, Davis. *Oscar Wilde: The Importance of Being Irish.* Dublin: Townhouse, 1995.

Cohen, William. "Manual Conduct in *Great Expectations.*" *ELH* 60 (1993): 217–59.

Colley, Linda. *Britons: Forging the Nation, 1707–1837.* New Haven: Yale University Press, 1992.

Craft, Christopher. *Another Kind of Love: Male Homosexual Desire in English Discourse, 1850–1920.* Berkeley: University of California Press, 1994.

Crompton, Louis. *Byron and Greek Love: Homophobia in Nineteenth-century England.* Berkeley: University of California Press, 1985.

———. "*Don Leon,* Byron, and Homosexual Law Reform." *Journal of Homosexuality* 8 (spring-summer 1983): 53–71.

Cvetkovich, Ann. *Mixed Feelings: Feminism, Mass Culture, and Victorian Sensationalism.* New Brunswick, N.J.: Rutgers University Press, 1992.

DeJean, Joan. *Fictions of Sappho: 1546–1937.* Chicago: University of Chicago Press, 1989.

Dellamora, Richard. "The Androgynous Body in Pater's 'Winckelmann.'" *Browning Institute Studies* 11 (1983): 51–68.

———. *Apocalyptic Overtures: Sexual Politics and the Sense of an Ending.* New Brunswick, N.J.: Rutgers University Press, 1994.

———. "The Ends of Man: AIDS, Kant, Derrida." In *Constructive Criticism: The Human Sciences in the Age of Theory,* ed. Martin Kreiswirth and Tom Carmichael. Toronto: University of Toronto Press, 1995.

———. "Male Relations in Thomas Hardy's *Jude the Obscure.*" *Papers on Language and Literature* 27 (fall 1991): 453–72.

———. *Masculine Desire: The Sexual Politics of Victorian Aestheticism.* Chapel Hill: University of North Carolina Press, 1990.

———. "Oscar Wilde, Social Purity, and *An Ideal Husband.*" Special issue, "Oscar Wilde and the 'Nineties." *Modern Drama* 37 (March 1994): 120–38.

Derrida, Jacques. *Archive Fever: A Freudian Impression.* Trans. Eric Prenowitz. Chicago: University of Chicago Press, 1996.

———. *Politics of Friendship.* Trans. George Collins. London: Verso, 1997.

———. "The Politics of Friendship." *The Journal of Philosophy* 85 (November 1988): 632–44.

Deutsch, Emanuel. *Literary Remains of the Late Emanuel Deutsch.* London: John Murray, 1874.

Dever, Carolyn. *Death and the Mother from Dickens to Freud: Victorian Fiction and the Anxiety of Origins.* Cambridge: Cambridge University Press, 1998.

Dickens, Charles. *Nicholas Nickleby.* Ed. Paul Schlicke. New York: Oxford University Press, 1990.

———. *Oliver Twist.* Illus. George Cruikshank. Ed. Peter Fairclough. Harmondsworth: Penguin, 1974.

———. *Oliver Twist.* Ed. Kathleen Tillotson. Oxford: Clarendon Press, 1974.

———. *Pickwick Papers.* Ed. James Kinsley. Oxford: Clarendon Press, 1986.

Dictionary of National Biography. Ed. Sir Sidney Lee. 2nd supplement. 3 vols. London: Smith, Elder & Co., 1912.

Disraeli, Benjamin. *Alroy.* London: Peter Davies, 1927.

———. *Coningsby or, the New Generation.* New York: Capricorn Books, 1961.

———. *Letters.* Ed. J. A. W. Gunn, John Matthews, Donald M. Schurman, and M. G. Wiebe. Vols. 1–6. Toronto: University of Toronto Press, 1982–2003.

———. *Lord George Bentinck: A Political Biography.* 9th ed. London: Longmans, Green, and Co., 1874.

———. *Tancred or the New Crusade.* New ed. 1877. Reprint, Westport, Conn.: Greenwood Press, 1970.

———. *Whigs and Whiggism: Political Writings.* Ed. William Hutcheon. London: John Murray, 1913.

Disraeli, Isaac. *The Genius of Judaism.* London: Edward Moxon, 1833.

Douglas, Mary. *Purity and Danger: An Analysis of Concepts of Pollution and Taboo.* Harmondsworth: Penguin, 1966.

Douglas, Roy. *The History of the Liberal Party, 1895–1970.* London: Sidgwick and Jackson, 1971.

Dowling, Linda. *Hellenism and Homosexuality in Victorian Oxford.* Ithaca, N.Y.: Cornell University Press, 1994.

————. *The Vulgarization of Art: The Victorians and Aesthetic Democracy.* Charlottesville: University Press of Virginia, 1996.

During, Simon. "Literature—Nationalism's Other? The Case for Revision." In *Nation and Narration,* ed. Homi K. Bhabha. London: Routledge, 1994.

Edel, Leon. *Henry James, 1882–1895: The Middle Years.* New York: J. B. Lippincott, 1962.

Edelman, Lee. "Seeing Things: Representation, the Scene of Surveillance, and the Spectacle of Gay Male Sex." In *Inside/Out: Lesbian Theories, Gay Theories,* ed. Diana Fuss. New York: Routledge, 1991.

Elfenbein, Andrew. *Byron and the Victorians.* Cambridge: Cambridge University Press, 1995.

————. *Romantic Genius: The Prehistory of a Homosexual Role.* New York: Columbia University Press, 1999.

Eliot, George. "Address to Working Men, by Felix Holt." In *Felix Holt, the Radical,* ed. William Baker and Kenneth Womack. Peterborough, Ontario: Broadview Press, 2000.

————. *Daniel Deronda.* Harmondsworth: Penguin, 1982.

————. *George Eliot's* Daniel Deronda *Notebooks.* Ed. Jane Irwin. Cambridge: Cambridge University Press, 1996.

————. *The Impressions of Theophrastus Such.* Ed. D. J. Enright. London: Everyman, 1995.

————. *The Journals.* Eds. Margaret Harris and Judith Johnston. Cambridge: Cambridge University Press, 1998.

————. *Letters.* Ed. Gordon S. Haight. 9 vols. New Haven: Yale University Press, 1954–1978.

Ellmann, Richard. "Henry James among the Aesthetes." *Proceedings of the British Academy* 69 (1983): 209–28.

————. *Oscar Wilde.* Markham, Ont.: Penguin, 1987.

Eltis, Sos. *Revising Wilde: Society and Subversion in the Plays of Oscar Wilde.* Oxford: Clarendon Press, 1996.

Encyclopaedia Judaica. Jerusalem: Keter Publishing House Ltd., 1972.

Fairbrother, Trevor. *John Singer Sargent: The Sensualist.* New Haven: Yale University Press, 2000.

Feldman, David. *Englishmen and Jews: Social Relations and Political Culture, 1840–1914.* New Haven, Conn.: Yale University Press, 1994.

Feltes, Norman N. *Literary Capital and the Late Victorian Novel.* Madison: University of Wisconsin Press, 1993.

————. *Modes of Production of Victorian Novels.* Chicago: University of Chicago Press, 1986.

Flynn, Thomas. "Foucault as Parrhesiast: His Last Course at the Collège de France (1984)." In *The Final Foucault,* ed. James Bernauer and David Rasmussen. Cambridge: MIT Press, 1988.

Forster, John. *The Life of Charles Dickens.* New ed., rev. 2 vols. New York: Dutton, 1969.

Fothergill, Brian. *Beckford of Fonthill.* London: Faber and Faber, 1979.

Foucault, Michel. *The Birth of the Clinic: An Archaeology of Medical Perception.* Trans. A. M. Sheridan Smith. New York: Vintage Books, 1975.

——. "The Eye of Power." In *Power/Knowledge: Selected Interviews and Other Writings, 1972–1977,* ed. Colin Gordon. New York: Pantheon Books, 1980.

——. "On the Genealogy of Ethics: An Overview of Work in Progress." In *The Foucault Reader,* ed. Paul Rabinow. New York: Pantheon, 1984.

——. *The History of Sexuality.* Vol. 1, *An Introduction.* Trans. Robert Hurley. New York: Vintage, 1980.

——. *The History of Sexuality.* Vol. 2, *The Use of Pleasure.* Trans. Robert Hurley. New York: Vintage, 1986.

Foucault, Michel, and Gilles Deleuze. "Intellectuals and Power." In *Discourses: Conversations in Postmodern Art and Culture,* ed. Russell Ferguson, William Olander, Marcia Tucker, and Karen Fiss. Cambridge, Mass.: MIT Press, 1992.

Freedman, Jonathan. "The Poetics of Cultural Decline: Degeneracy, Assimilation, and the Jew in James's *The Golden Bowl.*" *American Literary History* 7 (fall 1995): 477–98.

——. *Professions of Taste: Henry James, British Aestheticism, and Commodity Culture.* Stanford: Stanford University Press, 1990.

Freud, Sigmund. *The Standard Edition of the Complete Psychological Works.* Trans. and ed. James Strachey in collaboration with Anna Freud. 24 vols. London: Hogarth Press, 1971–1974.

Gabriel, Mary. *Notorious Victoria: The Life of Victoria Woodhull, Uncensored.* Chapel Hill, N.C.: Algonquin Books, 1998.

Gagnier, Regenia. *Idylls of the Marketplace: Oscar Wilde and the Victorian Public.* Stanford: Stanford University Press, 1986.

——. *The Insatiability of Human Wants: Economics and Aesthetics in Market Society.* Chicago: University of Chicago Press, 2000.

Galchinsky, Michael. *The Origin of the Modern Jewish Woman Writer.* Detroit: Wayne State University Press, 1996.

Gallagher, Catherine. *The Industrial Reformation of English Fiction: Social Discourse and Narrative Form, 1832–1867.* Chicago: University of Chicago Press, 1988.

Gallop, Jane. *The Daughter's Seduction: Feminism and Psychoanalysis.* Ithaca, N.Y.: Cornell University Press, 1989.

Gellner, Ernest. *Nations and Nationalism.* Oxford: Basil Blackwell, 1983.

Gilman, Sander L. *Freud, Race, and Gender.* Princeton, N.J.: Princeton University Press, 1993.

——. *Jewish Self-Hatred: Anti-Semitism and the Hidden Language of the Jews.* Baltimore: Johns Hopkins University Press, 1986.

Gladstone, William Ewart. *Bulgarian Horrors and the Question of the East.* Montreal: Lovell, Adam, Wesson, and Company, 1876.

Glendinning, Victoria. *Trollope.* London: Hutchinson, 1992.

Glover, David. "Bram Stoker and the Crisis of the Liberal Subject." *New Literary History* 23 (1992): 983–1002.

Goldberg, Jonathan, ed. *Reclaiming Sodom.* New York: Routledge, 1994.

——. *Sodometries: Renaissance Texts, Modern Sexualities.* Stanford: Stanford University Press, 1992.

Goldsmith, Barbara. *Other Powers: The Age of Suffrage, Spiritualism, and the Scandalous Victoria Woodhull.* New York: Knopf, 1998.

Graham, Wendy. *Henry James's Thwarted Love.* Stanford: Stanford University Press, 1999.

Habegger, Alfred. *Henry James and the "Woman Business."* Cambridge: Cambridge University Press, 1989.

Haggerty, George E. *Men in Love: Masculinity and Sexuality in the Eighteenth Century.* New York: Columbia University Press, 1999.

Haight, Gordon S. *George Eliot: A Biography.* Oxford: Clarendon Press, 1969.

———. *George Eliot's Originals and Contemporaries: Essays in Victorian Literary History and Biography.* Ed. Hugh Witemeyer. Ann Arbor: University of Michigan Press, 1992.

Halbertal, Moshe, and Avishai Margalit. *Idolatry.* Trans. Naomi Goldblum. Cambridge, Mass.: Harvard University Press, 1992.

Hall, Catherine. "Competing Masculinities: Thomas Carlyle, John Stuart Mill, and the Case of Governor Eyre." In *White, Male, and Middle-Class: Explorations in Feminism and History.* New York: Routledge, 1992.

Hall, Donald E. *Fixing Patriarchy: Feminism and Mid-Victorian Male Novelists.* New York: New York University Press, 1996.

Hall, N. John. *Trollope: A Biography.* Oxford: Clarendon Press, 1991.

Hallam, Paul, ed. *The Book of Sodom.* London: Verso, 1993.

Halperin, John. *Trollope and Politics: A Study of the Pallisers and Others.* New York: Barnes and Noble, 1977.

Hamer, David Alan. *Liberal Politics in the Age of Gladstone and Rosebery: A Study in Leadership and Policy.* Oxford: Clarendon Press, 1972.

Haralson, Eric. "The Elusive Queerness of Henry James's 'queer comrade': Reading Gabriel Nash of *The Tragic Muse.*" In *Victorian Sexual Dissidence,* ed. Richard Dellamora. Chicago: University of Chicago Press, 1999.

Harvie, Christopher. *The Centre of Things: Political Fiction in England from Disraeli to the Present.* London: Unwin Hyman, 1991.

Henry, Nancy. *George Eliot and the British Empire.* Cambridge: Cambridge University Press, 2002.

Heuman, Gad. *"The Killing Time": The Morant Bay Rebellion in Jamaica.* Knoxville: University of Tennessee Press, 1994.

Hills, Patricia, ed. *John Singer Sargent.* New York: Whitney Museum of American Art, 1987.

Hilton, Boyd. "Gladstone's Theological Politics." In *High and Low Politics in Modern Britain: Ten Studies,* ed. Michael Bentley and John Stevenson. Oxford: Clarendon Press, 1983.

Hirshfield, Claire. "Labouchere, *Truth,* and the Uses of Antisemitism." *Victorian Periodical Review* 26 (fall 1993): 134–42.

———. "The Tenacity of Tradition: *Truth* and the Jews, 1877–1957." *Patterns of Prejudice* 28 (1994): 67–85.

Hoare, Philip. *Oscar Wilde's Last Stand: Decadence, Conspiracy, and the Most Outrageous Trial of the Century.* New York: Arcade, 1997.

Holcombe, Lee. "Victorian Wives and Property: Reform of the Married Women's

Property Law, 1857–1882." In *A Widening Sphere: Changing Roles of Victorian Women,* ed. Martha Vicinus. Bloomington: Indiana University Press, 1977.

Hyde, H. Montgomery. *The Trials of Oscar Wilde.* New York: Dover, 1973.

Ignatiev, Noel. *How the Irish Became White.* New York: Routledge, 1995.

The Imperial Family Bible. Glasgow: Blackie and Son, 1848.

Jack, Malcolm. *William Beckford: An English Fidalgo.* New York: AMS Press, 1996.

James, Alice. *The Diary.* Ed. Leon Edel. Harmondsworth: Penguin, 1964.

James, Henry. "Anthony Trollope." In *The House of Fiction: Essays on the Novel,* ed. Leon Edel. London: Rupert and Hart-Davis, 1957.

———. *The Art of the Novel.* Boston: Northeastern University Press, 1984.

———. *The Complete Notebooks.* Ed. Leon Edel and Lyall H. Powers. New York: Oxford University Press, 1987.

———. "*Daniel Deronda:* A Conversation." In *Partial Portraits.* Ann Arbor: University of Michigan Press, 1970.

———. *Letters.* 4 volumes. Ed. Leon Edel. Cambridge, Mass.: Harvard University Press, 1974–84.

———. Preface to *The Tragic Muse.* London: Penguin, 1995. The text is that of the 1908 New York edition.

———. *The Tragic Muse.* New York: Dell, 1961. The text is that of the original edition, published in 1890.

James, Robert Rhodes. *Rosebery: A Biography of Archibald Philip, Fifth Earl of Rosebery.* London: Weidenfeld and Nicolson, 1963.

Jenkins, Roy. *Gladstone: A Biography.* New York: Random House, 1997.

Jones, Gareth Stedman. *Languages of Class: Studies in English Working Class History, 1832–1982.* Cambridge: Cambridge University Press, 1983.

Jordan, Mark D. *The Invention of Sodomy in Christian Theology.* Chicago: University of Chicago Press, 1997.

Joyce, Patrick. "The Constitution and the Narrative Structure of Victorian Politics." In *Re-reading the Constitution: New Narratives in the Political History of England's Long Nineteenth Century,* ed. James Vernon. Cambridge: Cambridge University Press, 1996.

Kamen, Henry. "The Secret of the Inquisition." *New York Review of Books,* February 1, 1996, 4–6.

Kaplan, Fred. *Dickens and Mesmerism: The Hidden Springs of Fiction.* Princeton, N.J.: Princeton University Press, 1975.

———. *Henry James, The Imagination of Genius: A Biography.* New York: Morrow, 1992.

Kaplan, Morris B. *Sexual Justice: Democratic Citizenship and the Politics of Desire.* Routledge: New York, 1997.

Karl, Frederick R. *George Eliot: Voice of a Century.* New York: Norton, 1995.

Katz, Jonathan Ned. *Love Stories: Sex Between Men Before Homosexuality.* Chicago: University of Chicago Press, 2001.

Kaufmann, David. *George Eliot and Judaism: An Attempt to Appreciate* Daniel Deronda. Trans. J. W. Ferrier. 1888. Reprint, New York: Haskell House Publishers, Ltd., 1970.

Kaye, Richard. *The Flirt's Tragedy: Desire without End in Victorian and Edwardian Fiction.* Charlottesville: University Press of Virginia, 2002.

Kennedy, Hubert. "Johann Baptist von Schweitzer: The Queer Marx Loved to Hate." In *Gay Men and the Sexual History of the Political Left,* ed. Gert Hekma, Harry Oosterhuis, and James Steakley. New York: Harrington Park Press, 1995.

Kettle, Arnold. *An Introduction to the English Novel.* 1951. Reprint, New York: Harper, 1960.

Kiberd, Declan. *Inventing Ireland: The Literature of the Modern Nation.* Cambridge, Mass.: Harvard University Press, 1996.

Kincaid, James R. "Anthony Trollope and the Unmannerly Novel." In *Annoying the Victorians.* New York: Routledge, 1995.

———. *Child-Loving: The Erotic Child and Victorian Culture.* New York: Routledge, 1992.

Kristeva, Julia. *Powers of Horror: An Essay on Abjection.* Trans. Leon S. Roudiez. New York: Columbia University Press, 1982.

Kucich, John. *The Power of Lies: Transgression in Victorian Fiction.* Ithaca, N.Y.: Cornell University Press, 1994.

Lacan, Jacques. *Écrits: A Selection.* Trans. Alan Sheridan. New York: W. W. Norton, 1977.

Lane, Christopher. *The Burdens of Intimacy: Psychoanalysis and Victorian Masculinity.* Chicago: University of Chicago Press, 1999.

———. "The Impossibility of Seduction in James's *Roderick Hudson* and *The Tragic Muse.*" *American Literature* 68 (December 1996): 739–64.

Lane, Lauriat, Jr. "The Devil in *Oliver Twist.*" *The Dickensian* 52 (summer 1956): 132–36.

Laplanche, Jean, and J.-B. Pontalis. *The Language of Psycho-Analysis.* Trans. Donald Nicholson-Smith. New York: Norton, 1973.

Lee, Vernon. "John Singer Sargent: In Memoriam." In *John Sargent,* by Evan Charteris. New York: Scribner's, 1927.

Linehan, Katherine Bailey. "Mixed Politics: The Critique of Imperialism in *Daniel Deronda.*" *Texas Studies in Language and Literature* 34 (fall 1992): 323–46.

Litvak, Joseph. *Caught in the Act: Theatricality in the Nineteenth-Century English Novel.* Berkeley: University of California Press, 1992.

———. "Consuming Jews." Paper presented at the "Victorian Consumption, Taste, and Fashion" conference at the CUNY Graduate Center, New York City, May 9, 1999.

Mahaffey, Vicki. *States of Desire: Wilde, Yeats, Joyce, and the Irish Experiment.* New York: Oxford University Press, 1998.

Mahaffy, John Pentland. *Social Life in Greece from Homer to Menander.* London: Macmillan, 1874.

———. *Social Life in Greece from Homer to Menander.* 2nd ed., rev. London: Macmillan, 1875.

Malthus, Thomas Robert. *An Essay on the Principle of Population.* Selected and introduced by Donald Winch. Cambridge: Cambridge University Press, 1992.

———. *An Essay on the Principle of Population.* Ed. Antony Flew. Harmondsworth: Penguin, 1970.

Marcus, Steven. *Dickens from Pickwick to Dombey.* New York: Simon and Schuster, 1968.

Marks, Elaine. *Marrano as Metaphor: The Jewish Presence in French Writing.* New York: Columbia University Press, 1996.

Markus, Julia. *Across an Untried Sea: Discovering Lives Hidden in the Shadow of Convention and Time.* New York: Knopf, 2000.

Marsh, Joss. *Word Crimes: Blasphemy, Culture, and Literature in Nineteenth-Century England.* Chicago: University of Chicago Press, 1998.

Marshall, T. H. and Tom Bottomore. *Citizenship and Social Class.* London: Pluto Press, 1992.

Marx, Karl. *Capital: A Critique of Political Economy.* Ed. Frederic Engels and rev. Ernest Untermann. Trans. Samuel Moore and Edward Aveling. New York: Modern Library, 1906.

———. "On the Jewish Question." In *Early Writings.* Trans. Rodney Livingstone and Gregor Benton. New York: Vintage Books, 1975.

McClintock, Anne. *Imperial Leather: Race, Gender, and Sexuality in the Colonial Contest.* New York: Routledge, 1995.

McConkey, Kenneth. "'Well-bred Contortions,' 1880–1918." In *The British Portrait, 1660–1960.* Woodbridge, Suffolk: Antique Collectors' Club, 1991.

McCormack, Jerusha, ed. *Wilde the Irishman.* New Haven: Yale University Press, 1998.

McKenzie, K. A. *Edith Simcox and George Eliot.* Oxford: Oxford University Press, 1961.

McMaster, Juliet. *Trollope's Palliser Novels: Theme and Pattern.* London: Macmillan, 1978.

McWhirter, David. "Restaging the Hurt: Henry James and the Artist as Masochist." *Texas Studies in Literature and Language* 33 (winter 1991): 464–91.

Medick, Hans. "Plebeian Culture in the Transition to Capitalism." In *Culture, Ideology, and Politics: Essays for Eric Hobsbawm,* ed. Raphael Samuel and Gareth Stedman Jones. London: Routledge, 1982.

Meyer, Susan. *Imperialism at Home: Race and Victorian Women's Fiction.* Ithaca, N.Y.: Cornell University Press, 1996.

Mill, John Stuart. *Essays on Literature and Society,* ed. J. B. Schneewind. New York: Collier Books, 1965.

Miller, D. A. *Bringing out Roland Barthes.* Berkeley: University of California Press, 1992.

———. *The Novel and the Police.* Berkeley: University of California Press, 1988.

Miller, J. Hillis. "The Fiction of Realism: *Sketches by Boz, Oliver Twist,* and Cruikshank's Illustrations." In *Dickens Centennial Essays,* ed. Ada Nisbet and Blake Nevius. Berkeley: University of California Press, 1971.

———. *Illustration.* Cambridge, Mass.: Harvard University Press, 1992.

Moon, Michael. *A Small Boy and Others: Imitation and Initiation in American Culture from Henry James to Andy Warhol.* Durham, N.C.: Duke University Press, 1998.

Mowl, Tim. *William Beckford: Composing for Mozart.* London: J. Murray, 1998.

Mullen, Richard. *Anthony Trollope: A Victorian in His World*. Savannah, Ga.: Frederic C. Beil, 1992.

Mullen, Richard, and James Munson. *The Penguin Companion to Trollope*. London: Penguin, 1996.

Murray, Douglas. *Bosie: A Biography of Lord Alfred Douglas*. New York: Hyperion, 2000.

Newall, Christopher. "The Victorians, 1830–1880." In *The British Portrait, 1660–1960*. Woodbridge, Suffolk: Antique Collectors' Club, 1991.

Nordau, Max. *Degeneration*. Trans. from the 2d German ed. Lincoln: University of Nebraska Press, 1993.

Nunokawa, Jeff. *The Afterlife of Property: Domestic Security and the Victorian Novel*. Princeton, N.J.: Princeton University Press, 1994.

O'Connor, Sean. *Straight Acting: Popular Gay Drama from Wilde to Rattigan*. London: Cassell, 1998.

Oliphant, Margaret. "The Grievances of Women." In *"Criminals, Idiots, Women, and Minors": Victorian Writing by Women on Women,* ed. Susan Hamilton. Peterborough, Ontario: Broadview Press, 1995.

Oliver, J. W. *The Life of William Beckford*. London: Oxford University Press, 1932.

Olson, Stanley. "On the Question of Sargent's Nationality." In *John Singer Sargent,* ed. Patricia Hills. New York: Whitney Museum of American Art, 1987.

The Oxford English Dictionary. 2d ed. Oxford: Clarendon Press, 1989.

Parker, Andrew. "Unthinking Sex: Marx, Engels, and the Scene of Writing." In *Fear of a Queer Planet: Queer Politics and Social Theory,* ed. Michael Warner. Minneapolis: University of Minnesota Press, 1993.

Parker, Andrew, Mary Russo, Doris Sommer, and Patricia Yaeger, eds. *Nationalisms and Sexualities*. New York: Routledge, 1992.

Parry, J. P. *Democracy and Religion: Gladstone and the Liberal Party, 1867–1875*. Cambridge: Cambridge University Press, 1986.

Pater, Walter. *Plato and Platonism: A Series of Lectures*. 1893. Reprint, London: Macmillan, 1910.

———. *The Renaissance: Studies in Art and Poetry: The 1893 Text,* ed. Donald L. Hill. Berkeley: University of California Press, 1980.

———. *Studies in the History of the Renaissance*. London: Macmillan, 1873.

Pearson, Hesketh. *Labby: The Life and Character of Henry Labouchere*. New York: Harper, 1937.

Pelham, Camden. *The Chronicles of Crime or, The New Newgate Calendar*. Vol. 2. London: Miles and Co., 1887.

Pellegrini, Ann. *Performance Anxieties: Staging Psychoanalysis, Staging Race*. New York: Routledge, 1997.

Pine, Richard. *The Thief of Reason: Oscar Wilde and Modern Ireland*. New York: St. Martin's Press, 1995.

Poliakov, Léon. *The Aryan Myth: A History of Racist and Nationalist Ideas in Europe*. Trans. Edmund Howard. New York: Basic Books, 1974.

———. *The History of Anti-Semitism*. Vol. 3, *From Voltaire to Wagner*. Trans. Miriam Kochan. New York: Vanguard Press, Inc., 1975.

Poovey, Mary. *Making a Social Body: British Cultural Formation, 1830–1864.* Chicago: University of Chicago Press, 1995.

Pope, Rebecca A. "The Diva Doesn't Die: George Eliot's *Armgart*." *Criticism* 32, no. 4 (1990): 469–83.

The Portable Folio Family Bible. Ed. the Rev. John Eadie, with the Commentaries of Scott and Henry and notes by the Rev. Walter M'Gilvray. Glasgow: W. R. M'Phun, 1851.

Potkay, Adam. "Beckford's Heaven of Boys." *Raritan* 13 (summer 1993): 73–86.

Potolsky, Matthew. "Pale Imitations: Walter Pater's Decadent Historiography." In *Perennial Decay: On the Aesthetics and Politics of Decadence,* ed. Liz Constable, Dennis Denisoff, and Matthew Potolsky. Philadelphia: University of Pennsylvania Press, 1999.

Potts, Alex. "Beautiful Bodies and Dying Heroes: Images of Ideal Manhood in the French Revolution." *History Workshop Journal* 30 (fall 1990): 1–21

———. *Flesh and the Ideal: Winckelmann and the Origins of Art History.* New Haven, Conn.: Yale University Press, 1994.

Prins, Yopie, *Victorian Sappho.* Princeton, N.J.: Princeton University Press, 1999.

Psomiades, Kathy. " 'Still Burning from this Strangling Embrace': Vernon Lee on Desire and Aesthetics." In *Victorian Sexual Dissidence,* ed. Richard Dellamora. Chicago: University of Chicago Press, 1999.

Pullen, J. M. "Malthus' Theological Ideas and Their Influence on His Principle of Population." In *Thomas Robert Malthus: Critical Assessments,* ed. John Cunningham Wood. Vol. 2. London: Croom Helm, 1986.

Raddatz, Fritz J. *Karl Marx: A Political Biography.* Trans. Richard Barry. Toronto: Little, Brown, 1978.

Ragussis, Michael. *Figures of Conversion: "The Jewish Question" and English National Identity.* Durham, N.C.: Duke University Press, 1995.

Ridley, Jane. *Young Disraeli: 1804–1846.* New York: Crown Publishers, Inc., 1995.

Rose, Jacqueline. *The Case of Peter Pan or the Impossibility of Children's Fiction.* Philadelphia: University of Pennsylvania Press, 1993.

Rose, Paul Lawrence. *Revolutionary Antisemitism in Germany: From Kant to Wagner.* Princeton, N.J.: Princeton University Press, 1990.

Roth, Cecil. "The Court Jews of Edwardian England." In *Essays and Portraits in Anglo-Jewish History.* Philadelphia: Jewish Publication Society of America, 1962.

Rowe, John Carlos. *The Other Henry James.* Durham, N.C.: Duke University Press, 1998.

Rubinstein, W. D. *A History of the Jews in the English-Speaking World: Great Britain.* London: Macmillan, 1996.

Saab, Ann Pottinger. "Disraeli, Judaism, and the Eastern Question." *International History Review* 10 (November 1988): 559–78.

Said, Edward W. *Culture and Imperialism.* New York: Vintage, 1994.

———. "On Repetition." In *The Literature of Fact,* ed. Angus Fletcher. New York: Columbia University Press, 1976.

———. *Orientalism.* New York: Vintage, 1979.

———. "Zionism from the Standpoint of Its Victims." In *George Eliot: Critical*

Assessments, ed. Stuart Hutchinson, vol. 3. Mountfield, East Sussex: Helm Information Ltd., 1996.

Salbstein, M. C. N. *The Emancipation of the Jews in Britain: The Question of the Admission of the Jews to Parliament, 1828–1860.* Rutherford, N.J.: Farleigh Dickinson University Press, 1982.

Savoy, Eric. "'In the Cage' and the Queer Effects of Gay History." *Novel* 28 (spring 1995): 284–307.

Schmidgall, Gary. *The Stranger Wilde: Interpreting Oscar.* New York: Dutton, 1994.

Schultz, Bart. "Truth and Its Consequences: The Friendship of Symonds and Henry Sidgwick." In *John Addington Symonds: Culture and Demon Desire,* ed. John Pemble. London: Macmillan, 2000.

Schwartz, Regina M. "Adultery in the House of David: 'Nation' in the Bible and Biblical Scholarship." In *Shadow of Spirit: Postmodernism and Religion,* ed. Philippa Berry and Andrew Wernick. London: Routledge, 1992.

Scott, Sir Walter. *The Heart of Mid-Lothian.* Ed. John Henry Raleigh. Boston: Houghton Mifflin, 1966.

Sedgwick, Eve Kosofsky. *Between Men: English Literature and Male Homosocial Desire.* New York: Columbia University Press, 1985.

———. *Epistemology of the Closet.* Berkeley: University of California Press, 1990.

———. *Tendencies.* Durham, N.C.: Duke University Press, 1993.

Semmel, Bernard. *George Eliot and the Politics of National Inheritance.* New York: Oxford University Press, 1994.

———. *Jamaican Blood and Victorian Conscience: The Governor Eyre Controversy.* Boston: Houghton Mifflin, 1963.

Sennett, Richard. *The Fall of Public Man.* New York: Knopf, 1977.

Shand-Tucci, Douglass. *The Art of Scandal: The Life and Times of Isabella Stewart Gardner.* New York: HarperCollins, 1997.

Shapiro, James. *Shakespeare and the Jews.* New York: Columbia University Press, 1996.

Shell, Marc. *Children of the Earth: Literature, Politics, and Nationhood.* New York: Oxford University Press, 1993.

———. *Money, Language, and Thought: Literary and Philosophical Economies from the Medieval to the Modern Era.* Berkeley: University of California Press, 1982.

Simpson, Marc. *Uncanny Spectacle: The Public Career of the Young John Singer Sargent.* New Haven, Conn.: Yale University Press, 1997.

Small, Ian. *Conditions for Criticism: Authority, Knowledge, and Literature in the Late Nineteenth Century.* New York: Oxford University Press, 1991.

Smith, F. B. "Labouchere's Amendment to the Criminal Law Amendment Bill." *Historical Studies* 17 (1976): 165–73.

Stallybrass, Peter. "Marx and Heterogeneity: Thinking the Lumpenproletariat." *Representations* 31 (summer 1990): 69–95.

Steiner, George. *No Passion Spent: Essays, 1978–1995.* London: Yale University Press, 1996.

Stevens, Hugh. *Henry James and Sexuality.* Cambridge: Cambridge University Press, 1998.

Stewart, Alan. *Close Readers: Humanism and Sodomy in Early Modern England.* Princeton, N.J.: Princeton University Press, 1997.

Stewart, R. W., ed. *Disraeli's Novels Reviewed, 1826–1968.* Metuchen, N.J.: Scarecrow Press, 1975.

Sutherland, John. *The Stanford Companion to Victorian Fiction.* Stanford, Calif.: Stanford University Press, 1989.

Swinburne, Algernon Charles. *Poems and Ballads.* London: John Camden Hotten, 1866.

Thompson, E. P. *The Making of the English Working Class.* Harmondsworth: Penguin, 1972.

Tracy, Robert. "'The Old Story' and Inside Stories: Modish Fiction and Fictional Modes in *Oliver Twist.*" *Dickens Studies Annual* 17 (1988): 1–33.

Trevor-Roper, Hugh. *A Hidden Life: The Enigma of Sir Edmund Backhouse.* London: Macmillan, 1976.

Trollope, Anthony. *An Autobiography.* Eds. Michael Sadleir and Frederick Page. New York: Oxford University Press, 1980.

———. *The Prime Minister.* London: Penguin, 1993.

———. "Public Schools." *Fortnightly Review* 2 (1865): 476–87.

Trumpener, Katie. *Bardic Nationalism: The Romantic Novel and the British Empire.* Princeton, N.J.: Princeton University Press, 1997.

Tucker, Irene. *A Probable State: The Novel, the Contract, and the Jews.* Chicago: University of Chicago Press, 2000.

Vernon, James. *Politics and the People: A Study in English Political Culture, c. 1815–1867.* Cambridge: Cambridge University Press, 1993.

Vicinus, Martha. "The Adolescent Boy: Fin-de-Siècle Femme Fatale?" In *Victorian Sexual Dissidence,* ed. Richard Dellamora. Chicago: University of Chicago Press, 1999.

Viswanathan, Gauri. *Outside the Fold: Conversion, Modernity, and Belief.* Princeton, N.J.: Princeton University Press, 1998.

———. "Raymond Williams and British Colonialism." *Yale Journal of Criticism* 4 (spring 1991): 47–66.

Walkowitz, Judith R. *City of Dreadful Delight: Narratives of Sexual Danger in Late-Victorian London.* Chicago: University of Chicago Press, 1992.

Wallace, Jo-Ann. "Technologies of 'the Child.'" Paper presented at the "Human Sciences in the Age of Theory" conference at the University of Western Ontario, London, Ontario, April 3, 1993.

Walton, Priscilla L. *Patriarchal Desire and Victorian Discourse: A Lacanian Reading of Anthony Trollope's Palliser Novels.* Toronto: University of Toronto Press, 1995.

Weiner, Marc A. *Richard Wagner and the Anti-Semitic Imagination.* Lincoln: University of Nebraska Press, 1995.

Weintraub, Stanley. *Disraeli: A Biography.* New York: Truman Talley Books, 1993.

Weiss, Timothy. "Walter Pater, Aesthetic Utilitarian." *Victorians Institute Journal* 15 (1987): 105–22.

Welsh, Alexander. *The City of Dickens,* 1971. Reprint, Cambridge, Mass.: Harvard University Press, 1986.

Wihl, Gary. "Novels as Theories in a Liberal Society." In *Constructive Criticism: The Human Sciences in the Age of Theory,* ed. Martin Kreiswirth and Thomas Carmichael. Toronto: University of Toronto Press, 1995.

Wilde, Oscar. *The Artist as Critic: Critical Writings of Oscar Wilde.* Ed. Richard Ellmann. New York: Vintage, 1969.

———. De Profundis *and Other Writings.* London: Penguin Books, 1986.

———. *An Ideal Husband.* In *The Importance of Being Earnest and Other Plays.* London: Penguin, 1986.

———. Review of Amiel's Journal and Lord Beaconsfield's letters to his sister. c. 1886? Unpublished mss. William Clark Memorial Library. Los Angeles, California.

———. *Two Society Comedies.* Ed. Ian Small and Russell Jackson. London: Ernest Benn Ltd., 1983.

Winckelmann, Johann Joachim. *History of Ancient Art.* Trans. G. Henry Lodge. 4 vols. in 2. New York: Ungar, 1968.

Wolfreys, Julian. *Being English: Narratives, Idioms, and Performances of National Identity from Coleridge to Trollope.* Albany: State University of New York Press, 1994.

Wood, Gordon S. "Tocqueville's Lesson." *New York Review of Books,* May 17, 2001, 46–49.

Young, Robert J. C. *Colonial Desire: Hybridity in Theory, Culture, and Race.* London: Routledge, 1995.

Zimmerman, Bonnie. "'The Dark Eye Beaming': Female Friendship in George Eliot's Fictions." In *Lesbian Texts and Contexts: Radical Revisions,* ed. Karla Jay and Joanne Glasgow. New York: New York University Press, 1990.

———. "'The Mother's History' in George Eliot's Life, Literature, and Political Ideology." In *The Lost Tradition: Mothers and Daughters in Literature,* ed. Cathy N. Davidson and E. M. Broner. New York: Frederick Ungar Publ. Co., 1980.

Index

abjection, feminine-identified, 59
aesthetic education, 153–77; in liberal political theory, 159
aesthetic politics, 153–77
aesthetics of existence, 196 n.5
aesthetic utilitarianism, 174
affiliation (versus filiation), 194 n.33; defined, 202 n.55
African-Americans, as internal Others in the United States, 173–74
agency: dependent upon "a diversity of views," 129; friendship as a mode of, 51; minority, after 1867, 121; neo-conservative meaning of challenged by Jacqueline Rose, 44–45; and patriotism during Napoleonic Wars, 34–35; as a political and religious concept, 16; problematic aspects of after 1867, 121–22; and self-fashioning, 176; working-class, 29–30, 34–35, 126
Alter, Robert, 18, 101, 204 n.34
Anesko, Michael, 216 n.17
anti-Semitism: against Disraeli, 68–69; in England in the 1870s and 1880s, 115–66; in England during World War I, 18; and "Jewish self-hatred," 206–7 n.29; of Karl Marx, 92–101; in *Oliver Twist*, 30; after World War I, 217 n.42
Apollo Belvedere, 63
Arendt, Hannah, 163
Aristotle, 75, 77, 123
Armstrong, Karen, 205 n.39
Arnold, Matthew, 2, 139–40; *On the Study of Celtic Literature*, 14–15, 184; opposes Home Rule for Ireland, 184
Ascham, Roger, 21
Asquith, H. H., 92
Augustine, Saint, 209 n.35
Austen, Jane, 57; *Mansfield Park*, 200–201 n.29

bachelor, status of, 164, 174

Bad Homburg (Germany), 145, 180
Balfour, Arthur, 23
Barham, Richard Harris, 47; "The Wondrous Tale of Ikey Solomons," 68
Bauer, Bruno, 205–6 n.10
Beckford, William, 4, 47, 53, 63–64, 67; and celibacy, 51; and Disraeli, 64–66; on male friendship as sexual, 199 n.10; obsession with William Courtenay, 49; on women's capability for friendship in marriage, 199 n.10. Works: *Episodes of Vathek*, 48, 65; *Italy: With Sketches of Spain and Portugal*, 64; "The Story of Prince Alasi and the Princess Firouzkah," 49–50; —, male relations in earlier version of, 199 n.10; *Vathek*, 48, 49, 53–54
Beer, Gillian, 214 n.51
Bentham, Jeremy, 38
Bentinck, Lord George, 70–71, 204–5 n.36
Bentley, Richard, 46
Berlioz, Hector, 133
Besant, Annie, 15
Beshant, Wendy, 134
Bible, the: as ground of English national identity, 6, 7, 148; and Oriental practices, 194 n.18
Bible-reading, as a form of masculine performativity, 6
Blake, Robert, 183
Blanchot, Maurice, 206 n.28
Bodichon, Barbara, 150
body: androgynous youthful male, 140; boy's, 26; divine, 63; and "embodification" (term of Disraeli's), 55, 57–58; Gladstone's concept of the body politic, 109, 115; monarch's, 56; national, 27, 56, 195 n.35; social, 27, 56
Boime, Albert, 171
Boldini, Giovanni, 155
Botta, Paul Emile, 107
Bourdieu, Pierre, 6

159, 177; affiliation and filiation in, 194 n.33; "aristocracy," 191; and autonomy, 182–83, 185–86; and "a diversity of views," 129; egoism as characteristic vice of, 105, 186; and emergent mass politics, 170; a "government of the best," 191; importance of individual choice in, 154–55, 176–77, 182–83, 185–86; and nation formation, 174; and the politics of scandal, 189; and progress, 104–5; and religious faith, 104; and sodomy, 182; tension between individual and group aspects of, 186; theater as characteristic art form of, 157, 163–64, 174, 176–77. *See also* aesthetic politics; aesthetic education; citizenship; desire, social; friendship; influence, political; sodomy

Demuth, Helene, 206 n.14

De Quincey, Thomas, 53

Derrida, Jacques, 21–22, 86, 194 n.33

desire: adult's for a child, 26–27, 29; between men and boys, 25, 50; pederastic, 48–51

desire, male-male, associated with fascist politics, 196 n.58

desire, social (term of John Kucich's), 104–5; and Disraeli's concept of democracy, 91; heterosexual, 120; and Marx and de Tocqueville, 207 n.8; sacrificed, 120–21, 124

desire between women, 157, 212 n.14; figured as monstrous, 212 n.14; and the social circle of Charlotte Cushman, 160. *See also* friendship

Deutsch, Emanuel, 138, 213 n.31

Dickens, Charles: assimilation of into the middle classes, 46; and Bob Fagin, 39–40; radicalism of in 1830s, 26; self-fashioning as a successful novelist, 46. Works: *Oliver Twist*, 25–46; —, anti-Semitism in, 30; —, and Chartist radicalism, 26, 30; —, and modern publishing, 25–26, 46; —, working-class agency in, 34; *Pickwick Papers*, 28–29

Dilke, Sir Charles, 167

Disraeli, Benjamin, earl of Beaconsfield, 63; accused of political idolatry by Gladstone, 104, 110; accused of posing as a sodomite, 107–8, 208 n.20; and anti-Semitism, 68–69, 88–90, 198–99 n.5; and William Beckford, 64–65; as dandy, 48; effeminacy alleged, 48, 198–99 n.5; and father's view of Judaism, 55, 69; friendships with young men, 23, 202 n.4; 210 n.53; as genius, 201 n.45; as impe-

rial subject, 47, 48; Jewish background in political rise of, 55; and Jewish leftists, 90; on Jewish self-hatred, 90; as offspring of secular Jews, 95–96; and the Ottoman Empire, 107, 109; and Sir Robert Peel, 70, 78, 82, 86; populist imperialism of, 55, 115, 201 n.29; and racial bias, 200 n.24, 205 n.43; self-fashioning of, 47, 56; and Suez Canal, 107, 111–12, 113; and women, 107, 108. Works: *Alroy*, 47–69; —, Jewish difference in, 69; —, idolatry of Alroy, 54; —, purity of Alroy, 53, 58; —, sodomitic innuendo in, 65–66; *Coningsby*, 56, 72; —, conciliates social differences, 118; —, racial theory in, 80; *Endymion*, 109; *Iskander*, 5; "Mutilated Diary," 56; *Sybil*, 72; *Tancred*, 70–91; —, and *Alroy*, 83–84

Disraeli, Isaac, *The Genius of Judaism*, 53, 55

Disraeli, Sarah, 88

Douglas, Lord Alfred, 92; accuses Wilde of having been "a diabolical influence," 180; friendship with Wilde, 179–80

Douglas, Mary, 59

Dowling, Linda, 1, 3, 159, 182, 213 n.40, 218 n.6

Drumlanrig, Viscount (oldest son of Queensberry), engagement and suicide of, 180–81, 187

During, Simon, 56, 57

Edward I, 209 n.31

Edward II, 66

Edward VII, 168, 180, 183

effeminacy, 5, 9; alleged of Disraeli, 48; alleged of Jews, 52; a regulating concept, 59; and sexual inversion theory, 52; and uxoriousness, 52. *See also* influence, political

Eliot, George, 127–52; on British imperialism, 214 n.58; and Oscar Browning, 214 n.59; and English nationalism, 69; friendships with women, 213 n.48; and gender-crossing, 131–34, 143; imperial entanglements of, 205 n.4; on Liberal attacks on Disraeli, 211 n.4; on male-male intimacy, 144; and mentor-protégé relations, 141–42, 214 n.51; on Oxford aestheticism, 130, 136–37, 140; on racial miscegenation, 144; radicalism of, 211 n.3; and Sappho, 135; and sexual inversion theory, 131–32; and Edith Simcox, 151–52; transgressive character of personal life of, 151. Works: "Address to Working Men, by Felix Holt," 211 n.3;

120–22, 124; theorized by Judith Butler, 210 n.53

Melbourne, William Lamb, second viscount, 107, 208 n.19

mentor-protégé relations (female), 141–42, 143

mentor-protégé relations (male), 27, 44, 45, 51–52; anxiety about, 62–63; and cultural transmission, 137–38

mentor-protégé relations (between a man and a woman), 128

Michelangelo, 179

Mill, John Stuart, 149; and the Jamaica Committee, 212 n.16

Millais, Sir John Everett, 156

misogyny, 49–50, 61–62, 65

money, as fetish-object, 211 n.56

monotheistic principle: in Disraeli, 82, 85; in Gladstone, 104, 110; versus idolatry, 85, 104, 110

Montaigne, Michel de, 21; on the impossibility of friendship in marriage, 189–90

Montesquiou-Fezensac, Robert de, count, 168, 169, 171

Moore, Thomas, 65

Murray, Douglas, 181, 218 n.14

Murray, George, 180

Newall, Christopher, 156

New Journalism, 216 n.17

Newman, John Henry, 15

Newman-Kingsley controversy, 4

The New Newgate Calendar (1841), 36–37, 68

New Poor Law (1834), 31

Nietszche, Friedrich, 174

Nordau, Max: on "ego-mania," 186; *Degeneration*, 76, 129

novel, the: aestheticist, 158, 216 n.17; altered conditions of production of in 1830s, 25–26; conciliating social differences, 5; crisis of realism in, 120, 126, 130; decadence and aestheticism in, 129–30, 136; defined in relation to the marriage plot, 210 n.43; as genre, 4–5; Gothic, 44, 45, 46; marriage plot of undermined by late Victorian degeneration theory, 144–45; naturalist, 162; Newgate or criminal, 31; and plot of upward mobility, 42–43, 46; realist, 57; "silver-fork," 202 nn.2–3; and social desire, 120–21. *See also* romance

Oastler, Richard, 30

O'Connell, Daniel, 85, 200 n.24, 209 n.35

O'Kell, Robert, 202

Oliphant, Margaret, 193–94 n.16

Oriental tale, 49, 52

Pappenheim, Bertha, 207 n.1

Parker, Andrew, 206 n.21

Parliament, oligarchic character of, 5, 22–23

Parnell, Charles Stewart, 167

Pater, Walter, 20, 139–40, 170; politics of, 213 n.40; *Studies in the History of the Renaissance*, 129–31, 156

patriotism: inculcated in Great Britain during Napoleonic Wars, 34–35; and Tory eighteenth-century politics, 56

Pearson, Hesketh, 167, 168

pederasty: and William Beckford, 48–51, 136; and cultural transmission, 137–38; in Sparta, 195 n.52; in Talmudic tradition, 138–39; Wilde's defense of, 179. *See also* friendship

Peel, Sir Robert, 12, 13, 70–71

Pellegrini, Ann, 209 nn.38–39

Peter Damian, 209 n.35

Pius IX (pope), *Syllabus Errorum*, 85

Plato, 75, 77; on democracy as a "government of the best," 191; and pederastic desire, 136, 179; *Phaedrus*, read by Eliot, 138; sublimating aspects of challenged by George Eliot, 136

plebeian culture, 34; defined, 197 n.29

Plutarch, 77, 152

Pocock, J. G. A., 193 n.2

Poliakov, Léon, 205 n.43

Poor Law Amendment Act (1834), 197 n.14

portrait painting, 154–56

Potkay, Adam, 50

Pozzi, Dr. Samuel, 171

Protectionist party, 89

Punch: on aesthetes, 4; on Disraeli's Jewishness, 68–69; on the Suez Canal, 111–12

purity, 204 n.28; and anti-Semitism, 31; of boys, 26, 148; brother-sister, 61; of childhood, 48–49; and Cruikshank's view of Oliver in *Oliver Twist*, 42–43; and Jewish tradition, 53; a preoccupation of Disraeli in *Alroy*, 58; and "the problem of purification," 26, 59, 196 n.5; and sexual abuse of children, 29, 39–40; an unrealizable ideal, 46, 51; and women's authority in politics, 188–89

Acknowledgments

The record of the writing of a book involves three maps. One is a map of reading. For me, writing this book has been an especially rich experience in discovering and assimilating the learning and thinking of others. With a view to assisting readers who share the interests that motivate this book, in "A Note on Further Reading," I offer a summary of my own routing through the writing of scholars such as Jonathan Boyarin, Daniel Boyarin, Mary Douglas, Moshe Halbertal and Avishai Margalit, and Patrick Joyce and other revisionary historians of the Victorian period. The second map is one of times, places, and people who have patiently, critically, and at times enthusiastically shared the questions and passions that have sustained this inquiry. The names of David DeLaura, Lauren Goodlad, Eric Haralson (how well I remember a conversation outside the Union Cafe in New York City in fall, 1998), Chris Lane, Jay Losey, John Schad, and Stephen J. Scanlan come immediately to mind. But there are many others, who will know how vital to me their responses and support have been. The third map is the record of the financial support that makes scholarly work possible.

For exchanges with listeners who have heard portions of the text delivered at various conferences, I am grateful. In particular, I would like to thank my hosts and the participants on the following occasions: the Psychoanalysis and Postcolonialism conference at George Washington University in the fall of 1995; the presentation of the Roger Henkle Memorial Lecture at Brown University in November 1996; the Wilde Days conference at the University of Birmingham (United Kingdom) in June 1997; a Victorian Faculty Seminar at CUNY Graduate Center in the spring of 1999; and the Victorian Subversions conference, organized by the Victorian Studies Association of Western Canada, at the University of British Columbia in September 2001.

I would like to express my continuing gratitude to the Social Sciences and Humanities Research Council of Canada for its financial support during the past decade. Without it, this book could not have been written. I owe a debt as well to the Guggenheim Foundation for the award of a fellowship, which gave me the time and leisure to research and write the Gladstone and Trollope portions of the book during a year as a visiting scholar in the Department of English at New York University in 1998–99. That year also changed the itinerary of the second half of this book. I would also like to thank the staff of the Clark and Young Libraries at the University of California at Los Angeles, where the final chapters were researched, written, and revised. I am grateful to the Clark Library for the grant of a research fellowship in the summer of 1998. Also, I would like to thank the staff of the Pratt Library at Victoria College of the University of Toronto for their friendliness and assistance on a daily basis.

I wish to acknowledge with thanks permission to reproduce in revised form as Chapter 2 of the present text the essay "Constituting the National Subject: Benjamin Disraeli, Judaism, and the Legacy of William Beckford," which originally appeared in *Mapping Male Sexuality: Nineteenth-Century England,* ed. Jay Losey and William D. Brewer (Rutherford, N.J.: Farleigh Dickinson University Press, 2000), 145–77.